A History of
Alma College

Where Plaid and Pride Prevail

Gordon G. Beld &
David C. McMacken

Charleston London
The History Press

Published by The History Press
Charleston, SC 29403
wwww.historypress.net

Front cover, top: Courtesy of Alma College Archives. All other cover photographs taken by Gordon G. Beld.

First published 2014

Manufactured in the United States

ISBN 978.1.62619.332.1

Library of Congress CIP data applied for.

Notice: The information in this book is true and complete to the best of our knowledge. It is offered without guarantee on the part of the author or The History Press. The author and The History Press disclaim all liability in connection with the use of this book.

For the thousands of Alma College students who have reached out to make a positive difference in the lives of others, thus making the world a better place for all of us.

CONTENTS

Contents

PREFACE

If Alma College is your alma mater, the pages that follow will bring back happy memories. If you're an Alma student now, they'll tell you what happened here before you arrived. If you're one of the thousands who have heard the skirling pipes and seen the swirling kilts at the colorful Scottish festival that takes place on the campus each spring, you'll learn how all that started. If you're one of those whose support has nurtured this wonderful place, you'll feel even better about having done so. If you have no connection with Alma College whatsoever, flip through these pages anyway, and who knows, you may decide to get connected.

The kinds of things that happened at Alma in the past aren't boring history. The people and events that come back to life on these pages are ones you're likely to talk about at a campfire with friends or a dinner table with family.

You'll see the college museum when it became a barracks for army trainees during World War I, and you'll learn about campus life during World War II when the grounds were taken over by navy recruits, one of whom later was among the best of National Football League coaches.

You'll discover that during one federal election, two former Alma students were candidates for the U.S. vice presidency.

You'll look on as Alma's women get a late start in intercollegiate athletic competition but soon outperform the men in collecting championship hardware.

Preface

You'll travel throughout the United States and abroad with Alma students as they explore other cultures and languages and reach out to make a positive difference in the lives of others.

You'll meet an Alma president who rescued the college from death, who presided over the construction of more than half the present major buildings, who made pancakes and served them to students.

You'll experience the thrills of Scot football during the years when the tiny Alma team tangled with the Irish—the ones at Notre Dame! Slow learners maybe, they did it four years in a row.

But enough of that. Read on. You'll find out, if you didn't already know, that Alma College is out of the ordinary. You may decide to get connected—or at least claim that you are.

ACKNOWLEDGEMENTS

The stories on the following pages couldn't have been written, of course, without the great contributions of many professors, students, administrators, trustees and philanthropists whose contributions through the years have built the reputation that Alma College has today. Many of them are mentioned on the following pages.

Besides our indebtedness to them, we are grateful for the assistance of several present Alma staff members who provided suggestions, found needed data and encouraged us.

President Jeff Abernathy enthusiastically embraced the idea for a volume of stories about Alma College and connected us with others who would make our necessary research and writing tasks enjoyable.

Communications Director Mike Silverthorn and Library Director Carol Zeile made sure we had everything we needed.

Viki Everhart, library technical assistant responsible for the college's archives, put our needs at the top of her priority list and spent much time and effort in making our work easier and more pleasant.

—GORDON BELD AND DAVID MCMACKEN

CHAPTER 1

A COLLEGE COMES TO ALMA

The year was 1886, and there was a lot happening. In Germany, Karl Benz drove the first true gasoline-powered automobile. On this side of the Atlantic, Geronimo was captured by U.S. troops. President Grover Cleveland presided at the dedication of the Statue of Liberty. And Coca-Cola went on the market in Atlanta.

Meanwhile, at Alma, the big news was the prospect of attracting an institution of higher education. In a meeting at Wright's Opera House in January of that year, citizens learned that the Eastern Michigan Normal School at Fenton was considering a move to Alma. Ammi W. Wright, the city's wealthiest and most influential resident, wasn't at the meeting, but he offered up to $25,000 to buy a site and build the necessary buildings. For that to happen, other Alma citizens were required to come through with support for the project, too. They did.

Three sites were suggested—two on State Street and another on Superior on the west side of town. After the west side site was selected, construction of two buildings was begun. They wouldn't be completed in time for use during a scheduled summer session of the normal school, of course, so those classes were held at the city's new Union School just east of the Pine River and south of Superior Street.

Cornerstone laying for the larger of the two buildings was to be on May 14, and three thousand outsiders joined Alma residents for the ceremony and a parade. It was a grand procession with Wright's Opera House Band

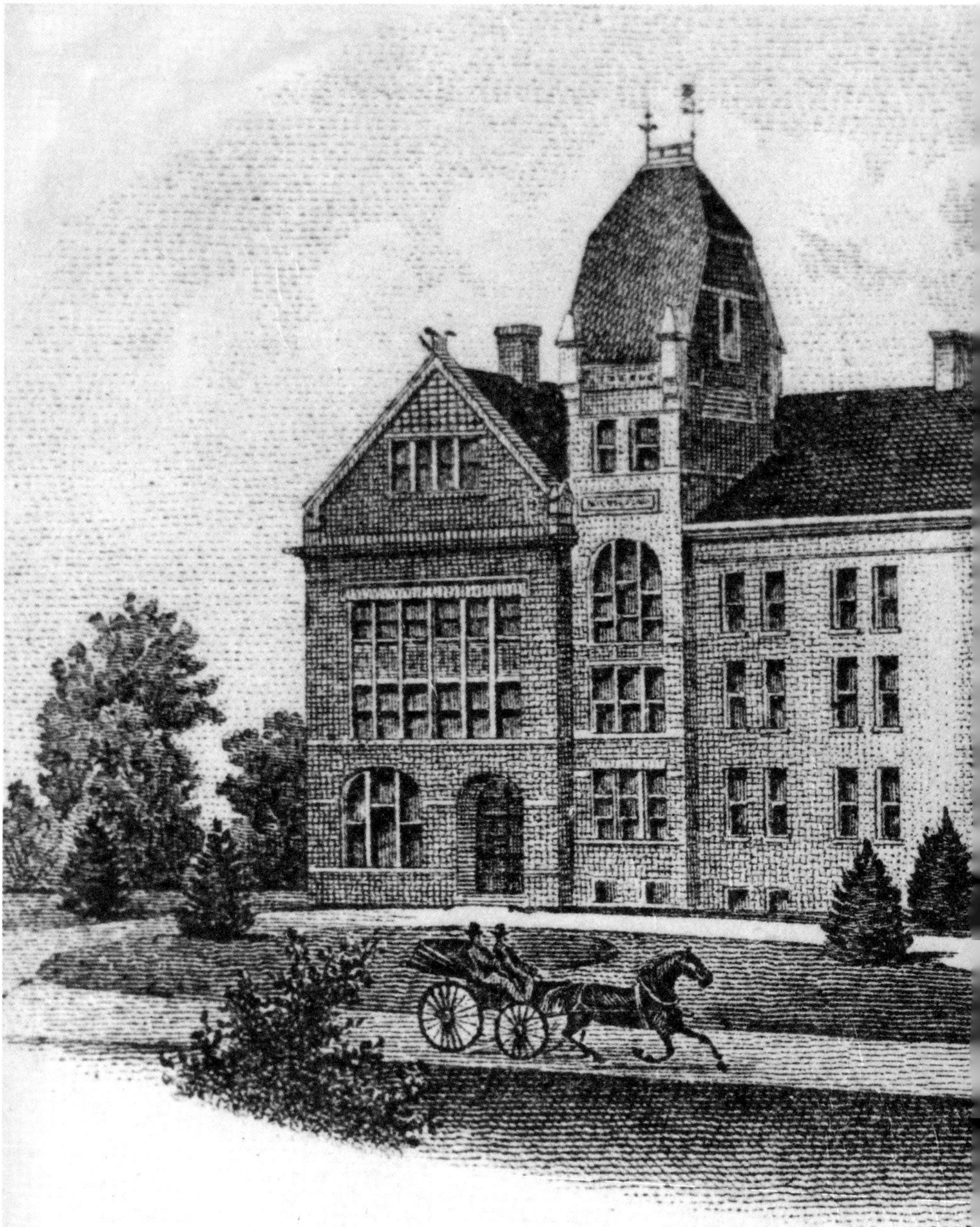

Recitation Hall (left) and Ladies Hall were used briefly by a normal school before Ammi Wright gave them to the Presbyterian Synod of Michigan to establish Alma College. Recitation Hall later became the Administration Building and then was Old Main. Ladies Hall was known to later students as Pioneer Hall. *Courtesy of Alma College Archives.*

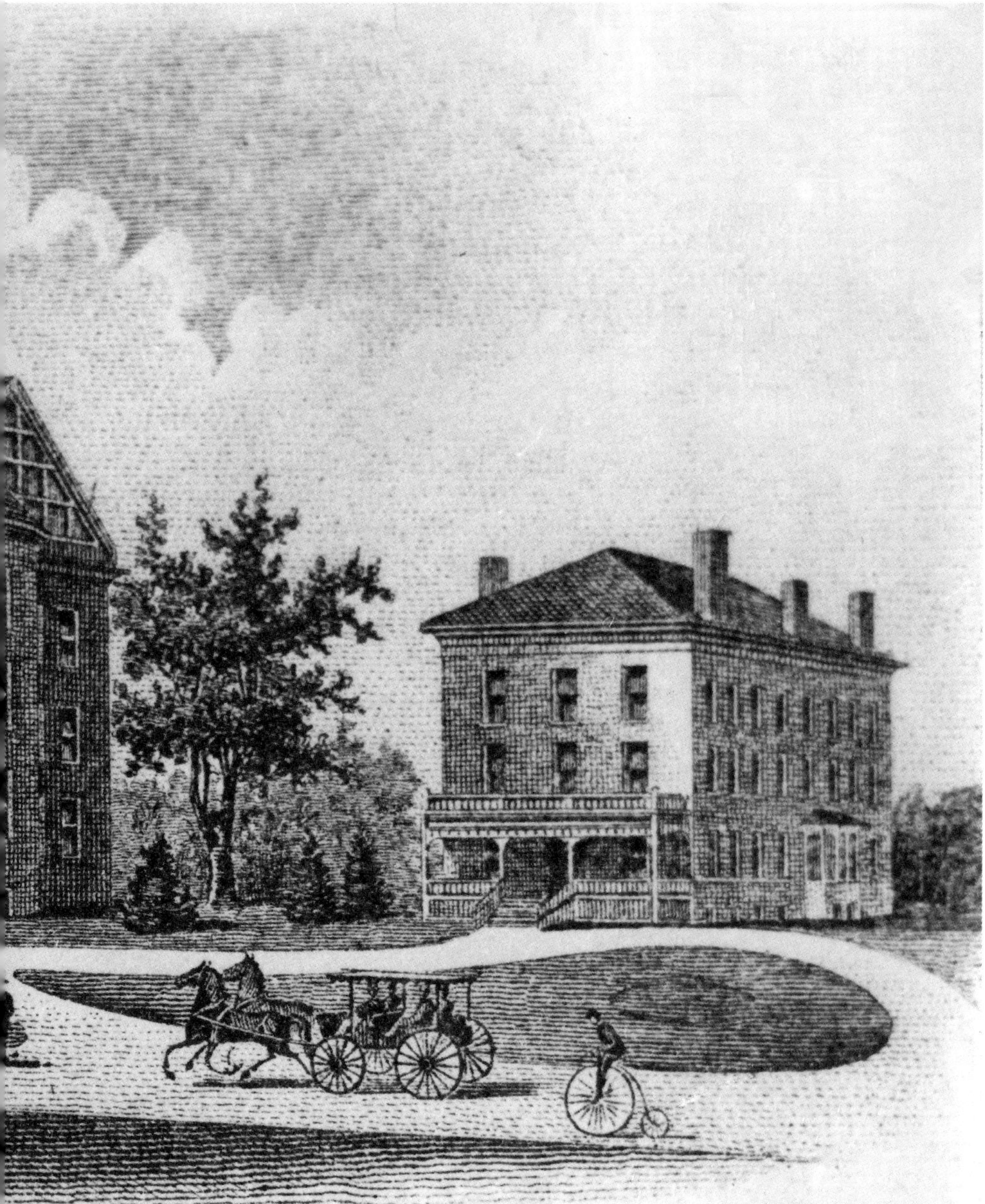

in the lead. Following were members of Alma, St. Louis and Ithaca masonic lodges; the Alma Fire Department; and many Alma citizens, some in carriages and some on foot.

The procession had just started north on State Street from Superior when lightning, thunder, wind and pouring rain scattered the crowd and the marchers. Eventually, the weather improved, and the march resumed. But it didn't get far. Another storm moved in, more severe than the first, and that brought the marching to a final halt. The ceremony for laying of the stone did take place later in the afternoon. However, historian Willard Tucker reported in his 1913 history of Gratiot County that "the address was delivered in the opera house."

During following weeks, construction continued and faculty members were hired. Summer classes for sixty-five students started in July at the Union School. Then in September, after the school's main building was completed and classes of the new normal school began, seventy students had hardly settled into their seats before rumors began spreading that Presbyterians were searching for a mid-Michigan site in which to locate a college. Hopes soared, and steps were taken in several communities to lure the new institution. Among them were Mt. Pleasant, Saginaw, St. Louis, Ithaca and Alma.

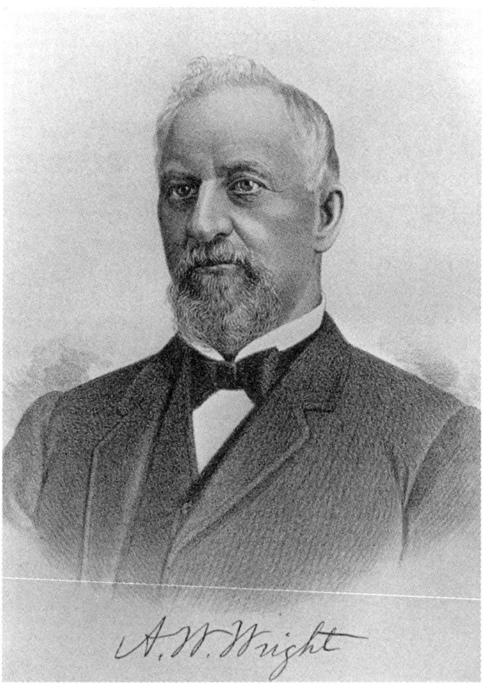

Ammi Wright gave the campus and first two buildings of Alma College to Presbyterians in 1886 and added other significant gifts in future years. *Courtesy of Alma College Archives.*

Again, the persistence of Ammi Wright prevailed. He held the deeds to the site and buildings of the normal school and offered them to the Presbyterians. None of the other contenders could come close to matching that. At the 1886 session of the Presbyterian Synod of Michigan in Westminster Presbyterian Church of Grand Rapids, members resolved, "We will, with God's help, establish and endow a college within our bounds." And that gave birth to Alma College.

The move, to be sure, was the action of just one denomination. But from the beginning, the development and growth of the new school resulted from an amazing ecumenical effort. Important contributions by members of other denominations made the synod's founding resolution a reality. Among them were five men—a proposer (then a Presbyterian but a graduate of a Methodist college and then a Congregational pastor), two persuaders (a Presbyterian and a Baptist) and two generous donors (a Presbyterian and an Episcopalian).

The proposer was August F. Bruske, pastor of Saginaw's First Presbyterian Church, who suggested at the 1885 synod meeting in Detroit that the group form a committee to decide whether it would be possible to create a Presbyterian college in Michigan.

One of the persuaders was J. Ambrose Wight, pastor of Bay City's First Presbyterian Church and chairman of the synod committee that was to consider establishment of a college. His evening sermon on October 18, 1885, told of the need for a Presbyterian College in Michigan. There was no immediate response, but five months later, a member of the congregation, Alexander Folsom, became the first of the generous givers when it was announced that he would donate $50,000 to establish an endowment fund for the school. A selfless as well as generous man, he apparently never had a portrait of himself made—at least, none has been found by his family association or libraries and historical societies in communities where he lived.

The other persuader, Theodore Nelson, was a rather unlikely candidate for involvement in a Presbyterian project. He was a Baptist minister as well as Michigan's superintendent of public instruction. His persuasive powers made Ammi Wright a generous donor when he pressured the wealthy Alma man to give the campus and two buildings to the college. When Wright was asked about Nelson's role in establishment of the college, he replied, "Well, he was always very generous in what he wanted me to give."

When classes began at Alma College, Nelson was its first professor of English. Before that time, he had served as acting president of Kalamazoo College, and after his service on the Alma faculty, he was named Kalamazoo's president. He completed his first term in that role in the fall of 1891, but as the next term began in 1892, he became ill and had to leave. He died on May 1 of that year at the Alma Sanitarium.

Bruske, Wight and Wright all were among the college's first trustees. Another was Russell A. Alger, governor of Michigan at the time and later secretary of war in the cabinet of President William McKinley and then a U.S. senator.

It was on September 14, 1887, that Alma's first students entered the main entrance to Recitation Hall, later known as the Administration Building and finally as Old Main. Thirty-four students registered to begin classes that day, and by the end of the fall term, there were sixty-three. Total attendance for the year was ninety-five.

This three-story main building had, on the first floor, a room for chapel services on one side of a central hallway with a lecture hall opposite. The second floor had a large room for commercial instruction and other classrooms. Another room served as the college's library. More classrooms were on the third floor, along with a botany laboratory. In the basement were a chemistry laboratory and a mailing room.

The other original building was Ladies Hall, a dormitory that in later years was known as Pioneer Hall. Also a structure with three floors, it was steam-heated. A first-floor dining room had seating for 140 persons, as well as two parlors. Forty sleeping rooms, with study rooms adjacent to each, were on the second and third floors. The heating plant, kitchen and a vegetable cellar were in the basement.

The college's first promotional publication, produced in June 1887, noted that the buildings were "on a rise of ground one-half mile west of the business center of the village, overlooking it and commanding a delightful view of fields and farms on every side." The campus had once been part of the farm of Dan Boyer, and at one time there was a blacksmith and gun shop where the first college buildings now stood.

The first phrase of the 1887 promotional piece was "In the Name of God, Amen," later Latinized "*In Nomine Dei, Amen*" and placed at the center of the college seal beneath an image of a pine bough symbolizing the lumbering operations of many early benefactors who made the college a reality.

—Gordon Beld

CHAPTER 2

BIGGER AND BETTER

Classes for the college's first students in 1887 had hardly begun before trustees decided two more structures were needed. Construction was begun on a separate boiler house to replace the heating unit in the basement of Ladies Hall, thus eliminating the danger of an explosion in that building. When completed, the heating plant's eighty-foot chimney often was used as a backdrop by student painters who climbed to the top and emblazoned their class years in white paint. The plant and its chimney were razed in the early 1970s to make room for the academic center.

Work started on the college's first library building in 1888, too. In June, college president August Bruske cleverly converted the cornerstone ceremony into a fundraising event. A special excursion train brought four well-filled coaches of guests from Saginaw and Bay City, and their procession from the depot to the campus was led by Wright's Opera House Band. After the cornerstone was laid, the crowd squeezed into the chapel room of the main building for comments by the president.

According to the local newspaper, Bruske, "in his own peculiar and effective manner, disclosed the real object of this pleasant gathering and, with many sallies of wit, in a very humorous way, made an earnest and importunate plea for the gold and silver necessary to the erection of the building." Before the chapel room doors opened again, pledges totaling $5,000 were secured.

The building opened early in 1889 with a collection of about two thousand books. The large reading room on the first floor had a cozy fireplace. On the

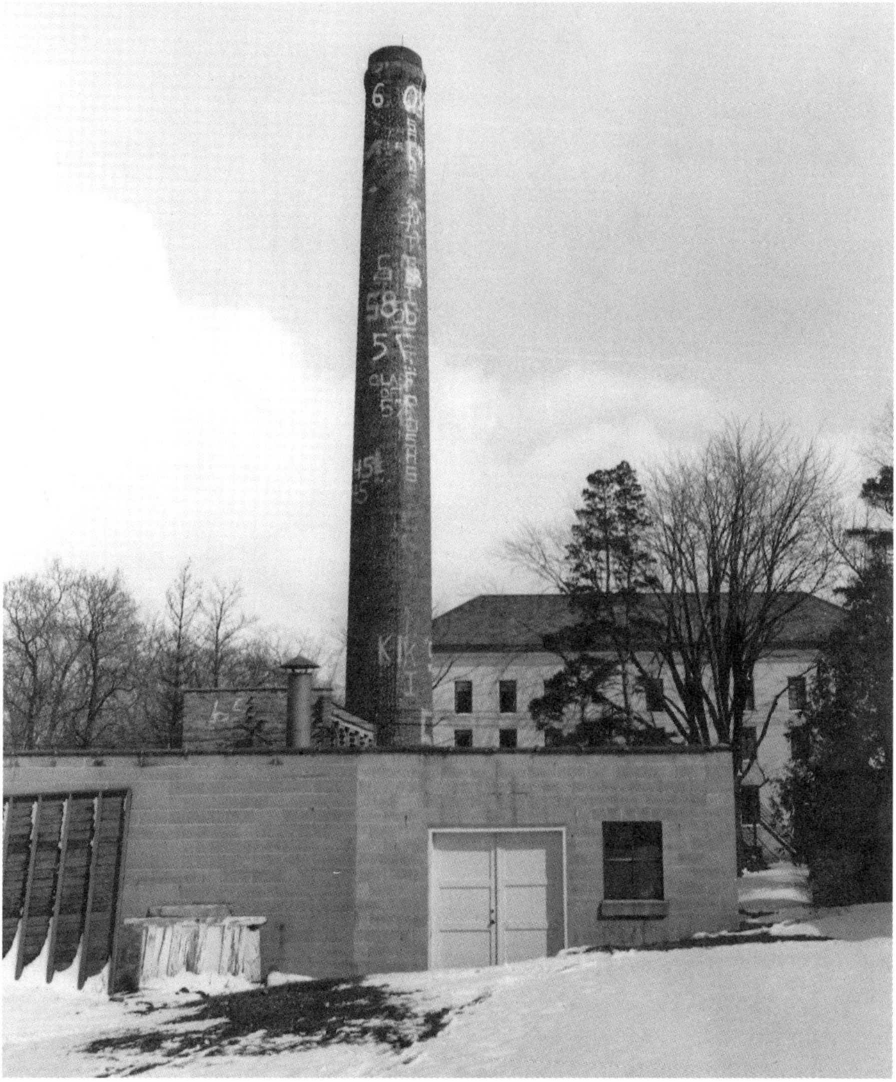

To remove the threat of an explosion from heating boilers in the Ladies Hall basement, a separate heating plant building was constructed in 1888. That solution, however, presented a new hazard—a tall smokestack that daring students climbed to paint numerals of their classes above those of others. *Courtesy of Alma College Archives.*

second floor was another big room, used initially as a gymnasium but later for other purposes.

Steps leading to the entrance were not as impressive. Made of wood, they sometimes disappeared when students lacked other targets for nighttime

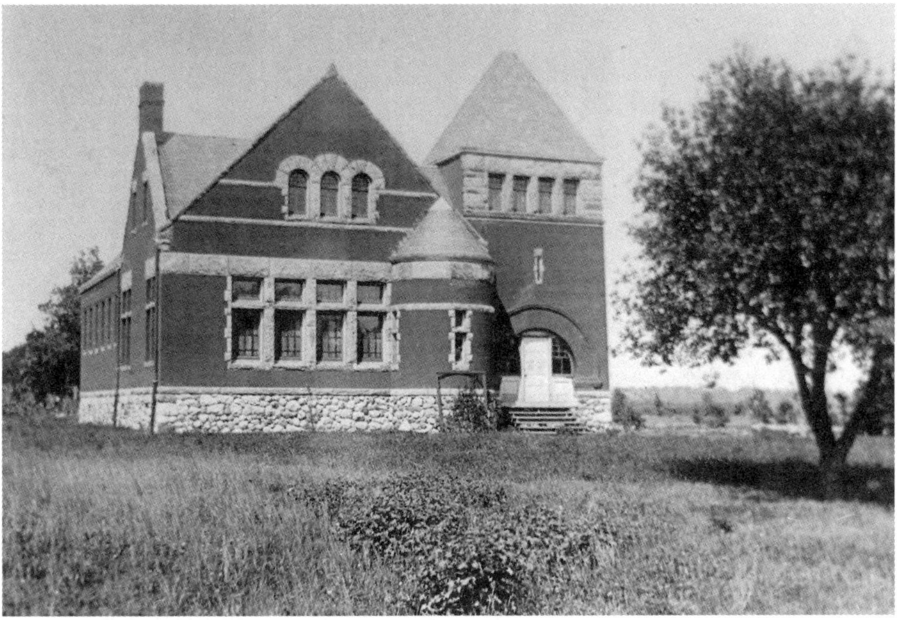

The college's first library, a structure of red brick and sandstone, had a large reading room with a cozy fireplace. Originally, it also had wooden steps at the entrance, and they sometimes disappeared at night. The problem diminished when President Bruske captured one of the kidnappers—and was eliminated when steps of concrete replaced those of wood. *Courtesy of Alma College Archives.*

pranks. That ended within a decade when a few young men who kidnapped the steps were encountered by President Bruske. He captured one and identified the others. Before another year passed, immovable stone steps replaced the old wooden ones.

In June 1894, ground was broken for another building, which included a museum that became home of specimens and artifacts the college had acquired. A window in one of the first-floor rooms had originally been used in the Michigan Building at the Columbian Exposition, held in Chicago in 1893. Of greater interest to many students, perhaps, was a sixty-five- by forty-foot gymnasium on the second floor. Built at a cost of $5,000, the structure was known to later generations as Folsom Hall.

The next addition to the campus came in 1899 when Mrs. Francis Hood and her son, Frank, gave funds to construct an entire building for use as a museum. Now the oldest structure on the Alma campus, Hood Building has served in many ways through the years. During World War I, when most of Alma's male students were members of the Student Army Training Corps, it was a barracks.

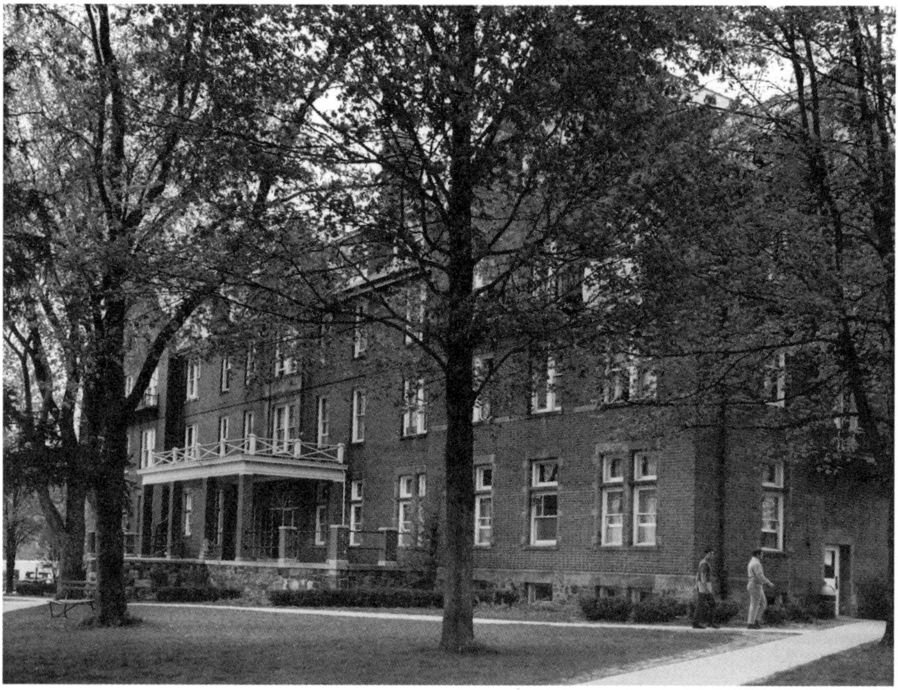

Wright Hall, a four-story dormitory for women, opened in 1902. Later, it was a men's residence before its demolition in 1976, when cost of heating and maintenance became excessive. A smaller, but better, Wright Hall was built on the site in 2005. That apartment-style dorm has design similarities to the first Wright Hall and utilizes solar panels. *Gordon Beld photo; courtesy of Alma College Archives.*

After the war, the building became a museum again, but later it was converted for use by the Biology Department and then for the Departments of Philosophy and Religion. After that, it was used for faculty and staff offices.

In 1900, a gift of land from Ammi Wright and his daughter, Mrs. Sarah Lancashire, expanded the campus to the south side of Superior Street. Wright also offered to build a dormitory on the site with rooms for about 100 women and a dining hall to serve 140 persons. Alma's young ladies moved into the four-story structure in 1902. The new building was known as Wright Hall.

When the women moved out, Ladies Hall became available for men—with a name change, of course. From that time, it was known as Pioneer Hall. Alma's male students previously had rented rooms in private homes.

Electric lights began to be installed in college buildings at this time, but the college library didn't get them until 1913.

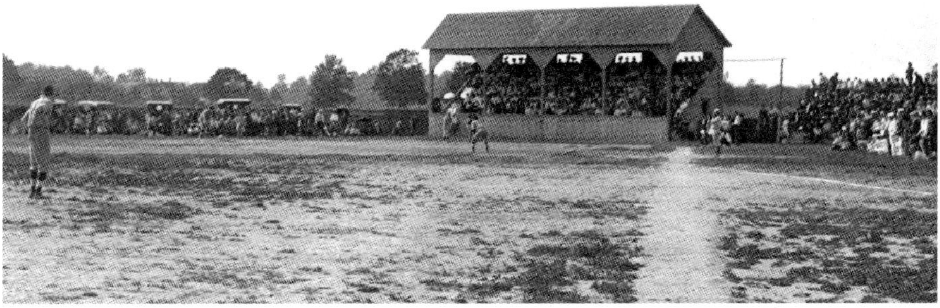

Alma College's first athletic facility, Davis Field, was a gift from Charles Davis of Saginaw. Its covered grandstand provided shelter from sun and rain for spectators at sporting events. It was here that Alma's baseball team defeated the University of Michigan, 4–1, in 1907. *Courtesy of Alma College Archives.*

While Wright Hall was going up, another gift made possible the development of an athletic field. The donor was Charles Davis, a Saginaw lumberman and banker. When completed, its football and baseball fields, tennis courts, quarter-mile cinder track and grandstand with seating for four hundred were surrounded by a high board fence.

An attractive gate was placed at the entrance to the field in 1912, thanks to an additional gift of $500 from Davis. When Bahlke Field became the college's principal athletic facility several years later, the brick-and-iron gateway was moved there.

Meanwhile, during the years of World War I, Davis Field went through tough times. In 1917, a fire, probably caused by careless smoking of neighborhood children, threatened the grandstand but was extinguished by the fire department. A year later, however, the grandstand was flattened by a tornado that also knocked down the fence on three sides of the field. The storm also blew out some windows in Wright Hall and shook plaster off walls at Pioneer. The local newspaper reported that the storm was "possibly caused by atmospheric disturbances due to the explosions in Europe."

In 1918, trustees approved a plan for future campus development, and three more buildings were constructed during the next few decades. The first was a gymnasium, which served as a memorial to the many men and women of the college and Gratiot County who served in military forces during the war.

Memorial Gymnasium's grand opening was in March 1923. Bleachers for 800 spectators were placed along sidelines of the playing floor. When used as an auditorium, with chairs on the floor, it accommodated 950 persons.

Eight acres were added to the campus when Mr. and Mrs. William Bahlke announced at the football banquet in 1923 that they were donating the property for use as a new athletic complex. Lack of sufficient funds stalled the start of development until late in 1926, and the first competition at the new complex was a football game another three years later. On the day it was dedicated, the college band went to the home of Mr. and Mrs. Bahlke and escorted them to the field.

Twenty years later, the field became the pre-season training site for the Detroit Lions. From early August until mid-September 1946, '47 and '48, the pro team worked out on Bahlke Field. The first exhibition game of each season was played at Bahlke in mid-August. Team members and their families were housed in Wright Hall, where they also had dining service.

Another acquisition in 1926 was the house of Jay Clizbe, who had bequeathed it to the college. The gesture was typical of the retired professor of religion who, during his sixteen years on the faculty, had, at his own request, accepted an annual salary of only $200 so as to help the college at a critical period of its history. Its new use was as a music building.

A brick house for the president was built at the corner of Superior and Maple Streets in 1927, replacing one at Superior and Philadelphia Avenue that had been acquired ten years earlier. That one had originally been owned by President Bruske. Today it is Smith Alumni House, headquarters of the college's alumni relations staff.

Dunning Memorial Chapel, a building that has become a symbol of the college and a mid-Michigan landmark, was constructed during the early years of World War II. Its octagonal white steeple topped by a twelve-foot bronze cross towers over the structure of Georgian architecture. Work on the building started in 1940, with hopes that it would be ready for use by commencement the next spring. However, government priorities for steel interrupted construction, and it was not dedicated until October 1941.

In 1949, college administrators were concerned that the peak of the tower of Old Main was showing signs of deterioration and in danger of falling on someone below. The executive committee of the board of trustees agreed and also believed the removal would improve the appearance of the building. Soon after the committee's decision, the top of the tower disappeared.

After the war, a spurt of building activity began in 1952 with construction of the Jerry Tyler Student Center, the first of three connected buildings at

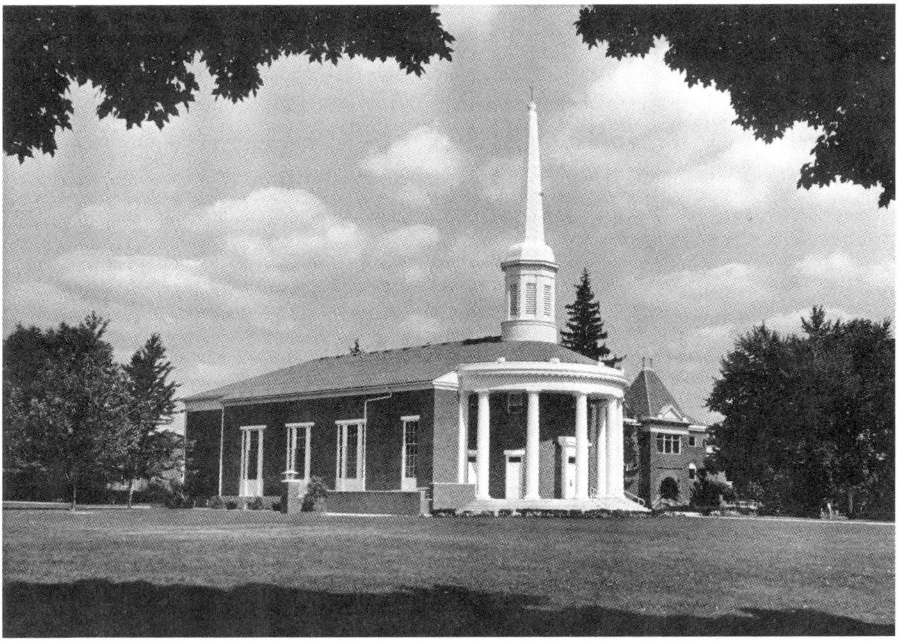

Dunning Memorial Chapel, constructed during World War II, was named for President John Wirt Dunning. The only Alma president who had been a student of the college, he retired because of ill health in 1942, and students requested that the building be named in his honor. *Gordon Beld photo; courtesy of Alma College Archives.*

the southwest corner of the campus. The building had an auditorium, a large lounge with a circular bay of windows and a central fireplace, a game room, snack bar, student post office and lounges.

That building had been completed only a matter of days in 1953 before work started on an adjacent structure, Van Dusen Commons. Its main dining room had seating for five hundred. A breezeway linked the two buildings.

A new headquarters for the college's top administrators was next on the building agenda. Annie Reid Knox, widow of Frank Knox, provided funds for a building that was completed in 1955. Knox, a member of Alma's first football team and the college's best-known alumnus, had been publisher of the *Chicago Daily News*, Republican candidate for vice president in 1936 and secretary of the navy during World War II. Besides offices of the president and others, Reid-Knox Administration Building had a large conference room containing several of Knox's personal items. Among them were the desk he used while at the head of the *Daily News* and his chair during days as a member of the cabinet of President Franklin D. Roosevelt.

In 1955, ground was broken for a new women's residence, which was connected to Van Dusen Commons. Completed the next year, it was named Mary C. Gelston Hall in honor of the college's first dean of women. She was a member of the faculty during the college's first two decades of operation. Construction of the building made the former women's dormitory, Wright Hall, available for use by male students.

Obviously, Alma's campus had experienced impressive improvements during the first seven decades of its existence. But the biggest building burst was yet to come. That would be during the administration of President Robert D. Swanson, which began in 1956.

—Gordon Beld

Chapter 3

STILL BIGGER, THE BOG

As additional buildings began to be constructed on the campus in the late 1880s, adequate facilities for instruction in most subject areas were provided. However, as far as Professor Charles A. Davis was concerned, something more was needed. Davis, Alma's first instructor of natural science, wanted an undeveloped tract where he could take his students for study and research. He found it twelve miles west of town.

In 1889, when Davis first took his students there, it was known to nearby residents as the Vestaburg Bog. Its location was near the Montcalm County community of Vestaburg, and at the center of the tract was a spongy floating mat bog surrounding a small lake. Around this was a distinct zone of spruce and tamarack that, in turn, was ringed by hardwoods.

After Davis left Alma to accept a position at the University of Michigan, Professor E.N. Transeau of the Biology Department took his students to Vestaburg by train during the first decade of the 1900s, and they walked to the bog.

Then the area was neglected until the 1940s, when Professor Ronald O. Kapp took his biology classes there to study. Research was limited, however, because scientific instruments could not be left behind without risk of vandalism. Since the college did not own the property, it could not erect protective facilities.

To rectify that situation, forty acres of the tract were purchased in 1964. During subsequent years, more acreage was added, and today its nearly two hundred acres are about twice the size of the main campus in Alma. It is now known as the Alma College Ecological Station.

Davis Lake at the center of the station is named in honor of Professor Davis. Writing about him in *Within Our Bounds*, Alma College's centennial history, Kapp said, "Perhaps no other Alma faculty member has achieved equivalent stature in his field."

Considered one of the most distinguished botanists, he also invented mechanical devices such as the Davis peat sampler. At Alma, he taught chemistry, botany, zoology, physiology, geology and physical geography. Despite that heavy teaching load, he published fifteen research papers while at the college. When he left Alma, he was replaced by two faculty members.

After he went to Ann Arbor in 1901, he completed his studies on the origin of peat that were begun at Alma. His three-hundred-page manuscript, "Davis on Peat," was published by the Michigan Geological Survey in 1907. Later, Davis served as a peat expert for the U.S. Department of the Interior.

Davis's example of extensive research set a pattern for later Alma educators who, often along with students, produced reports of their findings in biology and other disciplines as well.

Typical of the fascinating research projects conducted at the bog was a 1960s tree identification effort by Alma senior Jeanne Gilliam of Warren and Professor Kapp. Their observance of the trees required more than a stroll through the forest to check leaves and bark. They were interested in trees that lived as long as twelve thousand years ago. To identify them, they needed pollen. And it was to be found at the bottom of Davis Lake.

Their ultimate goal was to discover the kinds of vegetation in the area at various periods since the glacier that swept across North America thousands of years ago receded. To determine that, they needed to take samples from several levels of the thirty-three feet of sediment under about twenty feet of water at the bottom of the lake. Some probes were made from atop the floating mat that rimmed the lake, but it also was necessary to obtain pollen from the center of the lake.

Gilliam and Professor Kapp, along with two male students who helped with the more rugged aspects of the process, ventured out atop ice in the lake during the winter of 1965–66 to take samples. After chopping a hole in the ice, they placed a casing of two-and-a-half-inch pipe through it to the bottom of the lake. Into this they inserted a two-inch-diameter peat sampler attached to a section of one-inch pipe.

As the sampler was sent deeper into the sediment, additional sections of the narrower pipe were screwed into place, and when the sampler was raised to the surface, these sections had to be unscrewed. Each time the sampler

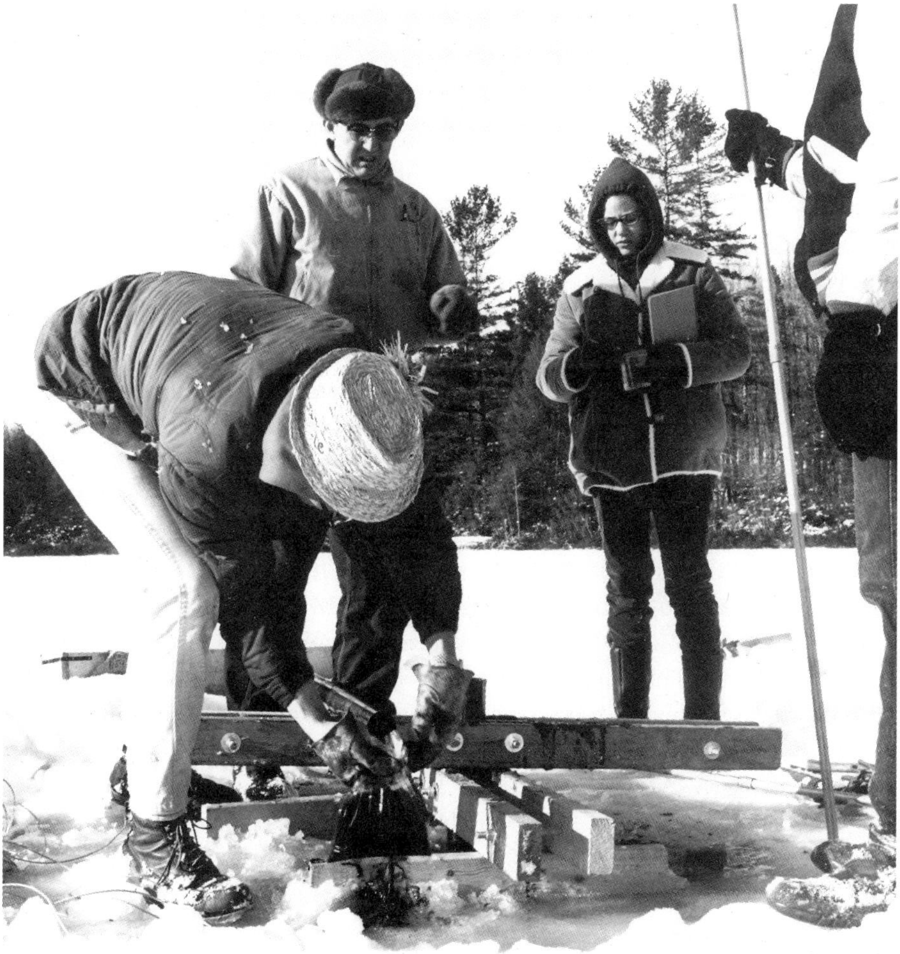

Atop the ice of Davis Lake, a student adjusts the wooden frame that will hold a casing through which a peat sampler will be inserted. The sampler is held by another assistant (right), while Professor Ronald Kapp and Jeanne Gilliam observe. Later lab analysis of the peat enabled Gilliam to determine the kinds of vegetation that had been at the site during the past twelve thousand years. *Gordon Beld photo; courtesy of Alma College Archives.*

was brought up, the sediment in it was forced into plastic bags, which were numbered to indicate the level from which it was taken.

Eventually, only sand came up in the sampler, and the researchers knew they had reached the point where a huge block of glacial ice melted 120 centuries ago. The last samples taken, of course, contained pollen of the earliest vegetation after the glacier melted.

The coldest and dirtiest part of the job was over, but Gilliam still faced the time-consuming task of identification. Back in a laboratory at Dow Science Center, she laid out the bags of sediment and took from each a small amount, which she bottled. To get samples with a concentrated amount of pollen, she treated the sediment with chemicals and whirled it in a centrifuge. This eliminated sand, marl, wood particles, other debris and water.

A few drops of each sample were placed on glass slides and, one by one, viewed with a high-power microscope. After counting the pollen grains at each level, she made a diagram to show the kinds of vegetation that grew in the Vestaburg area long before men were actually there.

Her efforts showed that many spruce trees grew soon after the glacier melted. A predominantly pine forest came next, and then the pines declined and oak trees increased greatly.

Gilliam and Professor Kapp completed the report of their research in time to present it at a session of the Michigan Academy of Sciences, Arts and Letters in April 1966.

Through the years, many other Alma students have conducted research projects at the station, which now includes a 1,600-square-foot research facility, 70-foot observation tower, 75-foot boardwalk to Davis Lake, trails and the Alma College Bird Observatory.

—Gordon Beld

Chapter 4

CHANGES IN THE CHURCH

Michigan's Presbyterians sensed the need for a college long before they founded Alma College. In 1837, they built a college in Marshall, Michigan, but it did not survive. Other denominational schools—Kalamazoo, Albion, Adrian, Hope, Olivet and Hillsdale—all predated the founding of Alma College. Many Presbyterian students attended the University of Michigan, but as that school grew more secular, the need for a Presbyterian College to train young men and women in Christian ministry became more obvious.

A committee reported to the Synod of Michigan in 1886 that the upper two-thirds of the state lacked educational opportunities above the level of the public school. Towns and villages were springing up in that developing part of the state, and Christian workers were needed. Soon the Synod declared its intention of starting a school in what then was considered the northern part of the state, an area now classified as central Michigan.

The establishing committee declared from the start that Alma College would not be strictly a sectarian institution, proselytizing students into Presbyterianism. It was declared to be a liberal arts college in the truest and traditional sense yet with a strong Christian foundation, "a college of high literary and scientific character permeated with the spirit of Christ." Thus, while it was not sectarian, Christian standards were powerfully present from the beginning.

In its youth, Alma College struggled with its identity as a Presbyterian school. Because it was geographically distant from the majority of large

Presbyterian churches in Michigan, it did not receive the financial support that was expected from them. Some churches thought of the college as the child of Presbyterians in the Saginaw Valley and continued to send their children to the University of Michigan. President August Bruske spent much of his time in southern Michigan attempting to persuade churches that Alma College was indeed the official Presbyterian college in Michigan, and they needed to fund it to keep the college open. He managed to raise some money for the school, but more importantly, he attracted students to the new institution.

Most of the school's early students considered themselves to be Christian, and the activities at Alma College reflected this. A writer for the school's newspaper, the *Almanian,* opined in 1898, "If the last Day of Prayer for Colleges was not a farce, as some boldly called it, the day was certainly less than it ought to have been. Of all days in the college year, this day should be the most sacred and holy." The day had been marred by a lack of solemnity.

The school, besides offering general programs, was preparing Presbyterian ministers and missionaries. In 1898, three young men—William Henry Long, John Bartlett Stevens and James Irving Crane—graduated and went off to seminary at Princeton University, a school with close ties to the Presbyterian Church.

The YMCA and YWCA were strong organizations in the early years of the college. In 1897, an Alma College delegation to the national YMCA convention in Lake Geneva, Wisconsin, traveled there on "wheels." Among the group who biked the distance were Professor John T. Ewing and the popular and irrepressible Frank Knox. YMCA members worked in local Sunday schools and, in the summer, served in churches in Michigan, Indiana and Wisconsin. The *Almanian* declared, "We trust the work will be blessed and the Master's kingdom extended thereby."

The Christian organizations on campus were influential and active. The YWCA in 1900 purchased and dressed forty-one dolls, which were sent to Detroit and Ann Arbor, where they were distributed among poor and sick children. The YMCA raised thirty dollars, a considerable sum at that time, for famine relief, to be sent to India through the Presbyterian Board of Foreign Missions. For the "Ys," evangelism of the world was the goal.

Miss Bernice Hunting, class of '91, went off on an investigative journey to Tripoli, so that she might establish herself there in the work of her choice while serving as a Christian witness. Clara Booth-McKee, '96, moved to Bankok, Siam, as a missionary. Richard Sidebotham, '96, sailed to Taiku, Korea. There he was attacked by a band of marauding robbers

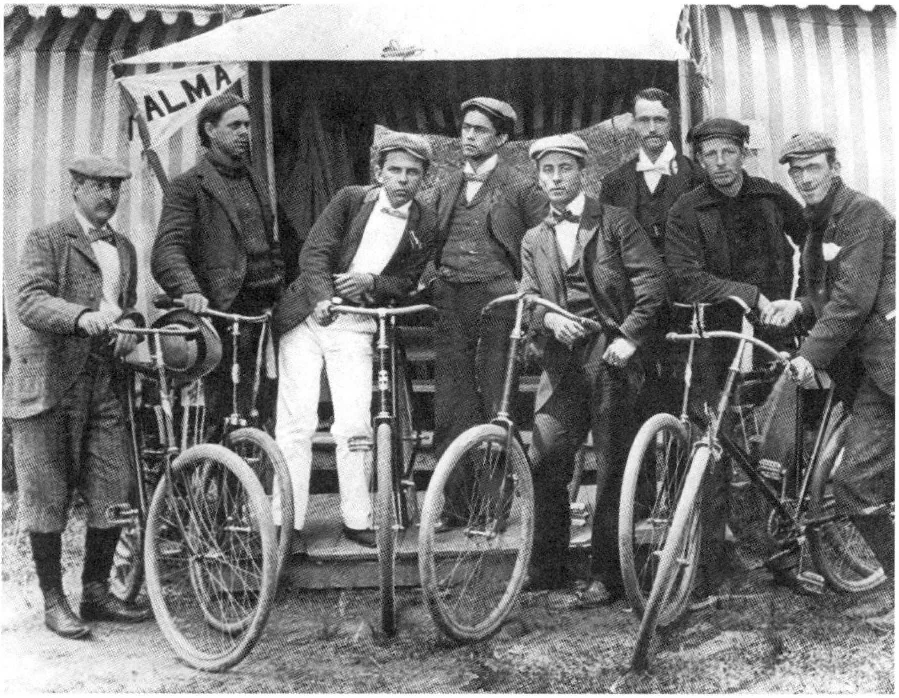

Biking from Alma to a YMCA conference at Lake Geneva, Wisconsin, in the 1890s was this group of students and Professor J.T. Ewing (far left). Frank Knox (second from right) later was editor and publisher of several newspapers, a vice-presidential candidate and secretary of the navy. *Courtesy of Alma College Archives.*

who took all his possessions and his clothing. Reportedly, he suffered no permanent injuries.

While the "Ys" were active Christian organizations at the college, other activities reflected the college's religious standards. Chapel, held in the Administration Building auditorium, was a daily requirement. The college prayer meeting was held weekly. It faded during the Great War but was revived in 1919, with the claim that "the importance of the prayer meeting cannot be emphasized too strongly."

Alma students were invited by Alma churches to attend Rally Day in October. Said the *Almanian*, "Coming as it does at the beginning of college, Rally Day brings an appeal to every student, which should be heeded. What a fellow starts out to do when he commences the year in school, he is likely to make his habit. If he starts out staying away from church, studying on Sunday, and being indifferent, he'll probably continue."

As it turned out, Rally Day was a booming success, with many students of varying denominations attending the churches of their choice.

By the 1920s, the compulsory chapel was being criticized as too confining and not offering the freedom that should be inherent in a liberal arts institution. The topics in the chapel services were as often secular as religious, but Reverend Gelston of Alma's First Presbyterian Church told students plainly that cheating in the classroom was no better than dishonesty in other parts of life. Besides speakers, chapel offered announcements, time for discussions and time for entertainments, such as dramas. The fervor of the old-time chapel services had faded.

Still, there were hints of the old standards. At Founders' Day, speaker Gerrit Diekema, president of the board of trustees of Hope College, criticized the liberal attitude of the University of Michigan toward the Bible and belief in the Godhead. He urged students and citizens of the state to rise in fullest indignation against this agnosticism.

By the 1930s, chapel was still a regular event, but many of the services focused on mundane rather than religious topics. One week, President Harry Means Crooks spoke on the need for reading and prayer. The next day, he talked about exams. Then Professor Roy Hamilton discussed the prospects of Alma College orators in competition. Finally, Crooks took another chapel session to emphasize the need to be a good reader.

The YMCA, after having faded away, was revived in 1930. In the spring, members were already discussing how to welcome incoming freshmen in the fall. The Geneva Camp student conference drew several Alma students in June 1930. It was designed for student workers, leaders, faculty members and pastors—all who were interested in helping college men with their problems.

In 1938, at his first chapel service, President John W. Dunning presented a new slogan for Alma College: "Alma—a laboratory for Christian living." Dunning said he took a view of Christ as a mortal who perfectly achieved the life of God. True religion, said Dunning, was not creedal opinion but the following of Christ. Dunning invited the men of the college to an informal discussion of religious problems. Even when he tried to entice them with dinner, only thirty showed up.

In the 1940s, Spiritual Emphasis Week was held annually in February. The Religious Life Committee offered some suggestions: allow students to select chapel speakers occasionally, sing more familiar hymns, introduce new hymns imaginatively and encourage students to read scripture, offer prayers and present religious dramas. They also urged a spirit of respect and quiet

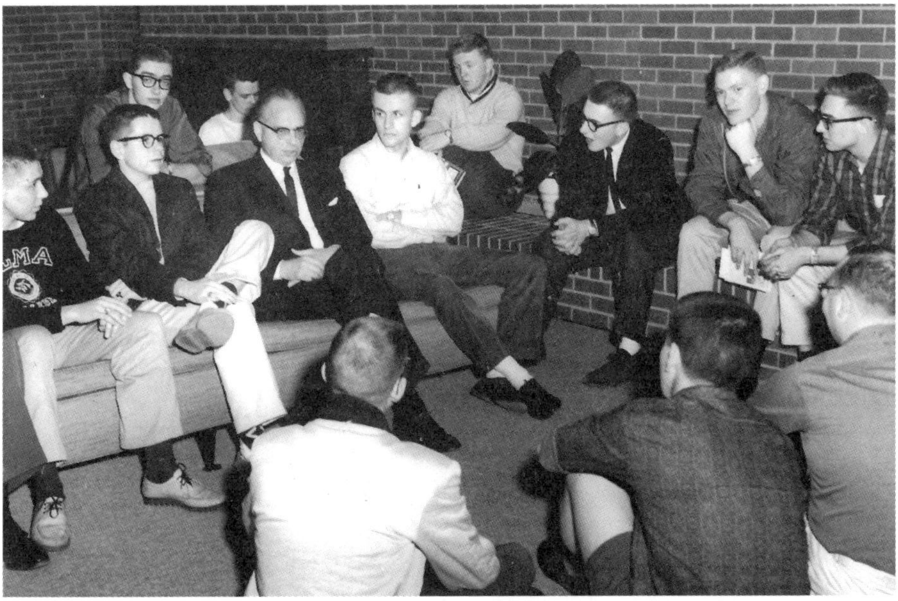

Religion in Life Week in 1961 featured eminent theologian Dr. D. Elton Trueblood, shown here as he meets with Alma men for a question-and-answer period after a chapel service. He referred to Alma College as a place of "great vitality." *John N. Scholl Photo; courtesy of Alma College Archives.*

at the beginning of chapel. Chapel was now being held in the new Dunning Memorial Chapel, named in honor of President Dunning.

Spiritual Emphasis Week in the 1950s reflected the school's strong religious foundations. The speakers were commonly pastors of large Presbyterian churches and were selected because they could communicate with young people. The annual event included sermons, fireside chats, personal conferences with the speakers and a skeptic's hour for discussion on challenging religious topics. The YMCA and YWCA were active on campus once again.

Religious activity was sponsored by the Alma Christian Association in the 1960s. Students were encouraged to perform Christian service by teaching in local Sunday schools, leading youth groups and leading devotions in nursing homes.

In his annual sermon in chapel, Professor J. Tracy Luke posed the question, "How do religious courses fit into an academic setting?" He argued for freedom of the individual to investigate. He said the religious life demanded a surrender to authority, and the intellectual life was to be a life of freedom. Both quests must be grounded in freedom. At a liberal arts college,

Dr. Luke explained, the freedom of religious and intellectual quests is the basic necessity for developing a mature individual.

In a similar light, Chaplain Cornelius Berry spoke of seeking the mind of Christ in the modern world. He promoted a new type of godliness. He explained that it was necessary to be active in the world and no longer claim that Christian discipleship was fulfilled just by being active in the church. He also said that the Bible was no longer regarded as a book of infallible laws for living. People needed to think intelligently about biblical concepts. He also pointed out that true Christianity in the modern world would be ecumenical. It is not acceptable to grow up in the church, said Berry, and pretend that other religions don't exist or have influence.

These bold statements regarding a new religious attitude reflected the general changing times in the United States in the 1960s.

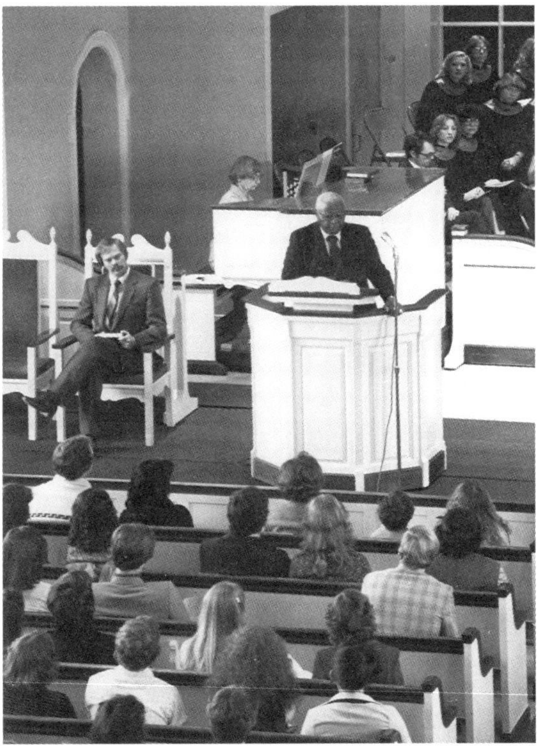

Reverend Martin Luther King Sr. was given a Distinguished Preacher award by Alma College in November 1980. He spoke at a packed Sunday chapel service and met students at a luncheon following the service. *Gordon Beld Photo; courtesy of Alma College Archives.*

Changes in compulsory chapel attendance policies and Bible course requirements opened Alma College to Catholic students. By 1985, Catholic students composed nearly a third of the student body. These students were served by Father Thomas Firestone, who offered mass every Sunday in the chapel.

The Fellowship of Christian Athletes was a new organization on campus in 1983, and it quickly garnered eighty-five members. It welcomed both male and female student athletes of all religious denominations and met each Monday evening in the chapel lounge.

One of the key features of the school's religious life in the 1990s was volunteerism. Under Chaplain Jesse Perry, students were encouraged to become involved in Habitat for Humanity, the Red Cross, the Commission on Aging, Big Brothers/Big Sisters, Youth for Christ, the Masonic Home and His Place Family Enrichment Center.

A major change in the religious affiliation of Alma College and the Presbyterian Synod occurred in 1970 when the charter was rewritten to call for the election of trustees by the board of trustees rather than by the Synod of Michigan. This change in control resulted from many changes in society and the church. Not as much funding was available to the college from churches, and government involvement in all levels of education challenged church-related colleges. Additionally, students at Alma College were coming from a variety of church and non-church backgrounds.

Over the years at Alma College, interpretation of Christian practices and teachings underwent a gradual metamorphosis. A denominationally diverse student body, as well as many secular influences, gradually moved the school from its conservative beginnings to a more liberal practice of Christianity.

—David McMacken

Charles Ernest Scott: Missionary

Charles Ernest Scott was perhaps the most famous missionary graduate of Alma College. He was an orphan adopted and educated by Charles and Mary Scott, a devout couple who were instrumental in establishing the Presbyterian church in Alma. He attended Alma College, where he was active in the YMCA, excelled in track and field and proved to be both a talented vocalist and prize-winning orator. He graduated from Alma College in 1898, briefly taught history in Alma public schools and was licensed to preach by the Saginaw Presbytery in 1902. Having received a scholarship, he attended seminary at Princeton University. During his Princeton days, he married Clara Heywood.

Even after he no longer lived in Alma, he never forgot his Alma roots. During summers, he returned to Alma and preached in churches in the Saginaw Presbytery. He studied abroad and in 1906 received his divinity degree from Princeton, one of his favorite professors having been Woodrow Wilson. The Scotts became the parents of Elizabeth Scott in 1906 while C.E. Scott was pastoring a church in Albion, Michigan. They had already been designated by the Presbyterian Church as missionaries to China.

During their early years in China, the Scotts became the parents of two more girls and two boys. As the children reached school age, they were sent to a school for foreign children. When Reverend Scott returned to the United States in 1914, he was already celebrated in Presbyterian circles for his effective leadership in the church's extensive mission work in China. While lecturing across the United States, he was asked to deliver the commencement address at Alma College. The college bestowed on him an honorary degree of doctor of divinity.

In 1917, he published China From Within, *a highly regarded book depicting the rise of Christian influence among many of the Chinese leaders. Scott was instrumental in establishing the North China Theological Seminary. In 1923, the family came home on furlough, and daughter Elizabeth stayed in the United States to attend Wilson College. Later she enrolled in Moody Bible Institute in Chicago. There she met a young man named John Stam. Feeling called to be missionaries to China, the two were married in China in October 1933. In September 1934, their little girl Helen Priscilla was born.*

By this time, a strong communist influence had grown in areas of China. On December 6, 1934, the Red Army troops entered the city where the Stams were living. With little warning, the Stams suddenly were captured in their house. The couple and their child were taken away and locked in the local prison. Prisoners were released to make room for them. When a soldier suggested that they kill the baby, one of the prisoners said, "Why kill her? What harm has she done?" Asked if he would die for the foreign baby, he nodded, and they hacked him to pieces on the spot. Baby Helen's life was spared.

A ransom of $20,000 was demanded by the communists. On December 7, John and Betty Stam were taken to the summit of a hill where, before a mocking crowd, they were beheaded. Baby Helen had been left on a bed, and thirty-six hours later, she was found unharmed. Chinese Christians spirited her across the country to safety, and she was called the "Miracle Baby."

The deaths of John and Betty Stam shook the Christian world in Europe and North America. Because of their martyrdom, seven hundred students at Moody Bible Institute and two hundred students at Wilson College consecrated themselves to Christian service. Reverend Scott wrote of his daughter and son-in-law, "The blood of the martyrs is still the seed of the church." The seed of Betty Stam's dedicated ministry grew from her father's childhood in Alma and education at Alma College.

—David McMacken

Chapter 5

The College and the Town

When the Central Michigan Normal School moved from Fenton, Michigan, to Alma in 1886, the two new buildings promised to the school were still under construction. Citizens were asked to house students who were from out of town, and a number of families took in student boarders. Once the ladies' dormitory was finished, the girls moved in. Men continued to live with town families.

Even though the normal school lasted for only one summer school session and a full year, the precedent had been set that drew the town and the institution together. As Alma College in 1887 succeeded the normal school, the men still boarded with town families. In general, the town was pleased to have Alma College, for students, professors and administrators would be spending a sizable amount of money for everyday living needs, and the students exuded youthful energy.

At first, Alma folks worried that the school would be a strictly Presbyterian institution whose chief purpose was to train ministers and missionaries and proselytize non-Presbyterian students. Assured that the new college was nonsectarian in its goals and that it would be a liberal arts college in the truest sense, the townspeople's concern diminished.

The town got used to having college students about, and they were a serious, mostly religious lot. The fact that they were able to attend a four-year college set them apart. Those who didn't need the four-year training entered several other programs that proved popular—commercial, music and art. The versatility of the programs was a strong selling point, and many Alma youths took advantage of the new college in their hometown.

Early on, it became clear that the survival of the college depended on whether the institution could balance its budget, and that was not easy. Alma citizen and business tycoon Ammi Wright, founder and devotee of the college, was regarded as one of Michigan's wealthiest men. Trustees often turned to him to rescue the school when liabilities outweighed assets. His wealthy lumbermen associates and friends in Saginaw and Bay City also chipped in when times were tough. The state synod was another source of income. Still, it was a struggle for the college to remain open, and once these men had passed on, the ready sources of income dried up.

In reaching out to the community, the college did not expect to receive many donations from the common citizen. Still, the city was supportive of the college, and in 1908, the editor of the *Almanian* made that clear. He reminded students that the city had helped fund a band the year before. Two years earlier, townsfolk had helped fund athletics, and in 1907, the villagers had helped pay for athletic honors trophies. He wrote, "That the college makes the town has been often remarked by those who have not put any serious thought on the matter, but that the town makes the college cannot be denied." He also suggested, "The typical college town is where the two, town and college, are one."

If large gifts had originally come from a few wealthy men like Wright, soon every penny and dime were important, no matter the source. As Alma College struggled into the twentieth century, the college president was often traveling, beating the bushes for funds. It helped that young men and young ladies became active in Presbyterian churches during summer break, preaching and assisting in Sunday schools. Their positive examples shook loose a few dollars.

The college also expanded its influence by offering off-campus classes in neighboring towns. Professors would board the train and travel to surrounding communities to offer a single class session or a series of sessions that would result in college credit. Alma College offered extension classes even before the Michigan Agricultural College began its celebrated extension programs.

Various college activities drew in Alma's citizens. As the college developed athletic teams, football and track being the most popular in the early days, locals became faithful supporters of the Maroon and Cream. The college's cultural influence was important, too, as speakers and musical groups attracted local citizens. Students often used Wright's Opera House downtown for theatrical productions. Many students attended the "College Church," the Presbyterian church three blocks from campus on Superior Street. The congregation was a mixture of townsfolk, college staff and college students.

Wars united the college and the Gratiot community, as evidenced by the Memorial Gymnasium, which the community financed and built to honor World War I casualties. World War II also drew the college and community together in a common goal shown by Red Cross work, war bond sales campaigns and the V-12 program for naval men that was housed at the college.

Still, a gradual gap had grown between the college and the town in the 1920s and '30s. Alma College became known to townies as "the college on the hill." The breach was not a deliberate thing. It seemed to happen during the struggles of the Depression. While the idea of the college being a world unto itself unfortunately had appeared, the faculty and staff remained very much a part of the community. Some professors were very active in local churches, civic organizations and community activities. Their children attended the local schools. They shopped with everyone else in local stores. Most were far from any ivory tower, but the sense of isolation seemed to prevail.

This sense of estrangement persisted until after World War II. At that time, the cooperation between town and gown engendered by the war was maintained when the Alma Chamber of Commerce pledged to help the college by encouraging students to enroll. The college, likewise, encouraged more community use of its facilities. The school made a deliberate effort to tap into the resources of the alumni, the church and the community.

The individual most responsible for bringing college and city together was the college's ninth president, Robert D. Swanson, who arrived in 1956. His efforts to draw in the community were purposeful and visionary. He joined and promoted local committees and organizations. Besides meeting with local businessmen and leaders, he instituted community breakfasts. About 150 people were invited to campus to have a meal with President Swanson and, in so doing, found out much about the college that perhaps they had not known. Swanson hosted between ten and fifteen breakfasts over a two-week period. These meetings generated goodwill and encouraged guests to consider the needs of the college.

Swanson effectively touted the advantages of an education at Alma College. Key movers in the college's public relations efforts during his administration

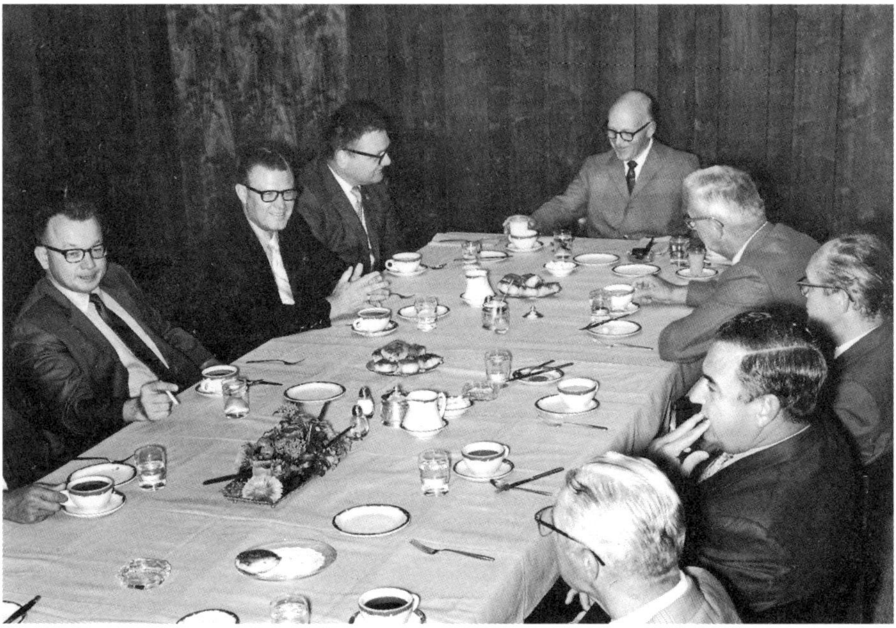

President Swanson met often with community leaders at on-campus breakfasts during which he updated them concerning college operations and needs and solicited their support. *Courtesy of Alma College Archives.*

were vice-presidents Harold "Hod" Vanden Bosch and Guile Graham. Estate planning was also developed. In community outreach, the college invited the citizens to use the library and gymnasium facilities. Grants allowed the college to initiate community education programs in twenty-six school districts. Some college courses were opened to the public at reduced rates. Recognizing the large number of alumni who remained in the Alma area, the Greater Gratiot Community Fund Drive was begun. Contributions from individuals, businesses and industries affirmed the importance of the college to the community.

Besides soliciting donations from a supportive community, the college returned its thanks through cultural and arts programs that drew many attendees from the community. Whether from college-produced theatrical or musical productions or from well-known performers and speakers brought in from outside, the cultural life of the community has been greatly enriched by the college.

Sporting events also attract a large number of community members. When the Scot football team takes the field at Bahlke Stadium, among the cheering spectators are many local fans.

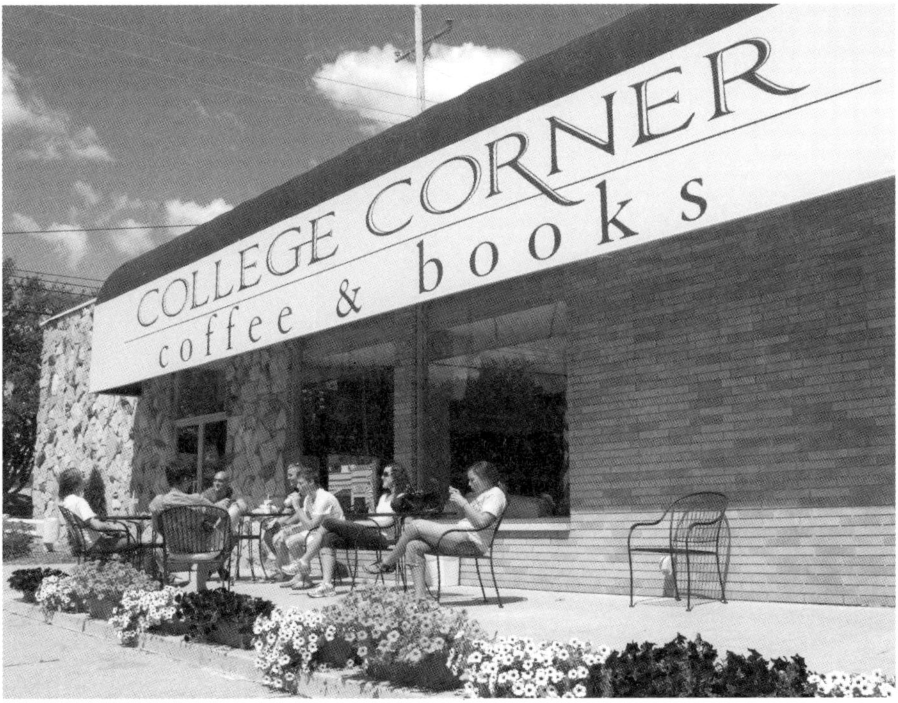

In an attempt to bring townsfolk and students closer together, the college purchased and renovated this former drugstore at the edge of downtown Alma and converted it to a bookstore and restaurant. It is now a popular gathering place for persons from the campus and the community. *Courtesy of Alma College Communication and Marketing Office.*

The blending of town and gown is part of the master plan of the college in the twenty-first century. The natural demarcation between the college and the downtown traditionally has been the railroad tracks that now run through an expanding campus. Stepping over that line, the college bought an abandoned drugstore off campus and installed the college bookstore there. A restaurant, popular with students and faculty as well as townsfolk, is also housed in the building.

The college also has moved to increase its enrollment, thus necessitating additional student housing. The college decided not to construct any more freestanding dormitories but to take advantage of unused space in the upper floors of buildings in the downtown area. Wright's Opera House Block, a large three-story business building that suffered a fire in 2010, has been rehabbed and repurposed into student housing.

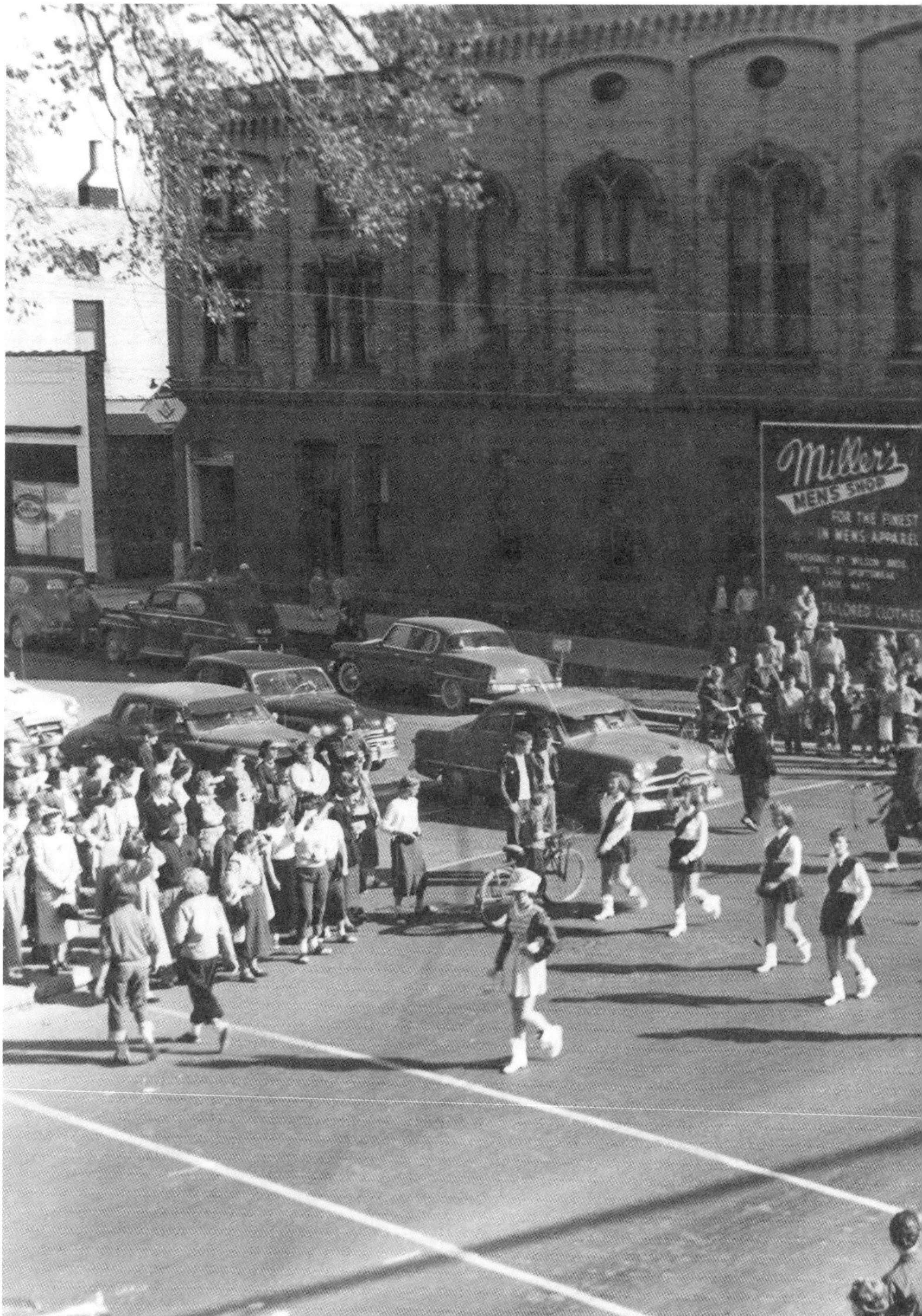
Miller's
MENS SHOP
FOR THE FINEST
IN MENS APPAREL
TAILORED CLOTHES

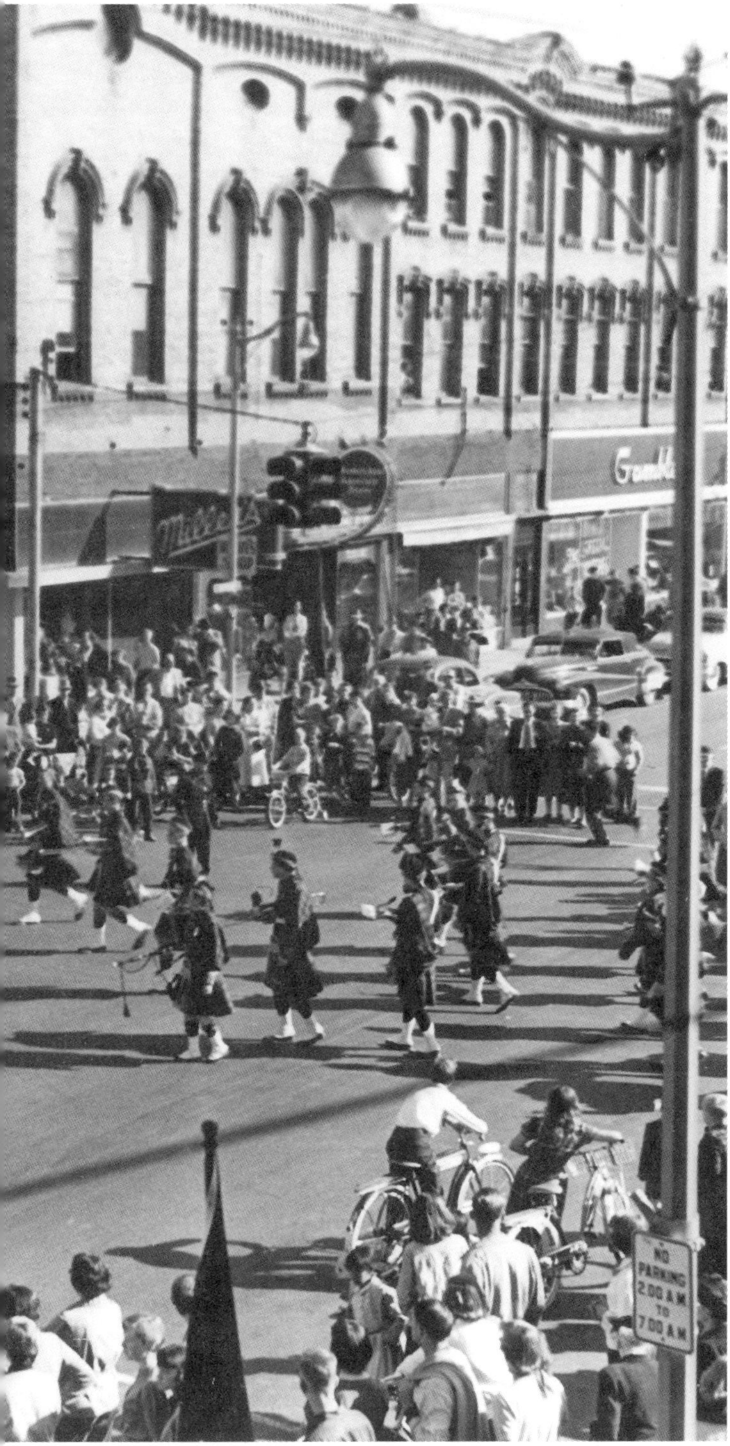

The Kiltie Band passes through Alma's principal downtown intersection during the 1953 homecoming parade. The building in the background is Wright's Opera House Block, where part of the 1886 cornerstone-laying ceremonies for the college's first two buildings were held. Though damaged by a 2010 fire, the opera house building has been restored. Its upper floors will provide apartments for Alma College senior honors students. *Courtesy of Alma College Archives.*

Through conscious efforts, Alma College has attempted to erase any barriers that have been raised between it and the town. Not wanting to be known as "the college on the hill," it has become unquestionably a vital part of the Alma community.

—DAVID MCMACKEN

CHAPTER 6

BEST OF THEM ALL

Many wise and energetic leaders have made major contributions that advanced Alma College to its present prestigious position. None, however, has yet matched the performance of Robert D. Swanson, longest serving president of the school.

In the mid-1950s, despite a recent surge of additions and improvements to facilities, the college was struggling. In search of a remedy, trustees hired a consulting firm. When its study was completed, the advice was to give up and let the institution die.

But trustees ignored the recommendation, and Dr. Swanson was invited to become the college's president. He had been a member of the faculty of Park College in Missouri, a pastor in Oklahoma and a navy chaplain during World War II. In 1956, he was vice-president of McCormick Theological Seminary in Chicago.

When he arrived on the Alma campus that year, he assured faculty members that he hoped for orderly change and development rather than revolution. Students loved his humility and friendliness and were impressed when he joined the younger freshmen in wearing a green "pot" like those they doffed at the command of upperclassmen. Though he was formally addressed by students and others as "Dr. Swanson," close colleagues called him "Bob." Eventually, in third-person references to him, however, the name used by all on the campus was "Swannie."

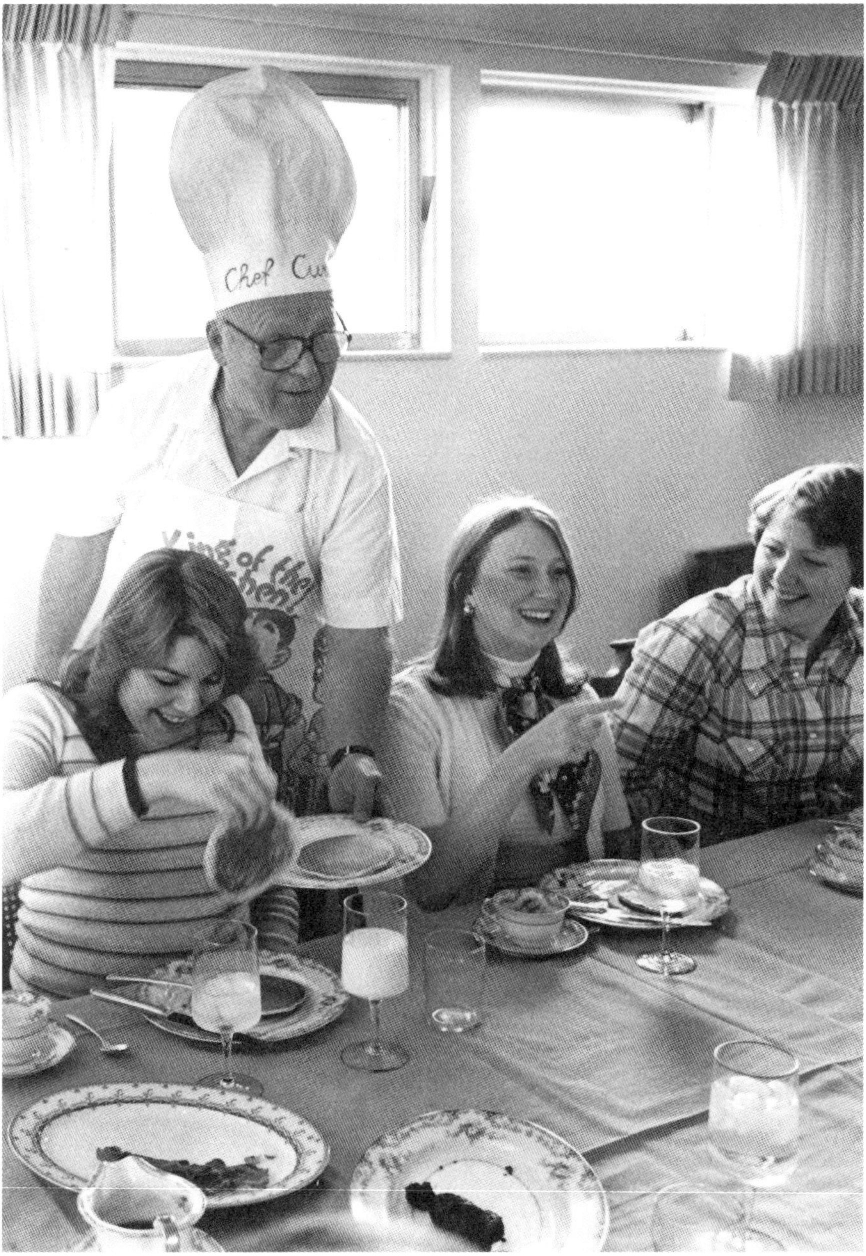

President Swanson's offer of the use of his home for a sleepover and a pancake breakfast, cooked and served by him, was the most popular entry in a 1978 auction at which students bid for items made available by members of the college staff. Proceeds of the annual auctions helped to fund the Africa Fellowship Program, which enabled Alma students to spend a year teaching in Nigeria. *Gordon Beld photo; courtesy of Alma College Archives.*

During the twenty-four years he served as Alma's leader, the college's enrollment grew from 657 to 1,212, and the faculty nearly doubled as well. Endowment increased from $375,000 to more than $12 million, and college assets went from $3 million to $33 million.

Academic quality soared, too. That began to happen shortly after Swanson came to Alma. Inadequate effort by students prompted him to shake up the campus one morning with the sudden announcement that more than sixty of them, a tenth of the student body, were being dismissed. Standards were raised, and before the end of Swanson's administration, a chapter of Phi Beta Kappa was established on the campus.

Facilities were greatly expanded as well. Half of the major buildings on the present campus were erected during his years of service. The first, Dow Science Center, was under construction by 1958. No other academic structures had been built since completion of the Hood Building in 1900. Completed in 1959, Dow had classrooms and laboratories for biology, chemistry, physics, geology, astronomy and mathematics; a planetarium; a three-hundred-seat auditorium; an amphitheater with seating for one hundred; and a greenhouse.

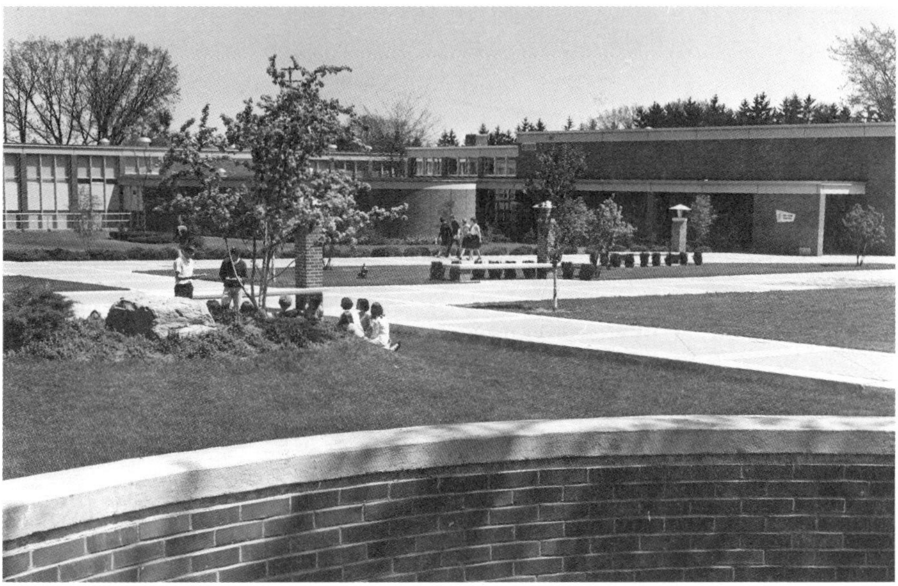

Completed at the edge of the central campus mall in 1959, Dow Science Center was the first building erected during the administration of President Swanson. More than half of today's principal campus structures were built during his presidency. *Gordon Beld photo; courtesy of Alma College Archives.*

Then work began on a new residence hall, the college's first to be built for men. Pioneer and Wright Halls had been used by men but were constructed for women. The new structure, Mitchell Hall, opened in the fall of 1960 and was named in honor of former dean of the faculty James E. Mitchell. It was the first of a quadrangle of residence and dining facilities to be built at the northwest corner of the campus. The second was another women's residence, Newberry Hall, which was completed the following year.

Another 1960 change erased the source of many memories of Alma alumni. The old smokestack at the college heating plant, emblazoned with class numerals by climbing student painters during the past half century, was torn down.

That summer, an addition to Van Dusen Commons provided more dining space for students and a public restaurant called the Heather Room, which quickly became one of central Michigan's most popular dining establishments. The room's motif and the uniforms of waitresses were Scottish.

In 1963, the old college library, which had served students and staff for three-quarters of a century, was razed, and construction of a new three-story learning and resource center was begun. Ready for use by the fall of 1964, it offered space for 120,000 volumes and also included classrooms, seminar rooms, offices and faculty carrels. Originally named Monteith Library in honor of John Monteith, first Presbyterian minister to reach Michigan, it was renamed Kehrl Building for Floyd A. Kehrl, who provided a major bequest.

The new library was one of several college facilities where photographers shot pictures for the 1966 Opel Kadett catalogue published by Buick Motor Division of General Motors Corporation. Featured in the publication were four new Opels and three professional models with a supporting cast of Alma students. To get the thirty-nine photos used in the catalogue, photographers clicked off more than four thousand shots during five days on the campus.

The other two buildings of the planned quadrangle of residence and dining facilities were ready for use by the fall of 1967. Bruske Hall, a four-story residence hall, named in honor of President August Bruske, was the first on the campus with rooms for both men and women who lived in separate wings of the structure. Hamilton Commons, a dining hall, named for President Roy Hamilton, provided seating for 570.

Also under construction at that time was a tri-level Physical Education Center with a gymnasium, a swimming pool, four handball courts, a dance studio, classrooms and offices. Three decades later, it was named Hogan

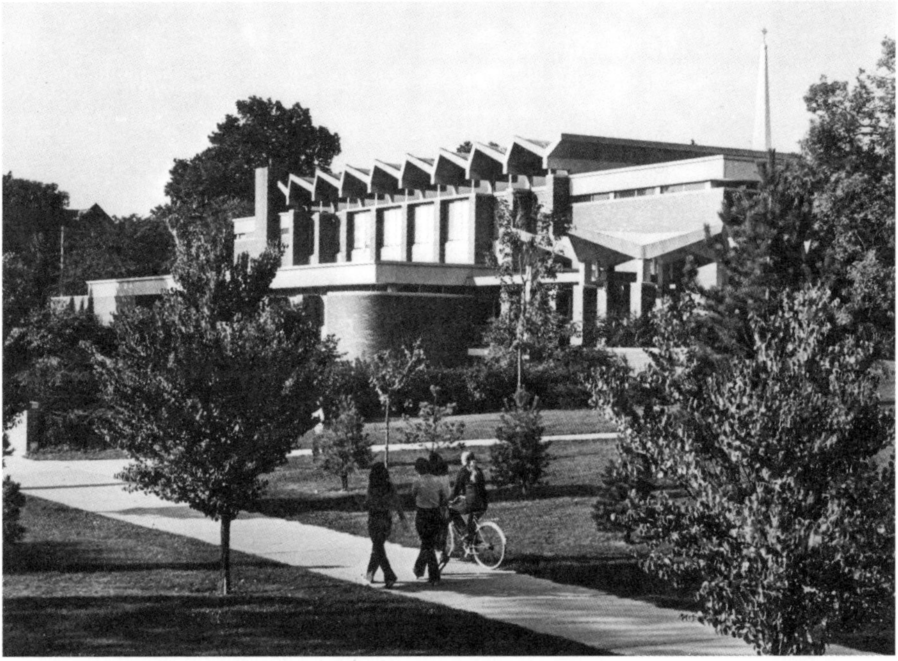

When a new library was planned in 1962, the college's senior class made the first contribution to the fund for its construction. Groundbreaking for what is now the Kehrl Building took place in June 1963, and it was ready for use by the beginning of the 1964–65 academic year. *Gordon Beld photo; courtesy of Alma College Archives.*

Center in honor of Romain and Helen (Kempf) Hogan, 1928 alumni, through a bequest by their son, James.

A shocking contrast to the rapid expansion of campus facilities came on a late winter morning in 1969 when smoke was detected in third-floor classrooms of Old Main, one of the two original college buildings. Flames soon broke through siding at the peak of the structure. Students joined faculty members in carrying out equipment and records until firemen arrived and prevented them from reentering. The fire spread rapidly through the old timber-frame, brick-faced building, and in little more than an hour, it was merely a pile of bricks and ashes. Faculty members stood helplessly and watched the flames devour nearly completed doctoral dissertations and notes that represented years of research, organization and writing.

Later that year, construction began for a complex of four new residence halls on the south side of Superior Street in what had been the Grove. The two-story units provided rooms for more than one hundred men and the same

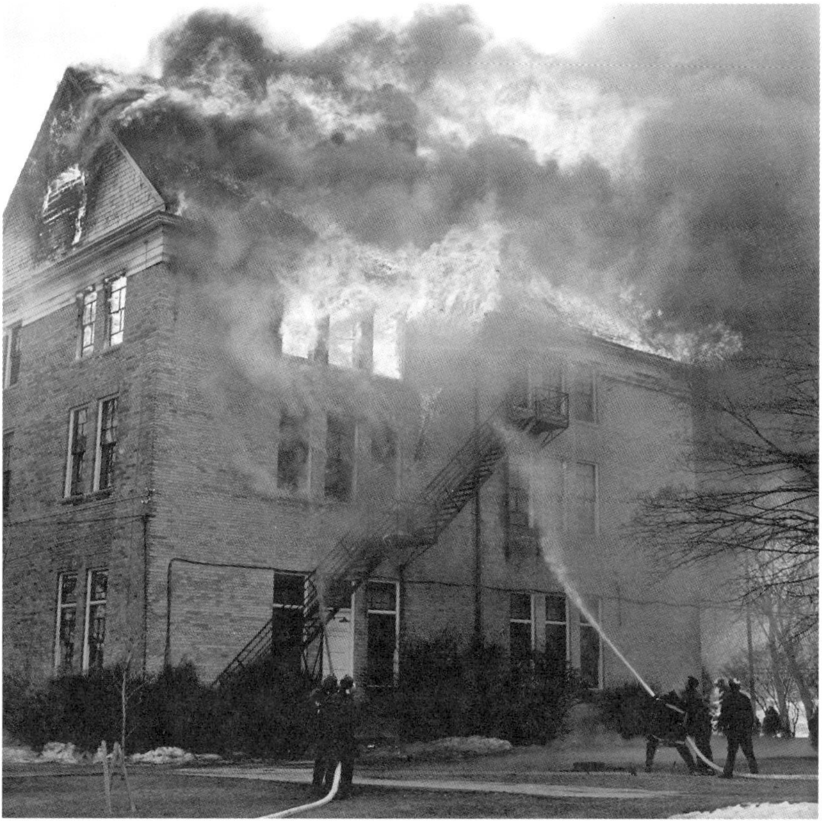

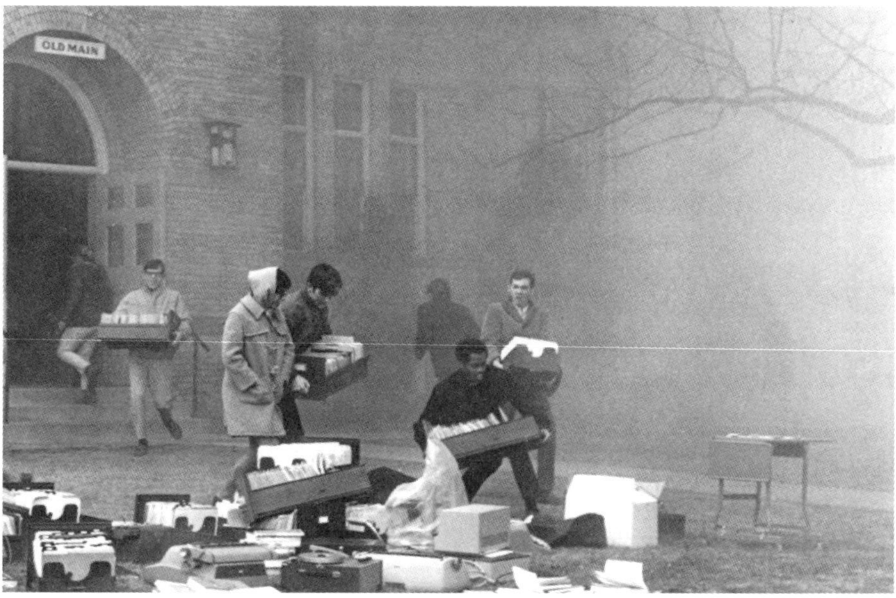
OLD MAIN

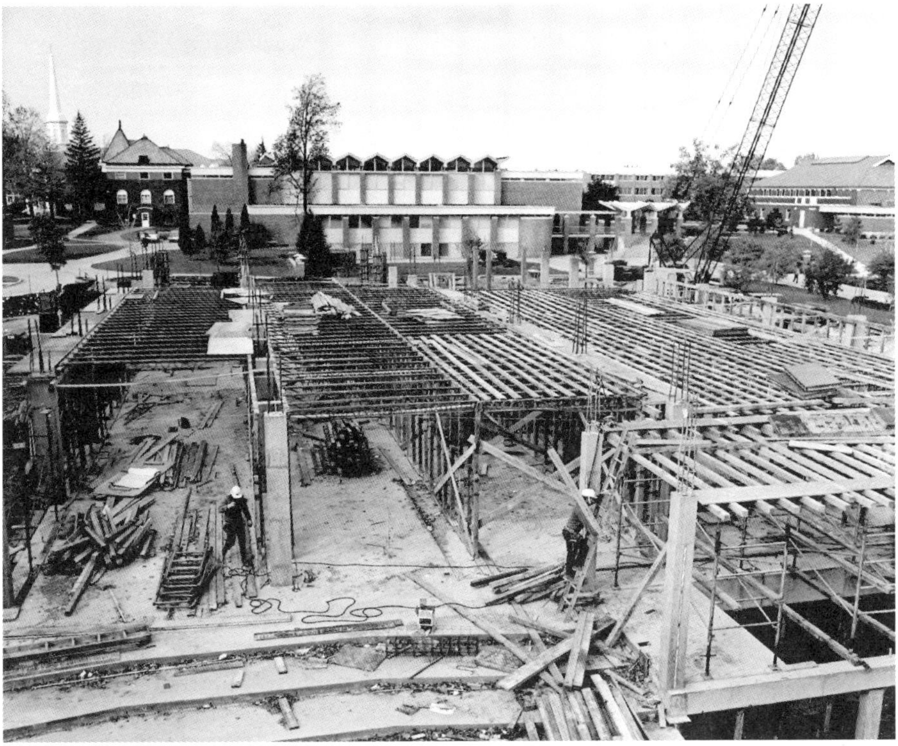

Construction of a new classroom and faculty office building to replace Old Main began in 1972 after several old buildings were leveled to make room for it. The new structure was named in honor of President Swanson and his first wife, Roberta. *Gordon Beld photo; courtesy of Alma College Archives.*

Opposite, top: An old friend suddenly disappeared in March 1969 when fire broke out in the attic of Old Main and, in little more than an hour, leveled the structure that had served Alma students for more than eighty years. *Gordon Beld photo; courtesy of Alma College Archives.*

Opposite, bottom: A few local naysayers suggested the Old Main fire wasn't accidental but might have been set by students as an antiwar protest like those happening on several campuses at the time. However, Alma's students dashed into burning Old Main and helped their professors salvage valuable documents and equipment until firemen arrived and barred them from the reentering building. *Gordon Beld photo; courtesy of Alma College Archives.*

number of women. The halls were named for four trustees whose combined service to the college totaled more than a century: Carl W. Bonbright, Reid Brazel, Walter F. Carey and Stephen S. Nisbet.

An innovative renovation, begun in December 1970, converted the old Memorial Gymnasium to an exceptional facility for art instruction. The building, with an addition at one end, provided studios for sculpture, painting and drawing; rooms for work with ceramics, wood, metal and plaster; a photo studio and darkroom; faculty offices; a small auditorium; and an outdoor work and display court. It was named Clack Art Center in honor of Hugh L. "Lee" Clack and his wife, the former Ann Carter, alumni who, with their four children, were killed in a Pacific Ocean airplane crash in 1957.

The dream of a new classroom and faculty office building, to replace Old Main, took a big step toward reality in June 1972 when three buildings at the construction site were razed. One was Pioneer Hall, Old Main's companion in the pair of original campus structures. The others were the old heating plant and Folsom Hall.

The new building was completed in time for use by students and faculty during the winter term of 1974, and two years later it was named the Roberta B. and Robert D. Swanson Academic Center in honor of President Swanson and his first wife. The building's many facilities include twenty-eight classrooms and sixty-one faculty offices.

A 1974–75 construction project added the Eddy Music Center to campus facilities. Alma's first building erected completely for music instruction, it includes a large rehearsal hall, practice studios, faculty offices and classrooms. Its name honors Mrs. Sara Eddy of Flint, whose estate provided a share of the construction funds. The center was renovated and improved in 2010 with an addition of more than four thousand square feet that includes a large lobby suitable for use as a gathering space at receptions and other events.

Since Wright Hall was no longer needed for housing students and couldn't be heated or maintained economically, it was razed in 1976. Three decades later, another Wright Hall was erected on the site, this one a smaller, sixty-bed facility. The new structure incorporated some of the design elements of the original.

Among other developments after President Swanson's retirement in 1980 were major changes to the Bahlke Field athletic complex. Consulting engineers reported in 1984 that the concrete home-side stands in the football stadium were deteriorating and were a potential hazard for football fans and spectators at Alma's Highland Festival. So they were razed, and the surfaces of the football and baseball fields were plowed up.

A new baseball field soon emerged in the place where the football field and stands had been. To the east, where the baseball field had been, a new stadium with a football field of artificial turf was constructed. Surrounding the field was a running track, the first one on the campus since the cinder track at Davis Field disappeared. The stadium, first in the Michigan Intercollegiate Athletic Association to have artificial turf, was ready for use when the college celebrated its centennial year in 1986.

Other post-Swanson-era construction added a performing arts center and a recreation facility. The Remick Heritage Center for the performing arts opened in 1993. Originally just called the Heritage Center, it was renamed ten years later in honor of Oscar E. Remick, who followed Swanson as president of the college. Concerts by Alma's band, orchestra, choir and dance groups are presented in its five-hundred-seat hall. The building also has an adjoining two-hundred-seat theater.

In 2001, completion of the Stone Center for Recreation provided four courts for tennis, basketball or volleyball. A suspended running track rims the facility. Other features of the center are a climbing wall and a multi-purpose room for activities such as fencing and martial arts classes. The building, which also has a variety of exercise equipment, was named for Alan J. Stone, who succeeded Remick in the presidency.

—Gordon Beld

A Tribute to Swannie

Editor's Note: Among those who were close associates of Robert D. Swanson is author Gordon Beld, who, at the time of the Alma president's death, was asked by college officials to share reminiscences of their days together. Following is his response as printed in the winter 2007 edition of *Alma Accents*, the college's alumni magazine.

Reminiscing about Bob Swanson is a pleasure. But finding adequate words to describe a man of his caliber is tough.

I'll always remember him as a great leader—one who led by example and who marched alongside his troops rather than in front of them. There was nothing ostentatious about Swannie. If you didn't feel comfortable in his presence, it was your problem—not his.

My first contact with him was a job interview at his Reid-Knox office during the summer of 1965. I'd been hoping, ever since the end of my undergraduate days at another MIAA school fifteen years earlier, to find a position in public relations at

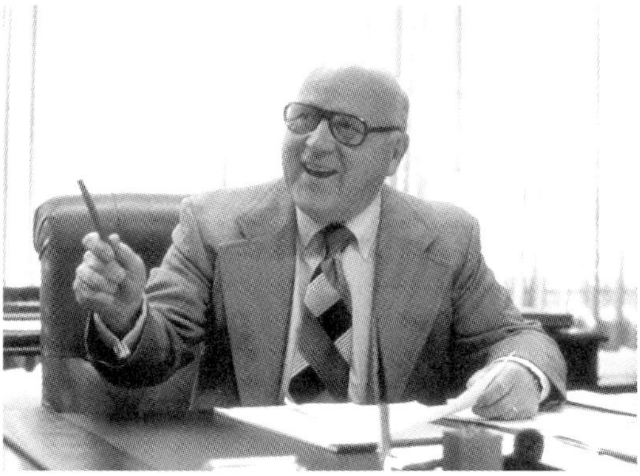

President Swanson greets a visitor to his office in Reid-Knox Administration Building. *Gordon Beld photo; courtesy of Alma College Archives.*

a small, church-related, liberal arts college. His job offer made a dream come true. And for the next fifteen years, while he and I were colleagues, the dream couldn't have been better. Who could ask for more than being an associate of Bob Swanson, a member of his Alma College staff and a resident of the Alma community?

It didn't take many days on the job to realize that he really didn't need anyone to help with public relations. He related to people better than anyone I'd ever met. He was a great speaker and writer with a marvelous gift of coming up with just the right words and phrases.

His magnetic personality drew to him several exceptional upper-level staff members who, like him, generated enthusiasm for Alma College and made it a better place. A little of Bob rubbed off on persons like Guile Graham, Hod Vanden Bosch, Steve Meyer, John Kimball and Ron Kapp. These co-leaders on Swannie's team helped him lift the college to its present prestigious position. I was blessed to work with, and learn from, all of them.

Bob never talked about his accomplishments, but soon after coming to Alma I heard from others about his role in resurrecting the college from the doorstep of death. In the mid-fifties, when trustees asked a consultant what to do about the struggling institution, he told them to let it die a merciful death. Instead, they hired Bob Swanson to turn things around. He certainly did. We're all familiar with the changes he inspired in quality of students and faculty, curriculum and campus facilities. It is he, more than anyone, who is responsible for Alma being what it is today.

Nevertheless, he combined genuine humility with his leadership skills. Students and staff alike regarded him as a friend. Among my fondest memories are the times, especially during my early years at Alma, when he'd spot me walking down the hallway past his office and call out, "Hey, come in here and have a cup of coffee."

He'd make me sit down, then go and get the coffee himself. We'd rarely talk about what was going on at the college. Rather he'd steer the conversation to something like world affairs, gardening or how things were going with members of my family. And when it was time to go back to work, he'd never be the one to end the break. I had to do that.

Though he was a much better writer than I, Bob never suggested how I should write a story—except once. That was when my daughter Dala received the Barlow Trophy, the college's most prestigious award. "No modesty," Swannie insisted. "You write the news release just like you would if it were somebody else's kid."

I don't recall him ever telling me how to do anything else. He wasn't one to complain. He was stingy with criticism. I never heard any come from him. But he was generous with praise.

Bob Swanson was the mold from which all leaders should be cast. I consider myself very fortunate to have known him and to have had the opportunity to contribute in a very small way to his efforts to make Alma College what it is today.

—GORDON BELD
Director of News Services and Publications, 1965–1989

CHAPTER 7

ALMA COLLEGE AT WAR

American involvement in wars has always been a strong challenge to colleges as young men were drawn into the conflicts through enlistments and the draft. Alma College was no exception. When wars came, the school pondered repeatedly how to adjust to a smaller student body, how to reschedule classes, how to deal with athletic schedules and how to accommodate government training programs. Sometimes it wondered how it would stay open.

The first war to influence Alma College was the Spanish-American War. The popular Frank Knox, a fireball on campus, left in April 1898 to enlist, and he took several other men with him. In Florida, he joined Teddy Roosevelt's Rough Riders. The Spanish-American War was short, and except for Knox's involvement, it did not strongly affect Alma College.

Not so with the Great War. Months before war was declared between Germany and the United States in 1917, it was assumed the United States would be drawn into the conflict, and Alma College was considering how the war would challenge the school and change its makeup.

President Harry Means Crooks attended a meeting of college presidents in Chicago, where the group resolved that military training would be instituted at all colleges and, if men left school and went to the armed forces, the schools might need to suspend athletics.

To make the military training official, the Alma College faculty voted that all male students would receive military drill and all female students

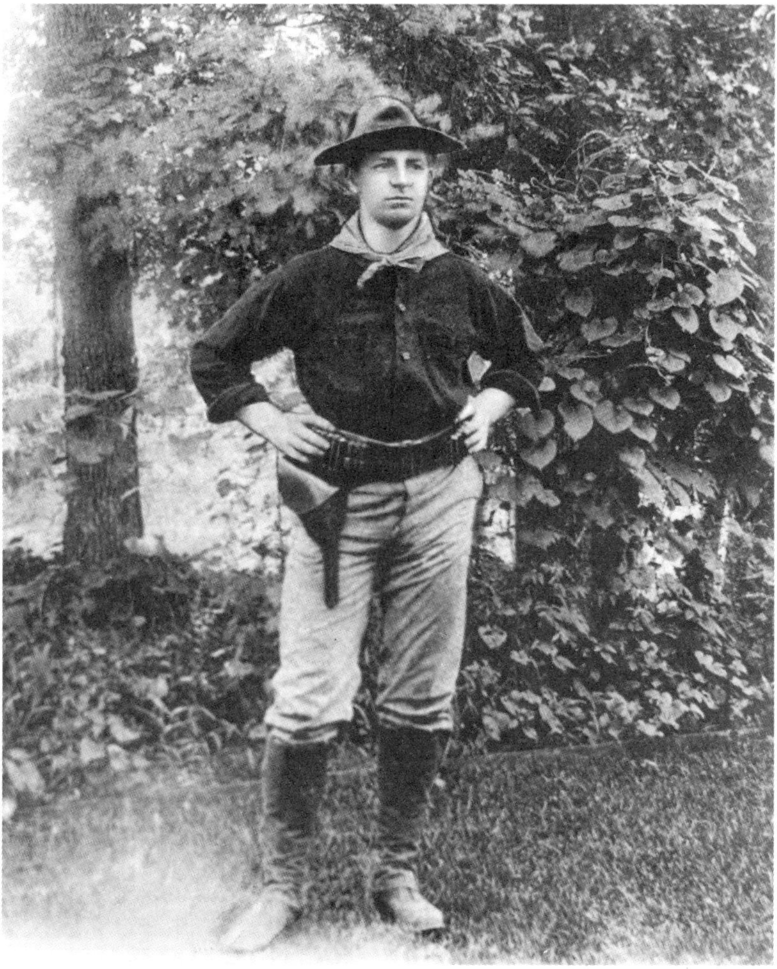

Alma senior Frank Knox quickly responded to the call to arms when the Spanish-American War broke out. He bicycled sixty miles from Alma to an army camp, where he learned more men were needed. After cycling back to Alma, he persuaded fifteen other students to enlist in the army with him. Shown here in uniform, Knox served with Theodore Roosevelt's Rough Riders in Cuba. *Courtesy of Alma College Archives.*

would engage in Red Cross work. The Michigan Intercollegiate Athletic Association (MIAA) still wished to continue athletics through the spring season, which was welcome news to many Alma citizens who were loyal fans of the college's baseball and track teams.

Military training at Alma began at once and was held three times a week. The school looked for a drillmaster to oversee the training, and coach

Harry Helmer was to have charge of the conditioning of the men until the drillmaster was appointed.

The request for young men to join the armed forces was compelling, and many enlisted. In May, President Crooks announced the suspension of athletics because so many schools in the conference had lost so many men to the war that sports schedules had been completely disrupted. Some athletes had joined the officers' reserve corps and expected to be called to Fort Sheridan. The loss of athletes would certainly weaken the baseball and track teams, and other young men were thinking of leaving school to help in farm work to generate food for the armed forces.

Still, when school resumed in the fall, Coach Helmer had many of his veterans back and expected to field a strong football team. By the end of the football season, the Maroon and Cream had taken the MIAA championship and was the only undefeated collegiate team in the state.

The euphoria of the moment, however, was soon overshadowed by the enlistments of H. "Speed" Narrance, football captain George Hebert, athletic manager Linton Melvin and *Almanian* manager Fred Holt. Eight more Alma College men joined them.

The faculty decided to give a series of science-oriented lectures that would benefit the men going into the army or navy and the women who would be dealing with food and fuel scarcity at home. Professor West of the Chemistry Department spoke on "Fuel and How to Save It," "Explosives, Ancient and Modern," "Poisons, Natural and Synthetic" and "Gases Used in War."

Commencement in 1918 was held on May 29, two weeks earlier than usual, to free up men for factory and farm work during the summer months. Of the 101 men who had enrolled at Alma College in September 1917, 49 had enlisted by the end of the school year. The college's service flag had 120 stars representing its men now in the country's service.

When school began in September 1918, male students who were at least eighteen and had enlisted could opt to join the Student Army Training Corps, which was instituted by the U.S. government. They would be provided with uniforms and equipment but, in their student status, would be regarded as on furlough and would receive no pay. They could be called up at any time. The government, however, recognized the value of the college-trained mind in creating a commissioned officer and wished to keep the men in school if possible.

In the fall of 1918, classes at Alma did not begin until October 2 so that the military training might be organized. By then the government had changed its policy. It was announced that for any physically fit young man

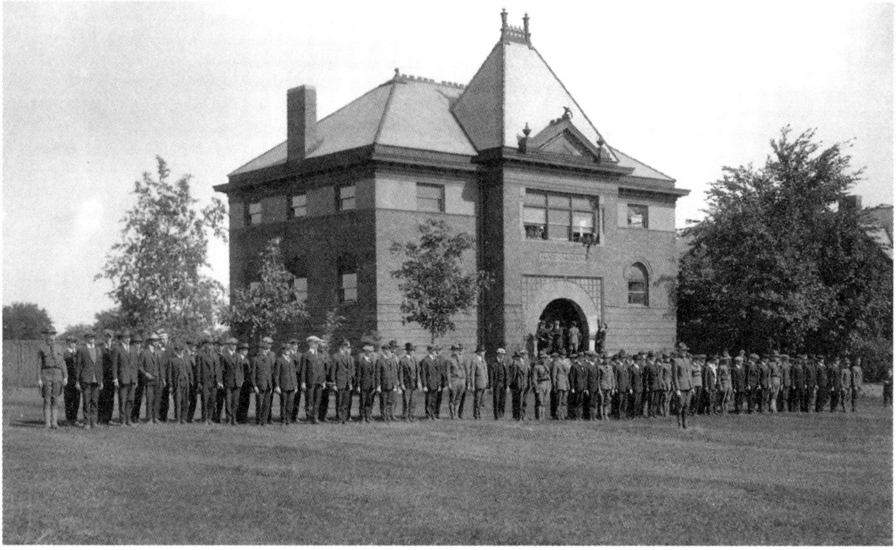

During World War I, the Student Army Training Corps included all able-bodied Alma College men who were at least eighteen and had enlisted. Sponsored by the government, the program was designed to attract men to college and prepare them to become commissioned officers. The response to the program was so great that Hood Museum, behind the long rows of trainees, was turned into a barracks. *Courtesy of Alma College Archives.*

who wished to attend college under the SATC, the government would pay his board, tuition and medical benefit and give him thirty dollars a month.

This splendid opportunity for college training attracted so many young men to Alma College that the Hood Museum had to be transformed into a barracks to house the recruits. It was assumed that men would be called up at three-month intervals for active service. Thus the year was divided into three-month terms.

The autumn of 1918 saw the arrival of an enemy as threatening as the Hun—a deadly respiratory infection dubbed the "Spanish influenza." Its casualties were great, and in mid-October, the Alma College campus underwent a quarantine. Lieutenant Robinson, in charge of the SATC, instituted a lockdown that prevented the flu from gaining even a toehold on the campus.

When the war ended on November 11, the city of Alma exploded in jubilation. At the college, the quarantine was abandoned as men of the SATC and the college girls joined the rest of the celebrants in a three-mile-long parade that traveled to Alma's sister city, St. Louis. It was announced that the SATC would be continued with emphasis on classwork rather than military training, but a week later, the government demobilized the SATC. Now college administrators wondered how many young men would not return to Alma College. Fear that the student body would shrink was allayed in the fall when Alma College attracted the largest freshman class thus far.

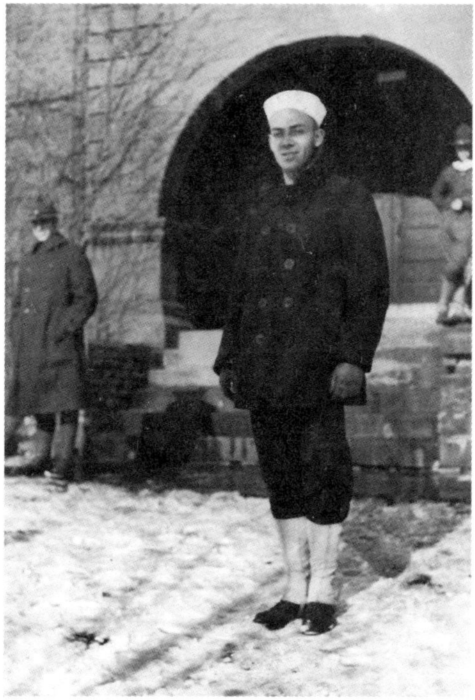

Verne Richards completed his college studies in 1918 and enlisted in the navy. An excellent athlete, he excelled in football, basketball and baseball. He is shown here at the time of a visit with friends on the Alma campus. *Courtesy of Alma College Archives.*

As the United States was drawn into World War II, the college knew that some of its young men would be leaving to fight. Even before Pearl Harbor, some college men joined the armed services. After Pearl Harbor, the reality of war turned the campus into a gloomy place. In regard to the draft, President John Dunning assured Alma College men that the school would try to have them deferred at least until graduation in June. He also warned students, "Don't enlist in any branch of service until you have thought the thing through carefully." He urged them to counsel with administrators or professors before making any decisions. The *Almanian* editorialized, "We don't want a war, but now that we have it we are going to do everything in our power to win that war and to earn the peace that is rightfully ours."

Naturally, it was very hard for students to concentrate on studies with many men sensing the need to enlist and others anticipating being drafted. Administrators proposed several plans to speed up education programs, allowing students to graduate in a shorter time without lowering graduation requirements. They finally decided to allow students to increase their academic load to seventeen hours per semester. Those with a "B" average could take twenty. An intramural program ensured that all students were engaged in healthful recreational activities.

By February 1942, a quarter of the male students had registered for the draft. The *Almanian* displayed recruiting advertisements from the U.S. Navy. The U.S. Army Air Corps advanced a plan that allowed enlistment but also permitted men to finish their educations. College reservists expected to be called up soon, as the demand for men exceeded enlistments. Soon the Air Corps reservists left for active service. It was common to be seated next to a male student one day and have him gone the next.

The war, sparking war bond sales and food rationing, made itself known to Alma College students in other ways. It became hard for students to travel home and back by bus on the weekends as military passengers took precedence, and students had to wait hours for a bus ride. Someone suggested shifting the weekly schedule to allow travel on weekdays rather than weekends.

The most serious of the challenges facing Alma College was very simple: with declining student enrollment, how could the college remain solvent? It is not an exaggeration to claim that Alma College in 1942 was close to shutting down. The college was carrying a debt of $120,000, and faculty members saw their salaries cut by 7 percent. Interim president Roy Hamilton urged that the board make a proposal to Secretary of the Navy Frank Knox, Alma's most famous alumnus, to secure a government training program for officers.

Through Knox's influence, Alma College, in the midst of a financial and nearly fatal crisis, became a location of the government's V-12 training program for navy and marine officers. The navy sent two lieutenants to investigate the college's buildings, grounds and technical equipment. Alma was one of five Michigan colleges selected for the training.

Potential trainees were given qualifying tests. Those who were accepted would become students while on active duty. They would be in uniform, receive military pay and be under military discipline. In July 1943, more than two hundred men arrived on campus to begin the new program. They were housed in Wright Hall, the women's dorm. Since many of the men's classes were regular college fare, a summer school was opened to other students who wished to attend and add credits. With their dorm already occupied, female students were housed wherever rooms were available.

The *Almanian* suggested how important the program was to the financial stability of the college: "It is an economic help in a time when numerous institutions of its type all over the country find the maintenance problem more difficult to solve than in normal times because of the drain on the student body." From July 1943 to October 1945, between 180 and 315 trainees were always on campus. The government was paying their college expenses.

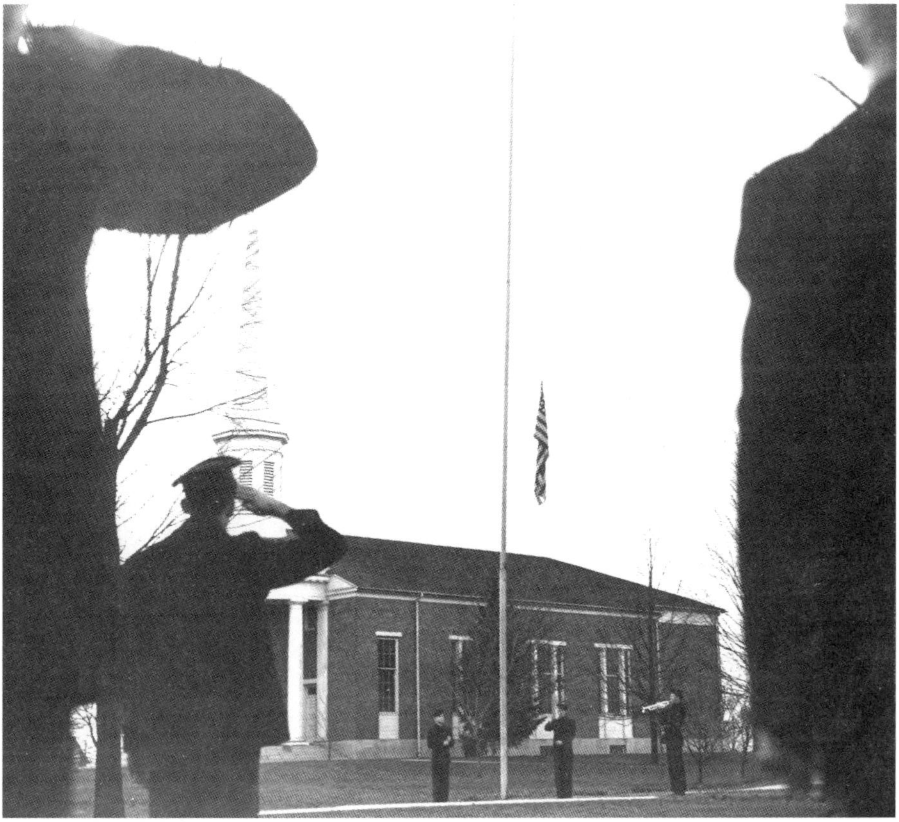

In an evening colors celebration on the Alma Campus, officers and men of the navy V-12 program salute as the flag is lowered. Help from Secretary of the Navy Frank Knox, a former Alma student, made it possible for the college to land a V-12 contract and bring navy officer candidates to the campus, thus keeping the college solvent during World War II. *Courtesy of Alma College Archives.*

Even before the V-12 program got underway, student athlete Jack Tait laid out an obstacle course to benefit naval reservists on campus. It involved running up the bleachers, jumping to the ground, climbing a fence, galloping through hopping racks, swinging on hand-over-hand bars fifteen feet above the ground, scrambling between posts and trees, jumping a series of hurdles, sprinting over an area and, finally, broad-jumping a fifteen-foot pond. Student Jack Heimworth covered the course in three minutes, fifty-one seconds.

Alma College was the first in the country to complete a contract for V-12 purposes. No one knew how the program would develop with both young

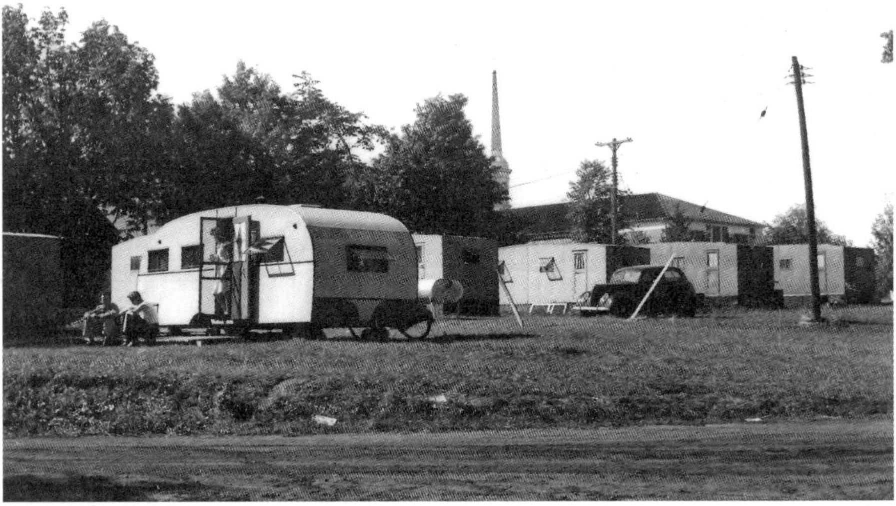

Temporary housing, including these house trailers, was needed after the war as veterans took advantage of the GI Bill. In 1947, twelve families were housed in trailers, and eight families occupied prefab houses on the campus. *Courtesy of Alma College Archives.*

military men and civilian students on campus and in the same classrooms. The summer school session went well. A new session and term that began in November had a rough time. Very deliberate action and careful planning smoothed the difficulties, and the classes and activities progressed. At the end of the term in February 1944, ninety young men left the college. Of these, fifteen were Alma College men who had completed enough credits for graduation, and the rest were apprentice seamen headed for further training to become junior officers. In March, ninety new sailors appeared on campus, some as transfers from other colleges and some as recent high school graduates. During the next two academic years, the military men accounted for a majority of the student body. In the last year of the program, 1945–46, the percentage had dropped to less than one-third.

The V-12 program had rescued the college at a crucial time, and it had prepared the school for the postwar influx of veterans who were taking advantage of the GI Bill. This anticipation became a reality in the 1946–47 school year, when postwar enrollment reached an unexpected high of 598.

When the Korean conflict began, the draft was in force, and in the spring of 1950, final exams for seniors were suspended. Of the men graduating, 70

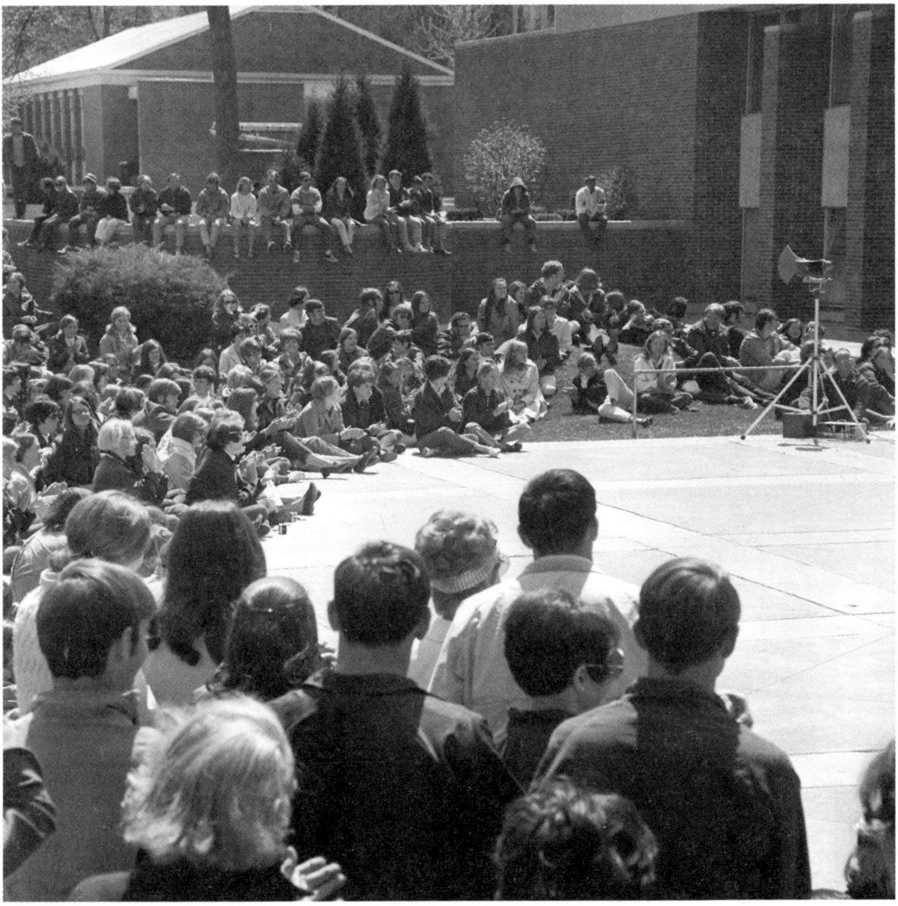

During the Vietnam conflict, student demonstrations and violence erupted on many college and university campuses. However, at Alma on Campus Day 1970, students and faculty met on the mall to conduct a civilized exchange of opinions about the war. *Courtesy of Alma College Archives.*

percent were facing induction into the armed services. This bending of the rules would remove pressure as the men prepared to leave college and enter basic training.

If students previously had accepted the deprivations of war in winning the peace, the Vietnam War told a different story. Sensing deception in the U.S. government regarding the war's progress, students on many campuses expressed their antiwar sentiments through demonstrations. At Alma College, a long-standing tradition, Campus Day, was suspended in 1970 so that a public forum might be held to discuss viewpoints on the war. Students and faculty took turns mounting the platform on the mall to express their opinions on U.S. action in Vietnam and Cambodia. This peaceful exchange was applauded by the local press. "The whole Gratiot community should be proud that students at Alma cared enough for others' rights to carry on reasonable protests," said Alma's *Daily Record-Leader*.

At regular intervals during its lifetime, Alma College has had to deal with the influence of war on its student body and, consequently, its financial stability. That it survived these challenges, especially during World War II, is a testimony to the determination of its administration and staff and the vicissitudes of wartime.

—David McMacken

CHAPTER 8

BATTLES ON THE CAMPUS

Two of the earliest traditions at Alma College involved competition between the freshmen and the sophomores. The annual flag rush was the attempt by freshmen to scale the flagpole and tear down the sophomores' flag. Also, the annual tug of war was held over the Pine River, with the winners pulling the losers through the water.

Flag rush was held at the very beginning of the year. Excitement was high on campus on the days when the freshmen were plotting how to take the sophs unawares and capture their flag. In 1908, the contest began on the Pioneer Hall veranda when a soph was attacked by six or seven freshmen. Soon the sophs hung their banner in Wright Hall, and the freshies quickly pulled it down. No one seemed to know when the "rush" actually was to start, and rules were instituted for the next year.

Flag rush required skilled planning. In the 1920 rush, the hostilities began with the capture of several sophs by the freshmen. Then some freshmen were captured by sophs and taken to Ithaca for safekeeping. A tussle broke out in front of the Paris Café in downtown Alma, but rules kept the men from knockdown, drag-out fights. In the end, the sophs successfully defended their flag from the charging freshmen, who were determined to reach and climb the pole.

By 1923, the flag rush had expanded into new territory. The frosh mobilized at Pioneer Hall at midnight and quietly and unobserved (they thought) went out across the athletic field, boarded a couple of Republic trucks and drove to Half Moon Lake, ten miles away. There they camped

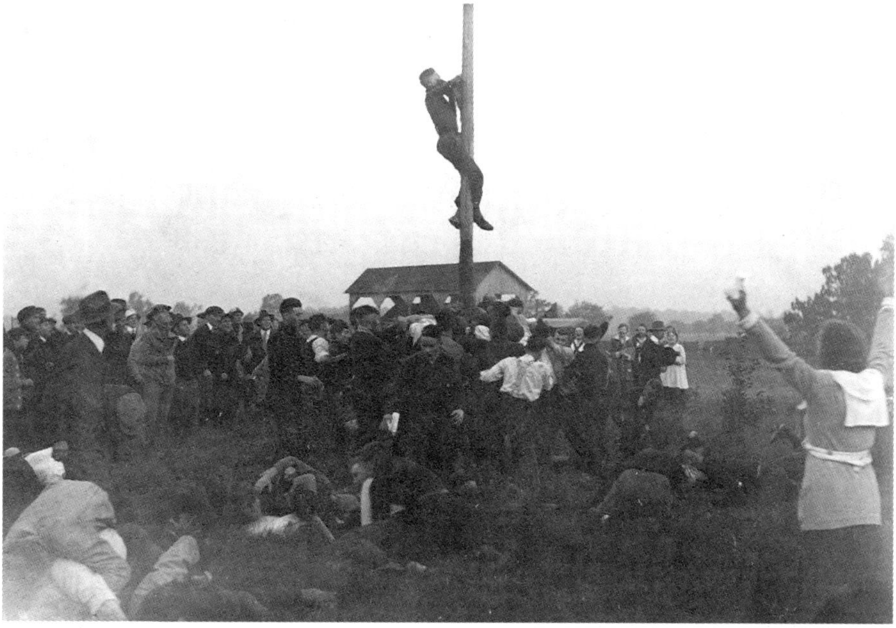

During the 1917 flag rush, the freshmen appeared, faces smeared with coal dust and determined to snatch the sophs' flag. Coach Harry Helmer gave the signal unleashing the forty-seven frosh, and soon "Rusty" Kelly shinnied up the pole while his buddies screamed, "Climb, Kelly, climb." With his jackknife, he cut down the brown and gold standard and descended victorious. *Courtesy of Alma College Archives.*

out the next day until their whereabouts were discovered. After a wild foray across several counties in an attempt to shake their sophomore pursuers, they finally took refuge at the mansion of Frank W. Ruggles, president of Alma's Republic Motor Truck Company. The sophs assumed that by now the frosh were so frightened of them that the sophomore flag was safe, so the second-year men went home for a night of peaceful sleep.

They had access to the trucks and the mansion because among the freshmen was Reed Ruggles, son of Frank Ruggles. The young men must have been impressed by the acres of gardens and the footbridges across the Pine River at the sprawling Ruggles estate on Alma's east side. It is no surprise that Reed was elected class president shortly after this event.

The following day, the men of both classes converged on the athletic field, cheered on by excited coeds. The frosh had ten minutes to capture the flag. The sophs were outnumbered, but they valiantly gathered around the pole and repulsed wave after wave of freshman bodies. One freshman reached the pole and scaled it. He touched the flag, but that was all. He was dragged

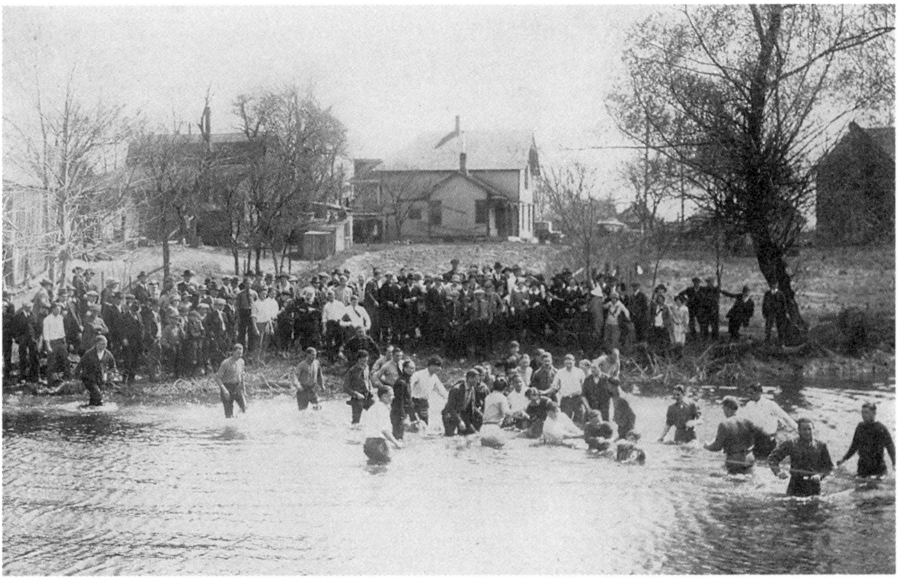

The college's 1912 tug of war, held on a Saturday afternoon, attracted an enthusiastic crowd of students and townsfolk to the banks of the Pine. There they watched a fifteen-minute seesaw battle between the freshmen and the sophomores. As neither side got pulled into the river, it was declared a draw. *Courtesy of Alma College Archives.*

down by the furious sophs. At the end of the ten-minute mêlée, the whistle blew, and the sophs cheered. They had successfully defended their flag.

The tug of war was held for many years at various places on the Pine River. The fact that in the earliest years of the competition the city was dumping its sewage into the river influenced the location of the contest. One time, the competition was cancelled because of trash, including broken glass, in the riverbed. Despite these risks, the tug of war was sometimes held near the swinging bridge behind the Republic Truck Plant. It was a polluted section of the river, but no one seemed to mind.

In 1908, the sophomores baited the freshies with large green bills posted around campus:

> *Ho! Ye! Freshies! Ye defenders of ye verdant green; ye scalers of the campus chimney; ye strutters about ye campus, ye class of 1911 challenge ye class of 1912 to a tug of war over Pine River, Saturday, October 10th at 3 p.m., said tug of war to be held below ye swinging bridge.*

Each side was to choose ten valiant men to anchor the ends of the rope. Three hours later, the response appeared:

> *We the soph exterminators, namely the Class of 1912, do hereby, this 8th day of October, accept the gladiators' challenge to a tug of war, the said tug of mighty beasts to be pulled off over the swirling waters of the Pine river, just below the swinging bridge.*

On Saturday, the grand official of the day, Mr. Carrithers of the college, fired his pistol, and the tug was on. After the men had exerted themselves with ten minutes of furious tugging, the bystanders could no longer contain themselves. Townspeople yelled and shouted, crowded up to the rope, sprayed the sophs and freshies with water and nearly cut off air to the sweating men. The tugging continued for an hour! Finally, the tug was called off at 4:10 p.m. with a pistol shot. The contest was considered a failure as neither side got "soused."

—David McMacken

CHAPTER 9

FAVORITE GATHERING PLACES

The tug of war became a long-standing tradition, and the proximity of the Pine River kept it going. The river itself, however, became an Alma College tradition, providing watery activities including swimming, casual canoeing and canoe races. Sometimes a small mixed group (carefully chaperoned by a college adult in the early days) would canoe to one of three Grassmeres—pleasant shady glens on the riverbank upstream, where the excursionists would spread their blankets, open their picnic baskets and enjoy a pleasant afternoon of eating and chatter.

The student newspaper *Almanian* rhapsodized, "In the warm spring afternoons and on Saturday, many students can be seen lazily drifting up and down the glassy surface of the Pine. The activity from paddling exercises the arms and gives a fine appetite to the wielder of the paddle. Who could ask for a more enjoyable afternoon than one spent on the Pine?"

Sometimes, students indulged in lengthy journeys on the river. In the spring of 1922, two couples, the men in sport coats and ties and the ladies in fancy dresses, hired a truck in Alma to transport their canoes upstream to the village of Sumner. They began their leisurely journey toward Alma, hitting and dodging stumps and portaging around fallen trees in the river. They lunched on the riverbank. The girls peeled potatoes, and the men made a campfire. The quartet dined on fried chicken, fried potatoes, buns, fruit salad, strawberries and cream, cake, olives and coffee. They washed and packed their dishes and were on their way again, singing, talking and laughing as they paddled along. Finally they came to familiar landmarks,

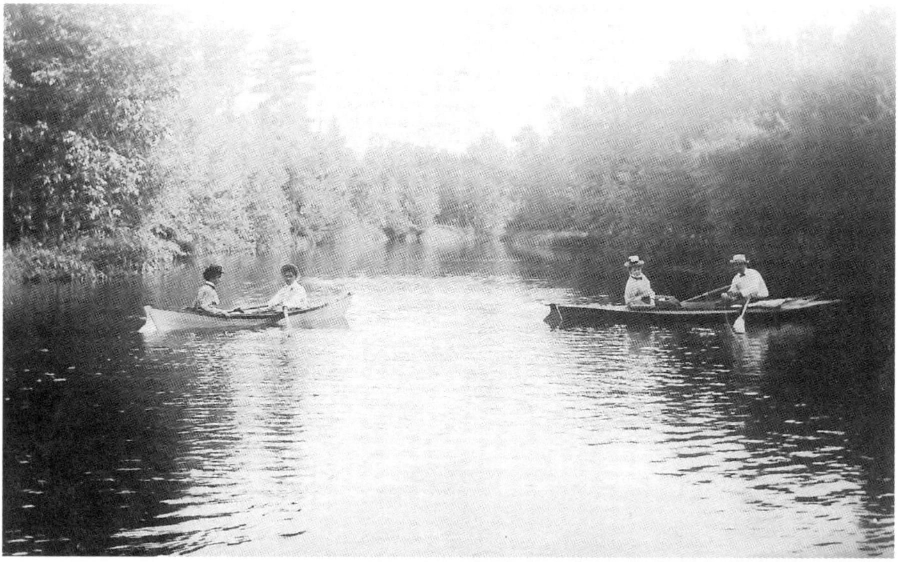

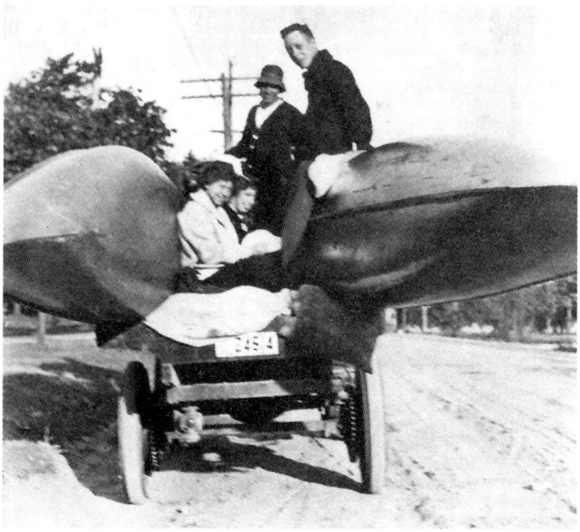

Above: Boating on the millpond and upriver was a favorite activity of many students. Two couples, dressed in their finery, enjoy a rowboat ride on the Pine. *Courtesy of Alma College Archives.*

Left: The easiest way to enjoy a long canoe ride was to truck the canoes upstream and then let the current do most of the work on the way back. Two couples and their canoes head out of Alma aboard a Republic truck to put in at the town of Sumner and enjoy a leisurely drift down the Pine. *Courtesy of Alma College Archives.*

the gravel pit, the cement bridge and the third Grassmere. There they went ashore and finished off whatever food remained in their basket.

In November 1923, after the river waters had begun to cool during the autumn season, three coeds—Misses Ritter, Keller and Hollweg—borrowed student Elmo McGlone's canoe and set out for the second Grassmere. Being somewhat inexperienced in the art of the canoe, Miss Hollweg decided she wished to trade places with Miss Keller in the middle seat. Miss H dropped her paddle in the water, and when she tried to retrieve it, they overturned into the chilly waters of the Pine. They splashed to the riverbank, where they had to remove some of their outer clothing and hang it to dry on bushes. The arrival of some boys proved an embarrassment to both parties. In the end, the girls returned to campus, and later McGlone got his canoe and his paddles back.

Often students would pack a picnic basket and walk down to the millpond and the college dock, where canoes were available, and paddle across to Turck's Woods, later Conservation Park. A favored spot allowed a campfire, and many a college student enjoyed the shady glade along the south side of the millpond.

In 1924, the annual men's breakfast was held on the banks of the Pine. Forty college men and their female companions took a fleet of canoes upstream to Three Pines, where they built cooking fires and fried ham and eggs. They also had rolls, coffee and doughnuts. Following a brief program and some leisurely lingering, they paddled back to the dock.

The river that provided pleasure in the tug of war and many pleasant afternoons of canoeing could also prove dangerous. In May 1907, three

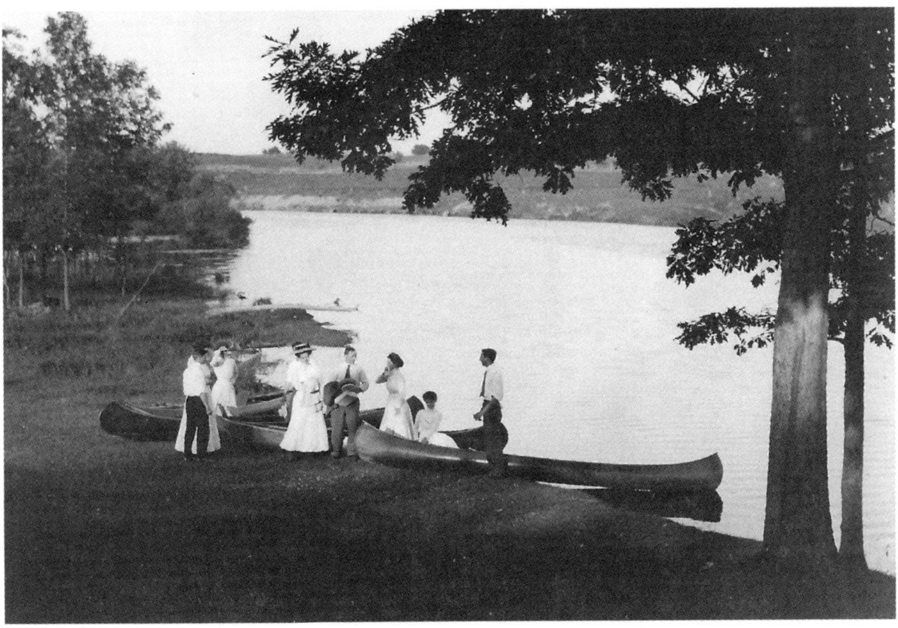

Four canoes have been pulled up at Three Pines, a favored picnic spot upstream for groups from Alma. *Courtesy of Alma College Archives.*

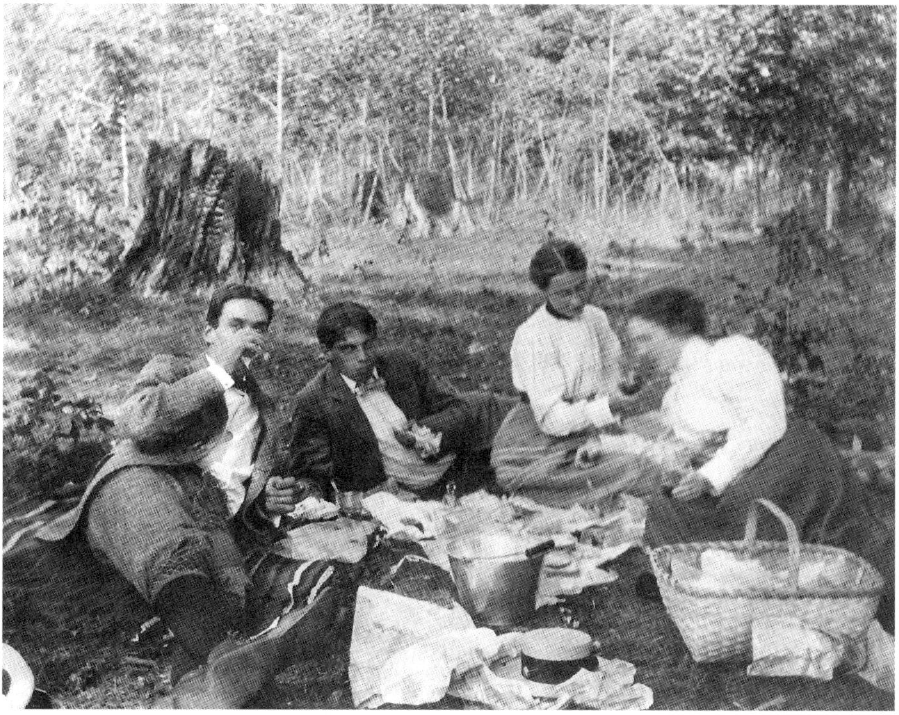

With the contents of their picnic basket spread on a blanket, these Alma students enjoy a meal on the banks of the river. *Courtesy of Alma College Archives.*

girls, sisters Grace and Addie Johnson and Beryl Inglis, decided to canoe to the first Grassmere. As they were upriver, it began to rain, and they turned around, taking shelter under Wolfe's Bridge. In turning the canoe around, it capsized, throwing all three into the water. Beryl Inglis could swim, and she clung to the overturned canoe. She ordered Addie to cling to the other end of the canoe. Grace's heavy clothes quickly became saturated and drew her beneath the water. The two girls screamed for help, and Ezra Wolfe ran to the bridge with a fishing pole. Grace had disappeared, and there was no way to find her. He was able to get Beryl and Addie to safety.

Townsfolk arrived in carriages and canoes with pike poles to help snag the body. An hour and a half later, Grace was pulled from the water, and it was recognized that she was dead when discovered. Grace's mother and sister Addie had come from Lapeer for a visit only the night before. Sadness descended on the campus.

The following year, the editor of the *Almanian*, reflecting on the recent drowning of Bert Henderson on the millpond, reminded students of Grace's drowning and observed that "the Pine River will be forsaken this spring." The gloom of these tragedies gradually wore off, and the river continued to be a favored recreational spot for college students.

Closer to campus than the river were two special locations used for outdoor activities. A lowland on the northeast side of campus became a special site for trysts and campfires. Consisting of fallen trees and brush, tall grass, a patch of swamp and a high grove of trees, it became known as the Jungle. In 1919, the frosh had their first experience in the Jungle, where they were taken for a hotdog roast. A few years later, one evening the men found the ladies missing from the dining room in Wright Hall. They, too, were having a weenie roast around a fire in the Jungle. The girls were enjoying dessert of cake and ice cream and the buzzing music of a ukulele when a storm arose. The ladies quickly packed their picnic baskets, folded their blankets, doused the campfire and scampered for Wright Hall.

On the south side of Superior Street, on land not yet part of the campus, was a pleasant wooded area known as the Grove. In the seclusion of its leafy shade many a couple met. In 1927, the new President's House was built amidst the trees, removing some of the charm of this shady spot. These two special locations live on in the college's Alma Mater Hymn:

> *Memory holds a cherished picture:*
> *Jungle, Grove, and campus fair.*
> *Sons and daughters, ever faithful,*
> *Hail thee one beyond compare.*

Another early tradition for Almanians occurred when men and women exchanged annual visits to their dorms. Pioneer Hall, the men's dorm, was made spick and span, for the ladies would be peering into the men's rooms. To tidy up, the lads carted many boxes of various items into the cellar. In the annual coed edition of the *Almanian*, the girls labeled Pioneer Hall "Home for Likable Young Men." They were eager to visit the digs of those likable young men who welcomed the ladies, served punch and exchanged autographs in their little albums. If the coeds wondered just what went on in the men's dorm, their visit may have done a poor job of satisfying their curiosity.

Wright Hall, the ladies dorm, because of its size, was often opened at the beginning of the year with a reception welcoming faculty, students and friends. This event was "to further the social life and the general atmosphere of friendliness for which Alma College is so well known." As a mixer, numbers were given to both men and ladies to match and find a partner with whom to sit while enjoying refreshments.

At the second-annual open house in 1909, children's toys were placed in the fourth-floor attic; swings, teeter-totters, roller skates, carts and bicycles were available to guests. Some men bumped the rafters when swinging high. Daisies were given to visitors as the open house ended. After groans of disappointment, the men soon discovered, to the delight of all, that the daisies were made of ice cream.

At the 1921 Wright Hall open house, the male guests marched through the halls peering into the rooms. Then there were quiet desertions and unnoticed slippings away as certain favored ones dropped out to visit certain favored rooms. The other guests wandered through the hall. Memory books were signed, each signer being rewarded with a piece of candy. At last it was time for the men to leave. Another Wright Hall open house had come and gone.

—David McMacken

Chapter 10

Happy Days

First there was Arbor Day, then College Day and finally Campus Day. It was the same day with different names, and it started as a day off from classes while students tidied and beautified the campus.

Arbor Day 1904 included student celebrations, the annual tree planting and a great display of school spirit. Each class planted its special tree. The sophomores, to earn the distinction of being first, had planted their tree at 2:00 a.m.

In 1910, Arbor Day developed into College Day and was designed to "make Arbor Day a pleasing and beneficial holiday." Whether most students considered the day particularly pleasant is debatable. Activities began with a program that most likely didn't excite many students. There were seven lectures and recitations, mostly about trees and the importance of the college.

According to administrators, it was to be "a day which would become an Alma tradition." Maroon and cream was floating everywhere, and students were encouraged to wear the college colors. The college invited citizens to visit campus to celebrate or help with the events of the day. One of those events involved male students climbing ladders and trimming trees. A landscape architect from Philadelphia had drawn a master plan for the campus, and the boys also planted new trees according to the map.

It soon became evident that College Day was intended to be a cleanup day using free student labor to remove debris and clutter that had accumulated during the winter. Male students were issued tools

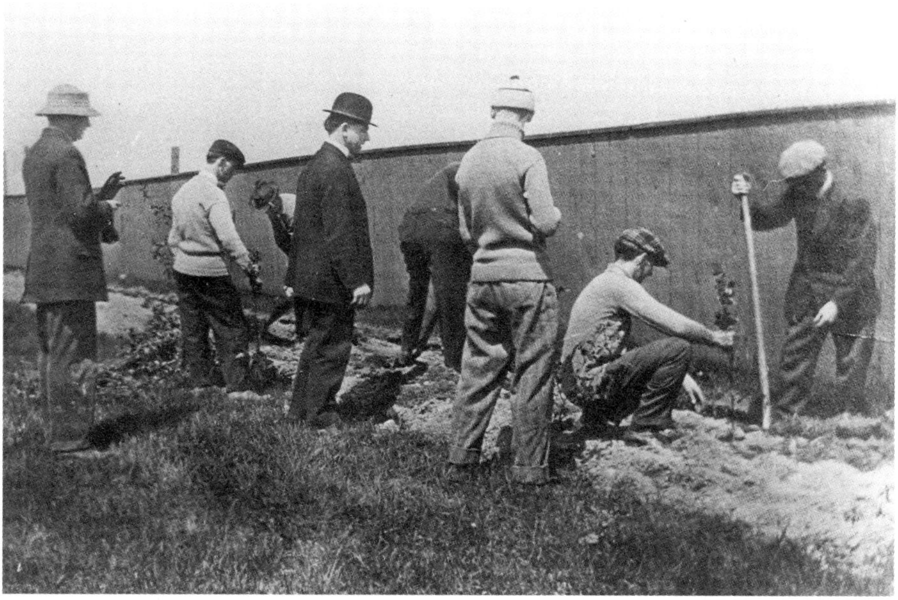

While College Day was an escape from books, male students were asked to clean up the campus and improve the landscaping. These men are planting bushes and trees according to the master plan devised by landscape architect A.B. Yeomans. *Courtesy of Alma College Archives.*

and garden implements and assigned areas of the campus that needed attention. Women cleaned the interiors of residence halls.

College Day on May 2, 1911, was designated as a jubilee because President Bruske had promised a celebration when enrollment broke three hundred. The jubilee may not have provided the merriment the name implied. Regular classes were followed by a literary program in chapel. This was followed by the girls' gymnasium drill on campus. At lunch, the swipes (student waiters) appeared in paper soldier hats like ones children make, and they marched to tables with the trays of food. The afternoon was devoted to tree trimming and beautification. Those men who had tired of the outdoor activities and had disappeared were rousted out, even those who were spending a few hours with their steadies.

Not long after College Day was inaugurated, tools began to disappear—or, at best, required gathering up by college staff. At lunch time, some of the young men would lay their tools down and then, after deciding they'd had enough of College Day, fail to return to work. Thus, the holiday ended in 1922, though tugs of war and other interclass competitions continued through the spring months of 1923 and '24.

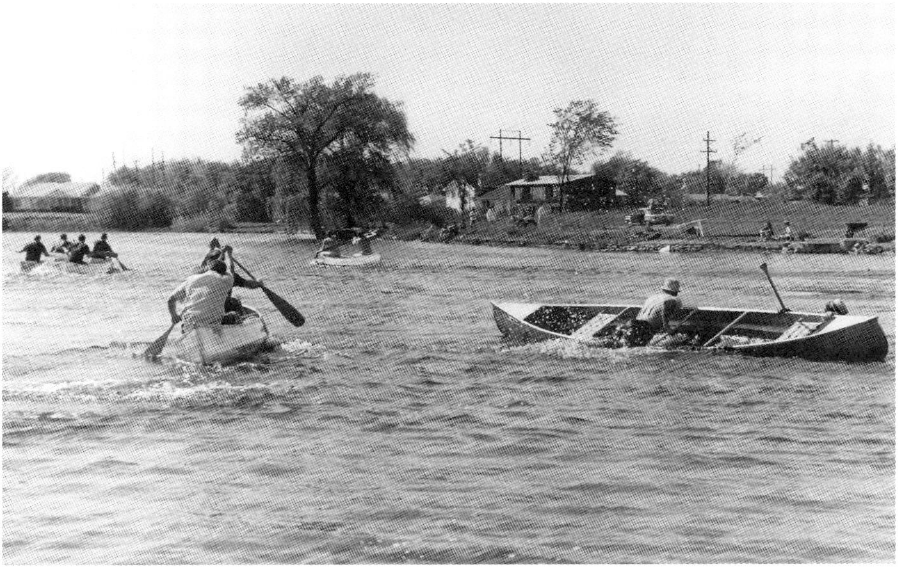

College Day became Campus Day, complete with entertaining activities like crowning a queen and canoe races on the millpond. Enthusiastic paddlers sent canoes flying, with a few experiencing a plunge into the Pine River. *Courtesy of Alma College Archives.*

In 1925, the spring day away from books and lectures was revived, and College Day was now called Campus Day. That year there was a tug of war, the senior-faculty baseball game, an interclass track meet and a picnic and a dance in the evening. Activities of that kind continued for many years, and by the 1960s, the most exciting competition involved pushcart races around neighboring streets and canoe races on the Pine River. The last tugs of war involved an artificial pond on campus rather than the polluted river.

A Queen of Scots was crowned at the 1934 Campus Day, and at later springtime holidays, her successors were known as Campus Day queens.

After the 1970 pushcart competition and crowning of the queen, students set aside frivolity and assembled on the campus mall for a serious exchange of opinions concerning American involvement in the Vietnam War. It was the last official Campus Day.

Dreary winter days were broken up when Snow Carnival started. It had a rather brief run between its beginning in 1959 and its ending after the 1974 event. Nevertheless, during its comparatively short existence, it did enable students to set aside books for a day midway between the year-end holidays and springtime's Campus Day.

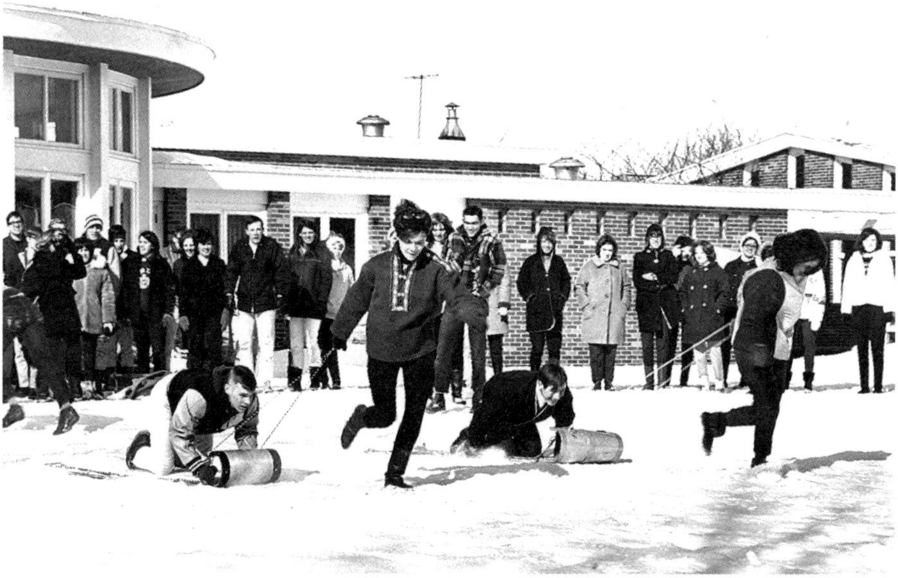

Toboggan races were only one feature of Snow Carnival. Snow sculptures, a holiday queen and an all-campus snowball fight added to the delight of a midwinter day off from classes. *Gordon Beld photo; courtesy of Alma College Archives.*

Among Snow Carnival's popular competitive events were toboggan races—not downhill but rather across level areas of the campus with one student riding the craft and another pulling it. Sometimes the puller was male and the passenger female. Often the roles were switched. At some snow carnivals, there were interfraternity hockey games, and at one event, faculty members battled students on the rink with brooms substituted for hockey sticks and a basketball replacing the puck. Free-for-all snowball fights also added to the excitement. Sometimes there were sleigh rides and evening programs or concerts.

There always was competition in snow sculpture, too, with work on the entries beginning during the afternoon preceding carnival day when student sculptors filled wastebaskets with water and snow to create the slush that would soon become a cool creation. Shovels were used to form the rough outline of the image, and spoons were the tools used for the finishing touches. In 1966, the winner of the snow sculptures were the Delta Sigma Phis with their gigantic St. Bernard made of packed snow. The theme was "Winter in Europe," and the informal dance was labeled "Alpine Adventure." Attendees were urged to wear ski clothes. The traditional all-campus snowball fight sent a fusillade of white missiles flying through the Alma College air.

The last Snow Carnival was in 1974, but five years later, an abundance of snow prompted Alma students to stage a one-day revival of the once-popular event. That day featured a cross-country ski race, snow sculpture competition, skating party, campus dance and the Snow Bowl—a football game between two sorority teams in foot-and-a-half-deep snow at Bahlke Stadium. Only the wind chill factor—eighteen below zero—was lower than the 0–0 score in the game between the girls from Alpha Theta and Alpha Zeta Tau.

Since the early 1900s, homecoming weekends have thrilled both Alma students and the alumni who return to renew friendships and revive memories. First mention of a "homecoming" in the *Almanian* told of an effort to encourage alumni to return to the campus for the November 14, 1914 football game against Olivet that would be followed by a banquet in the evening. A 1927 article in the student paper noted that the traditional "Hobo Parade" would be switched that year to an "Old Time Parade" in keeping with an observance of the college's fortieth anniversary.

A later feature of homecoming celebrations was the snake dance. This sinuous celebration had originated with the old Pajama Parade that was a wild and popular event in the 1920s. The Pajama Parade would erupt unannounced in an evening, and college men would run through downtown wearing only pajamas and nightshirts. They would raid stores that were still open, getting free cigars, cake and ice cream. Frosh were forced to get down in the street and race peanuts, propelled by their noses. Then the frosh put on a rowdy talent show at the Strand Theatre. The party ended with the men in their nightclothes parading back to campus to serenade the coeds in Wright Hall. The men formed an "A" in front of the dorm and sang "Good Night, Ladies." By 1937, the Pajama Parade had declined, and the newspaper columnist likened it to a "pink tea, compared to what it was in the old days." The Pajama Parade was revived only briefly in later years, but the snake dance version of the wild evening survived.

Homecoming as it is thought of now began in 1938, and it developed into one of the premier celebrations at Alma College. The 1938 homecoming included Parent's Day. It marked two firsts: the choosing of Alma's first homecoming queen—Carra Jones, Midland freshman—and the appearance of the Kiltie Band in their new kilts featuring the McPherson tartan. Miss Jones was crowned at the Friday night pep rally by football team captain Bob Devaney. The queen and her court of four ladies were attired in

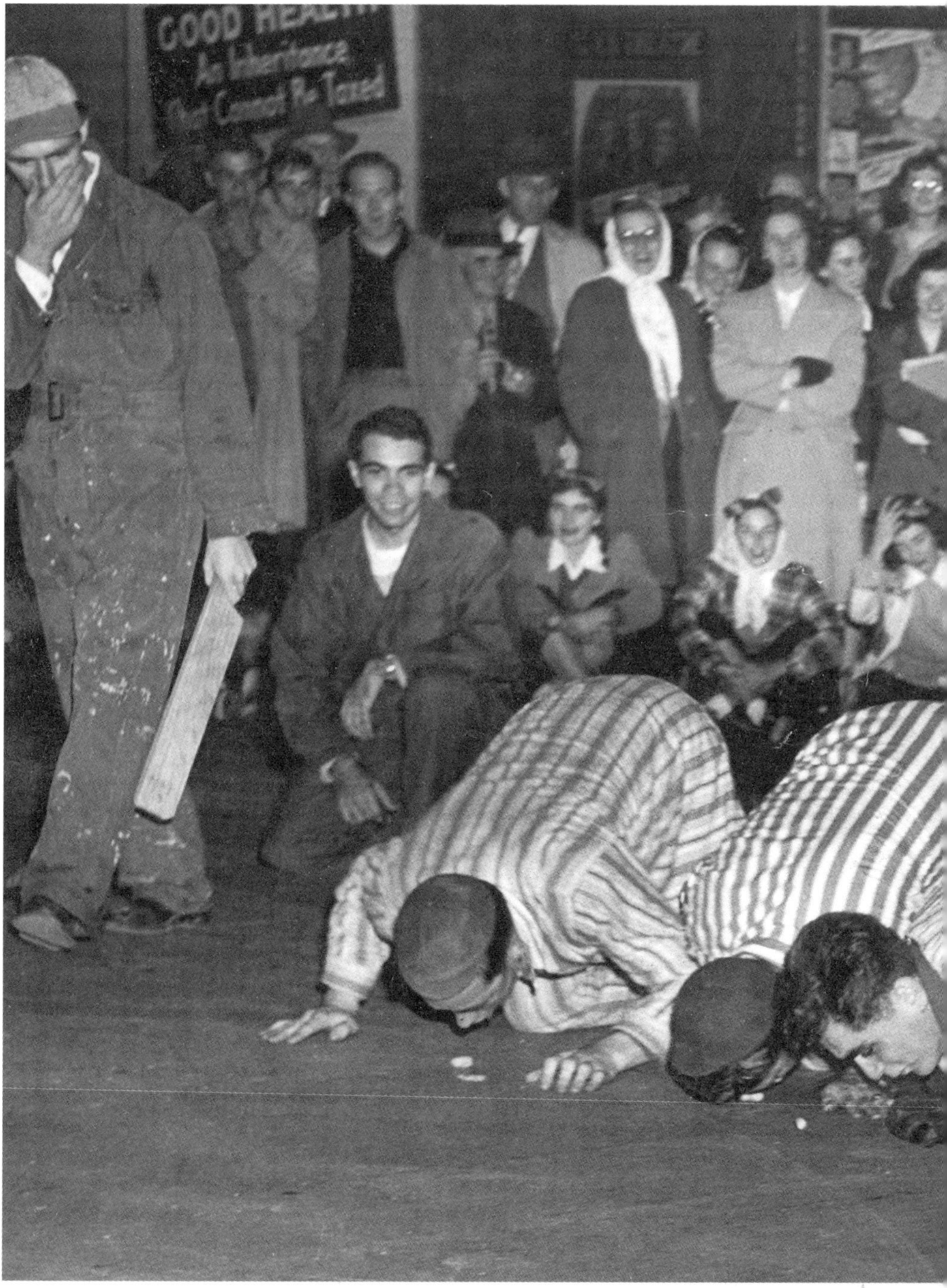
GOOD
An Inheritance
Cannot Be Taxed

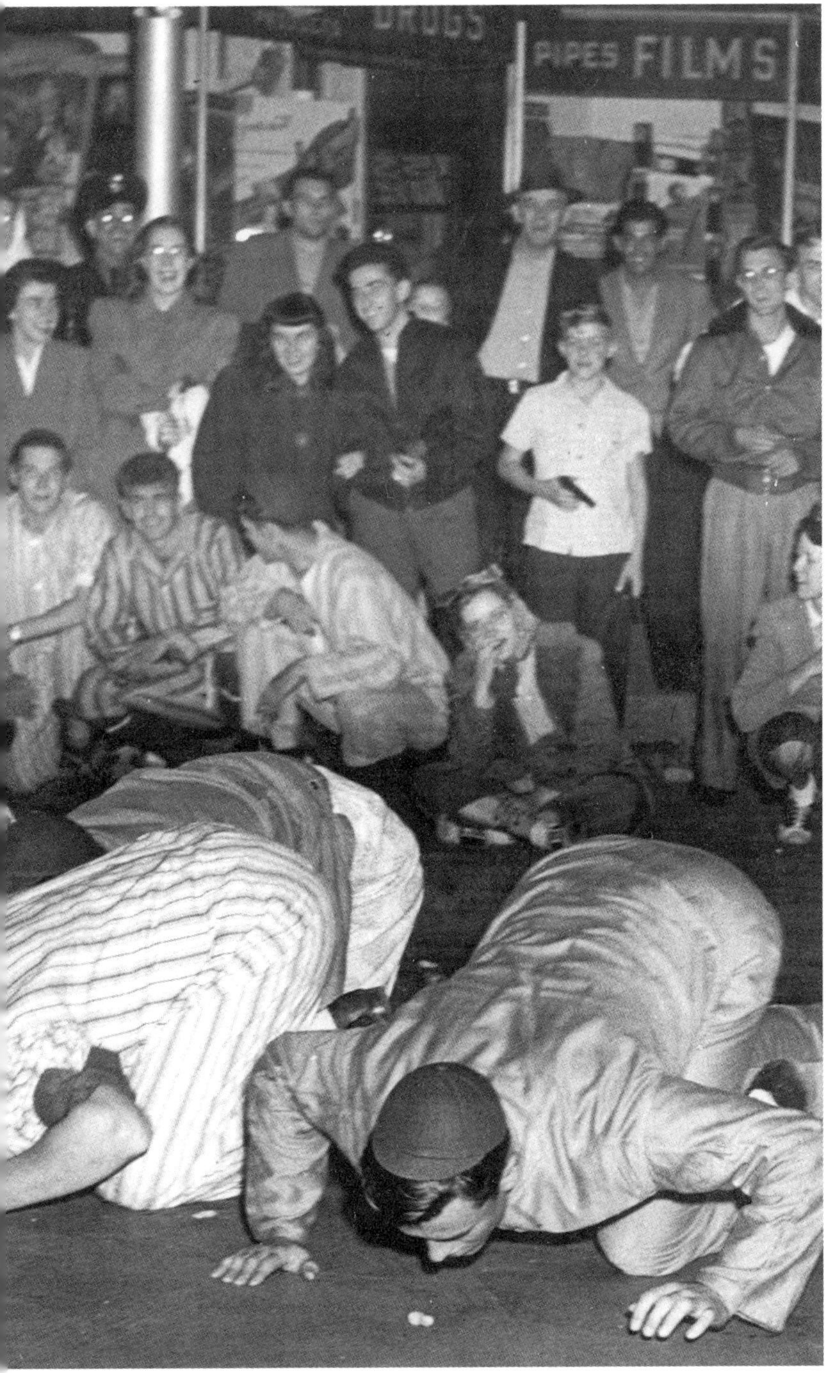

In the 1950s, Campus Day resurrected an early feature of the men's Pajama Parade. At Alma's main intersection, frosh were required to race peanuts propelled by their noses. The race attracted a gathering of amused students and townsfolk. *Courtesy of Alma College Archives.*

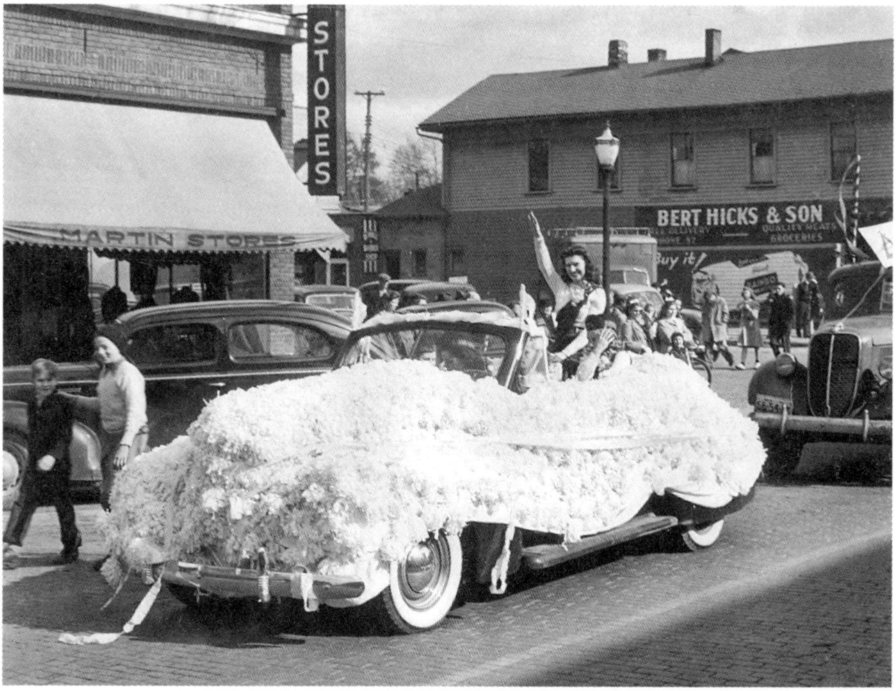

Alma's 1938 homecoming featured the new Kiltie Band and Carra Jones, the first homecoming queen. She was crowned at the Friday night pep rally by football team captain Bob Devaney. Here, she and her court ride in the homecoming parade in a 1939 Buick convertible. *Courtesy of Alma College Archives.*

sportswear, and they wore corsages. In the homecoming parade, they rode in a 1939 Buick convertible. At intermission during the Saturday night dance, everyone went out of the gym and watched the freshman burn their pots, the ceremony marking the time when the yearlings were accepted into the traditions of Alma College. Unfortunately, the Hillsdale College's gridders whumped the Scots 20–0.

Homecoming 1965 was typical of the fall celebration. A pep rally including the pep band, bonfire and snake dance was held on Friday evening. On Saturday, the parade got underway at 11:00 a.m. from Alma High School. The nine floats, queen's float included, along with the Kiltie Band and several high school bands, moved down Superior Street to the college. In the afternoon at Bahlke Field, the Scots hosted—and lost to—the Olivet Comets. Frat houses and residence halls were open, and sororities held teas. The Alumni Buffet was held at 5:30 p.m., and the film *Death of a Salesman* ran in the Dow Auditorium at 7:30 p.m. The

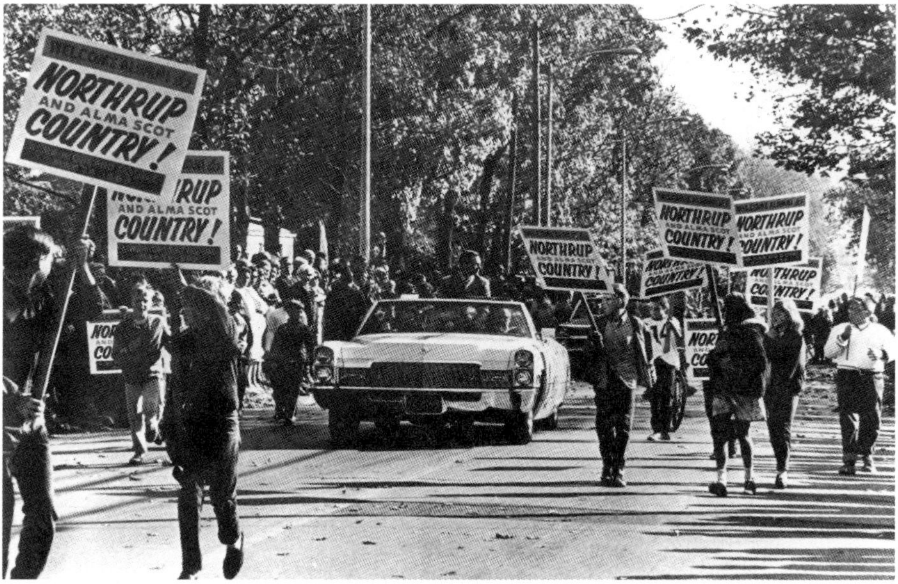

The hero of the 1968 World Series, Detroit Tiger Jim Northrup, was also the hero of the Alma College homecoming parade a few days later. He returned to his alma mater to receive more accolades for his triple in game seven that resulted in two runs and a trophy-taking victory over the St. Louis Cardinals. *Gordon Beld photo; courtesy of Alma College Archives.*

homecoming dance began at 9:00 p.m. On Sunday, the chapel service featured the well-known Reverend Louis Evans of the First Presbyterian Church of Hollywood, the largest Presbyterian church in the world.

For alumni, students and townsfolk, the 1968 homecoming was especially thrilling. Just twelve days after Jim Northrup and his bat propelled the Detroit Tigers to victory over the St. Louis Cardinals in the World Series, the Tiger hero was back at his alma mater for a grand reunion with other Scot players, coaches and fans. In game six of the series, Northrup banged out a bases-loaded home run during Detroit's ten-run third inning. The 13–1 victory tied the series at three wins each. Then in the seventh inning of the decisive seventh game, with the Tigers trailing 1–0, he slammed a triple with two men on to score the game-winning runs for a 4–1 win and the World Championship. The hero of the hour rode in a convertible in the homecoming parade waving to cheering students and townsfolk.

—DAVID MCMACKEN

CHAPTER 11

AT THE END AND UP FRONT

At the conclusion of each academic year on Alma's campus, two special events have proved to be the most fulfilling for students throughout most of the college's history. One is the annual honors convocation, at which many awards for scholarship and service are presented. The other is commencement, when students receive their degrees and the congratulations of family and friends.

Only three students graduated at the college's first commencement in 1891, and a total of only twenty degrees were awarded at the first five graduation ceremonies. Since then, thousands more have left the campus with degrees in hand and set out to make a better life for themselves and a better world for others.

Commencement, of course, is a rather bittersweet affair. Coupled with the joy of having completed years of study successfully is the realization that many close friendships formed at Alma are coming to an end—or, at best, are going to be long-distance relationships. Nevertheless, happiness outweighs the sadness of departure during most graduation days.

However, in the aftermath of Alma's 1905 commencement, it was tragedy rather than joy that prevailed. Guests assembled in the basement dining room of Wright Hall after the ceremony for a celebratory dinner and then left for their homes throughout the state. About two weeks later, reports of illness reached the college, and it became apparent that food contamination was responsible. A week later, twenty-five persons were reported to be suffering, and before a month passed, there were forty.

The first to die was Althea Soule, an Alma resident who had completed studies in the college's kindergarten program a year before. She returned to Wequetonsing in northern Michigan after attending the 1905 commencement and died during a Sunday evening at the hospital in Petoskey.

Early the next day, Herbert Wilcox, another 1904 graduate, died. Though his home was in Alma, he had moved for the summer to Pinconning, where he planned to serve its Presbyterian church after his first year of study at Princeton Seminary.

On Tuesday, the life of Hazel Garland of Alma ended. She had just completed her course of study in the kindergarten program and planned to begin teaching at Owosso that summer.

Charles Chapman, one of the 1905 graduates, followed the others in death. He had studied at Alma after graduating from Mason High School and taking a few courses at Olivet Academy, and he began suffering from the food poisoning soon after entering business at Ithaca.

About a week later, the next to die was Mrs. L.E. Butler of Caro, mother of one of the 1905 graduates who, according to the *Almanian*, "received highest honors."

On August 28, the sixth person to be victimized by the contamination was Professor Joseph W. Ewing, a trustee and promoter of the college in its early days and a member of the college's original faculty. His son, faculty member John T. Ewing, and his grandson, Ernest, also suffered from the food poisoning but survived.

The cause of the contamination could not be determined, according to the *Almanian*, which reported:

> *The source of the siege will never be known. Skilled physicians from all parts of the state have failed to attach the blame to any particular thing. That the banquet concealed the germs is certain, but beyond that it is a mystery. Perhaps it is well that it should remain as such, though the knowledge of the cause would relieve many an anxious mind. At any rate, it was proven beyond a doubt by state authorities that local conditions were in no way at fault.*

Spirits of those present at a later commencement also were dampened—but not by tragedy. The culprit in 1967 was rain. At that time, graduation ceremonies were held on the lawn in front of Dunning Memorial Chapel, and that Saturday in June was a hot and humid day. At the outset of activities, during the procession of graduates, lightning flashed and rain began to fall

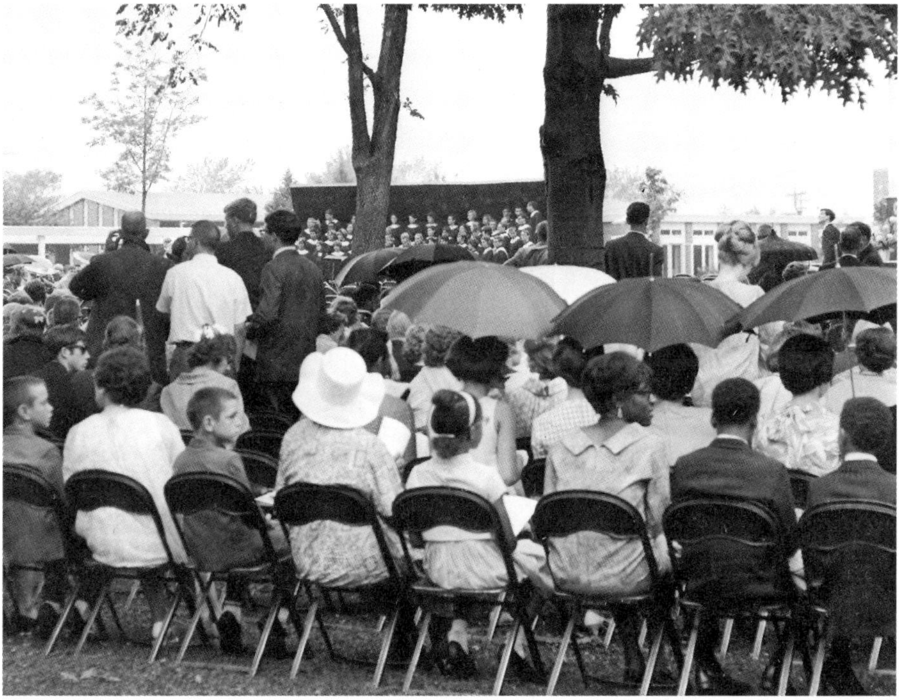

Umbrellas provided shelter from drizzle on a hot, humid morning in 1967 as the crowd listened to the college choir at commencement. Thunderstorms forced those present into Dunning Memorial Chapel twice during the ceremony, and it finished there. *Gordon Beld photo; courtesy of Alma College Archives.*

heavily. Members of the audience fled into the building for shelter, taking up so much of the space that many graduates and faculty members were unable to find a place to sit or stand.

Heat in the building was almost unbearable, so when the storm passed, the ceremony continued outside. But moments later, another deluge broke out. Several discouraged visitors had left by this time, so there was just enough space for the crowd to return inside, where the program continued and degrees were conferred.

The climax of honors convocation, the other special program at the end of each academic year, is presentation of the Barlow Trophy, Alma's most prestigious award for graduating seniors. Three students are nominated for the honor, which is conferred on the basis of scholarship and leadership. Votes by the faculty and student government determine the winner. Names of the recipients are engraved on a large silver bowl, which is kept on display at the college, and each Barlow winner receives a miniature version of the bowl.

A grant from Joel Barlow, 1929 *summa cum laude* graduate of the college and a Washington, D.C. attorney, established the award, and it was first presented in 1949. Another gift in 1982 created the Faculty Barlow Awards, which are presented along with cash honoraria to two faculty members each year.

Had an award such as his been presented in his senior year, Barlow surely would have been the winner. Besides his stellar performance in classrooms, he was active in and a leader of several organizations. He served as editor of the *Almanian* and president of the glee club, student council and two fraternities. He also was on the debate team and twice was winner of the college's annual oratorical contest.

Four years after his graduation from Alma, he served as a volunteer to help vice-president-elect John Nance Garner plan the inauguration of Franklin D. Roosevelt.

Later, as a partner in the law firm of Covington & Burling, he was among the nation's top tax attorneys. A member of the exclusive Burning Tree Country Club, he hobnobbed with other presidents—playing golf with Dwight Eisenhower, singing with pianist Harry Truman and serving on a tax reform committee for John Kennedy.

The pageantry of Alma's commencements and convocations was enhanced in the late 1960s by creation of an impressive ceremonial mace that has been at the head of processions to those events ever since.

The world's earliest maces were weapons—clubs with heavy heads to which sharp spikes of flint or volcanic glass might be attached. These devices, which could cut deeply as well as deliver powerful blows, were used as early as the Upper Paleolithic period, about 40,000 to 10,000 BC, when humans still lived in caves and agriculture had not yet developed.

Eventually, when maces ceased to be useful in combat, kings and warlords removed the spikes and replaced them with precious jewels and metals. They became symbols of authority and leadership, and they still are used for that purpose today. Among institutions that have them, besides those of higher education, are the United States Senate and House of Representatives.

Alma's mace is a six-foot-long piece of black walnut on which were carved symbols pertaining to the college's history, traditions and relationships. It was designed by Kent Kirby, a member of the Alma faculty from 1962 to 1990, when he retired as chairman of the Art and Design Department.

At the top of the mace is a four-sided mandorla or bud shape, which surrounds a cross. Use of a Tau Cross, according to Kirby, was dictated by the way the mandorla is shaped. He added that the pomegranate motif on the mandorla shafts symbolizes linking of the Old and New Testaments.

Among Old Testament accounts mentioning the fruit are those of God ordering Moses to put embroidered pomegranates, with golden bells between, at the bottom of the high priest's robe (Exodus 28:33–34) and of Solomon depicting pomegranates on the capitals of the two pillars at the front of the temple he built in Jerusalem (1 Kings 7:16–20). According to Jewish tradition, the pomegranate is a symbol for righteousness, and many Jews eat pomegranates on Rosh Hashanah.

For many Christians, pomegranates are symbols of the resurrection and the hope of eternal life. In Christian art, the bursting of the seeds of this fruit are likened to Christ's rising and leaving the tomb. Paintings of Mary and the baby Jesus by Botticelli, Leonardo da Vinci and Raphael include a pomegranate as a demonstration of this symbolism.

Just below the mandorla on the Alma mace is a circular field on which are carved figures reworked from engravings by sixteenth-century German artist Hans Sebald Beham. They represent the seven original liberal arts—Rhetorica (rhetoric), represented by a speaker; Dialectica (logic), a winged figure holding a scale of balances; Musica (music), seated with a harp; Astrologia (astronomy), attempting to hold a star; Geometria (geometry), with a compass; Arithmetria (arithmetic), holding a slate with numbers on it; and Grammatica (grammar), holding a slate with alphabets. Each of the seven figures is set in an archway separated by columns, which, according to Kirby, refer to classical knowledge and antiquity.

Farther down the shaft is a pentagon, on the five faces of which are carved the seals of the college, the Presbyterian Church, the State of Michigan, the United States and the United Nations.

A Scottish shield motif carved on the lower portion of the mace's shaft is symbolic of Alma College's link with Scotland through its affiliation with the Presbyterian Church.

After completing his design, Kirby started searching for a talented woodcarver who could bring the mace to reality. On a fishing trip to northern Michigan, he learned of Robert Hellem, a carver whose workshop was in a small former store at Manistee. Kirby stopped there to become acquainted and was impressed. Hellem had been carving for about twenty years, the first fifteen of them at American Seating Company's Grand Rapids plant. Transferred to a branch of the company in Mississippi, he stayed in the South for only a year before returning to Michigan to do a carving for

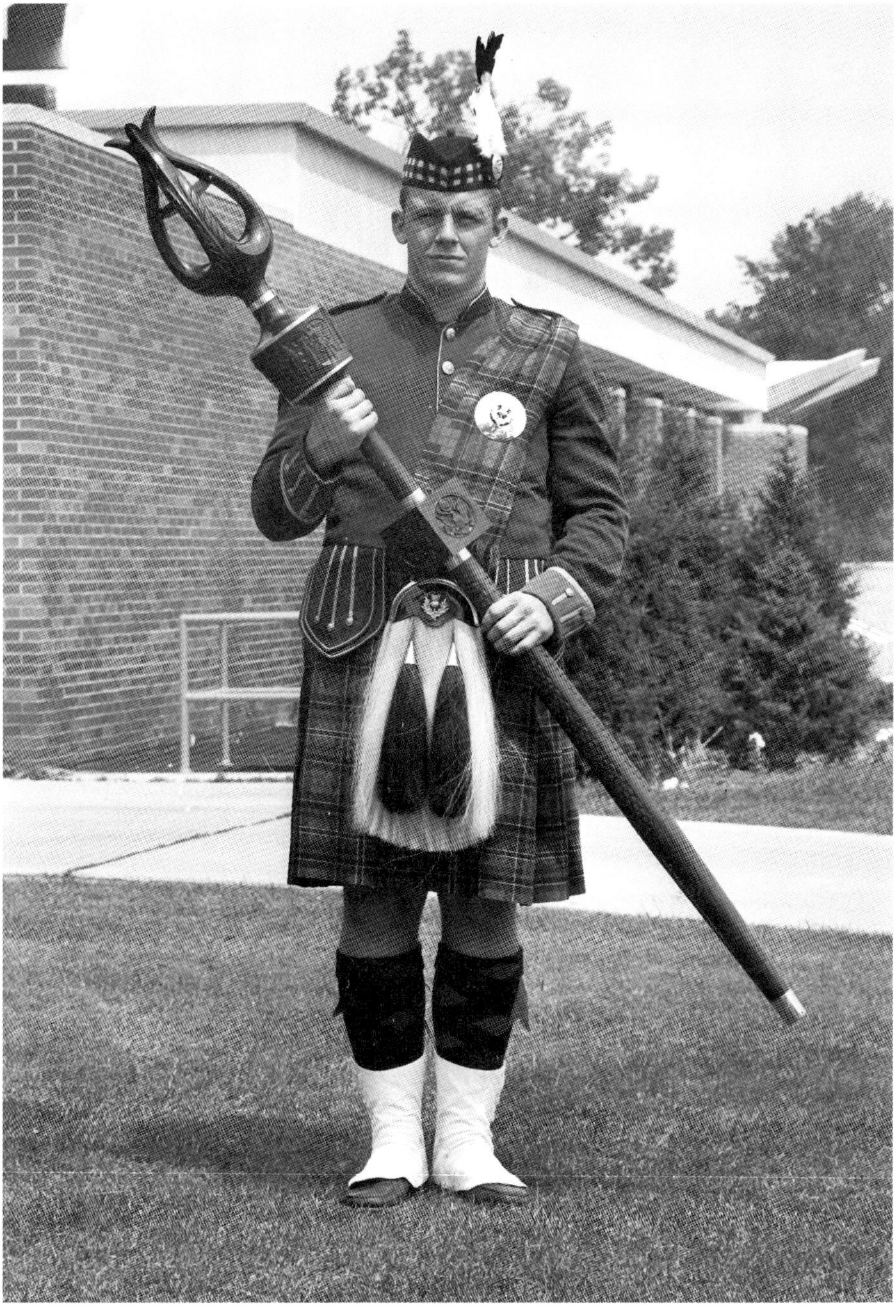

Heavy and husky All-MIAA lineman Ken Mitchell carried the college's new mace for the first time at the 1968 commencement ceremony. Nobody made any smart remarks about the "skirt" he was wearing. *Gordon Beld photo; courtesy of Alma College Archives.*

DeRaniera Studios of Detroit. That job was completed in seven months, and he then opened his own studio in Manistee.

After his first meeting with Hellem, Kirby returned with his drawings to discuss the mace project in greater detail. Hellem was soon at work, and after six weeks, the mace was ready.

The bearers of ceremonial maces at most colleges and universities that have them usually are high-ranking members of the faculty or administration. At some institutions, even the chancellor or president carries the mace at the head of academic processions. However, at Alma, the honor of carrying the mace to convocations and graduation ceremonies has always gone to a student.

First to lead an Alma campus procession with the mace was Ken Mitchell, who preceded faculty members and graduates to the college's 1968 commencement. A burly three-time All-Michigan Intercollegiate Athletic Association lineman for the Scot football team, he had no difficulty toting the heavy piece. And nobody made any cracks about the plaid kilt that he wore either.

—Gordon Beld

Chapter 12

A Changing Curriculum

When it was founded, the purpose of Alma College was clearly twofold: to provide education for potential ministers and missionaries and at the same time to provide a general education to young people who would move into many fields of endeavor. Over the years, the college constantly attempted to adapt to the changing world but also adhere to its founding principles. Its changing curriculum reflected this response.

By 1910, under President August Bruske, the college provided six programs of study: the College; the School of Pedagogy, for teachers; the Academy, for students who had not completed high school; the Commercial School; the School of Music; and the School of Art. These courses of study all reflected to some degree the needs of students in higher education.

High school graduates seeking admission to Alma College were required to present fifteen high school credits in English, mathematics, history, science, foreign language (two years of Latin) and electives.

The entrance exam included written paragraphs on prescribed works popular or well known: *Silas Marner, Pilgrim's Progress, Ivanhoe, The Merchant of Venice,* etc. The Latin test required sight-reading both prose and verse passages. And so the testing continued through the various disciplines. Students possessing a certificate stating they had graduated from the Academy were automatically accepted into the College program.

Graduation from the College program demanded 120 semester hours of work. In general, the required courses were typical: English, six hours; mathematics, eight hours; history, six hours; laboratory science, six hours;

philosophy, six hours; Bible and theism, seven hours; elocution (speech), two hours; physical training, two hours; and foreign language (Greek, Latin, German, French), sixteen hours.

Behind this curriculum was the assumption that many students would go on to graduate school in areas of law, medicine, engineering, teaching and Christian work.

Male students were encouraged to obtain physical education credits by playing on college teams: football, baseball, track, tennis and cross-country. From November to April, the freshmen and sophomores were involved in marching, calisthenics and work on the horse, bars and ladders. An athletic fee provided a private locker and free admission to all sports events.

In 1912, the college dropped the Commercial School and the first two years of the Academy. More youth were completing at least several years of high school, so the Academy concentrated on eleventh- and twelfth-grade work. It was no mark against a student that he or she had not completed high school, for many students had dropped out to go to work to support families or because no one in their families saw the benefits of attending college.

Alma College experienced unprecedented growth in 1912. Many students who had intended to stay for only one or two years decided to stay for their entire college careers and graduate from Alma. The school established an Alma College Fellowship, whereby one student a year was chosen to be supported for graduate work. Harlow Whittemore had graduated in 1908, but in 1912, he was chosen as the first "fellow." His field of interest was landscape architecture.

August Bruske, the beloved Prexy, resigned in 1912 and was succeeded by Thomas Blaisdell, scholar and author of several textbooks. Blaisdell continued to promote Alma as Bruske had. In selling the college to high school students, the catalogue stated, "Alma is a small college with a well-trained, experienced, efficient body of instructors. You will make no mistake by going to Alma if an education is what you are seeking."

The catalogue pointed out that Alma College provided a kindergarten program for prospective teachers. Not many colleges in the country offered such training. The kindergarten program emphasized the ideas of Friedrich Froebel, originator of the kindergarten. The ladies in the program even had their own club, the Froebel Society. The catalogue firmly averred, "Today the really successful teacher must be a college graduate." It also pointed out that teacher training would allow young women to support themselves in a respectable career. Trained teachers were in great demand, and all education graduates could expect to be hired. The kindergarten program flourished until 1920, when other education courses replaced it.

President Blaisdell, in his inaugural speech, heralded a bold concept among Christian colleges. He declared, "The renaissance of the Denominational College must be a triumph of 'progressivism' over 'conservatism'...The Denominational College must take its stand formally against tradition and insist on its right to think and plan for itself." He also asked for a red-blooded energy from students, the kind of energy seen too seldom in ministers.

The president suggested that women's education was suited to make "superlatively efficient homemakers." He claimed that not much college work was aimed at achieving this goal. In place of the traditional classes, he intended to introduce work that would develop better mothers, better wives and better homemakers. How this proclamation was received is not recorded, but for the most part, female students of that time would have agreed with his plan.

Warning against behavior common at many universities, he specifically cited instructors who smoked and drank with students and laughed at dirty stories. But the new instructor, he stated, would consider his influence on students more important than any personal satisfaction. How the "new" instructors reacted was not recorded either.

In appealing to the outlying communities, Alma College began offering extension courses on evenings and Saturdays in 1912. This was a radical form of education, but the college was trying to serve persons who could not attend regular classes but craved skills and learning. Classes were conducted in neighboring communities once a week. The art classes included drawing, applied design, bookbinding, stenciling and basketry. Other classes included music, storytelling and children's literature, debate, German, algebra, geometry, chemistry and the handling of exceptional children.

Blaisdell's emphasis was on curriculum, and he insisted that the courses being offered had to be justified by need. Thus, in 1913, the Academy was eliminated.

By 1914, the college was advertising that it could provide students with proper preparation to go on to professional schooling in such areas as medicine, dentistry, pharmacy, engineering and law.

In the early years of the college, the academic load for most students was five courses, which met for "recitation" three times a week. The day began at 8:00 a.m. and concluded at 4:15 p.m. Most testing was done at semester's end. Faculty graded students on a one-hundred-point scale, and seventy-five was set as "passing." Faculty determined grades using A through E.

After serving three years as president, Blaisdell resigned to take a position in the East. He was replaced by Harry Means Crooks, a former school administrator, newspaper editor and college president. Crooks had the privilege of guiding Alma College through the struggles sparked by both the Great War and the Great Depression.

Alma College was accredited by the North Central Association in 1916, beginning one of the longest unbroken periods of accreditation in Michigan. President Crooks was able to institute the sabbatical for faculty, although complications engendered by World War I and the Depression of the 1930s kept this privilege from being put into practice. The faculty was poorly paid and had no retirement plan or health insurance. A pension plan was begun in 1919, and then the issue of salaries was approached. Faculty salaries gained deserved raises of 20 percent in 1919 and 10 percent in 1920. This was influenced, perhaps, by the immense wealth in the city of Alma, which resulted from the phenomenal growth of Alma's Republic Motor Truck Company. The city's public schools were generously supported by taxpayers, and the contrast in compensation between the public school system and the college was significant.

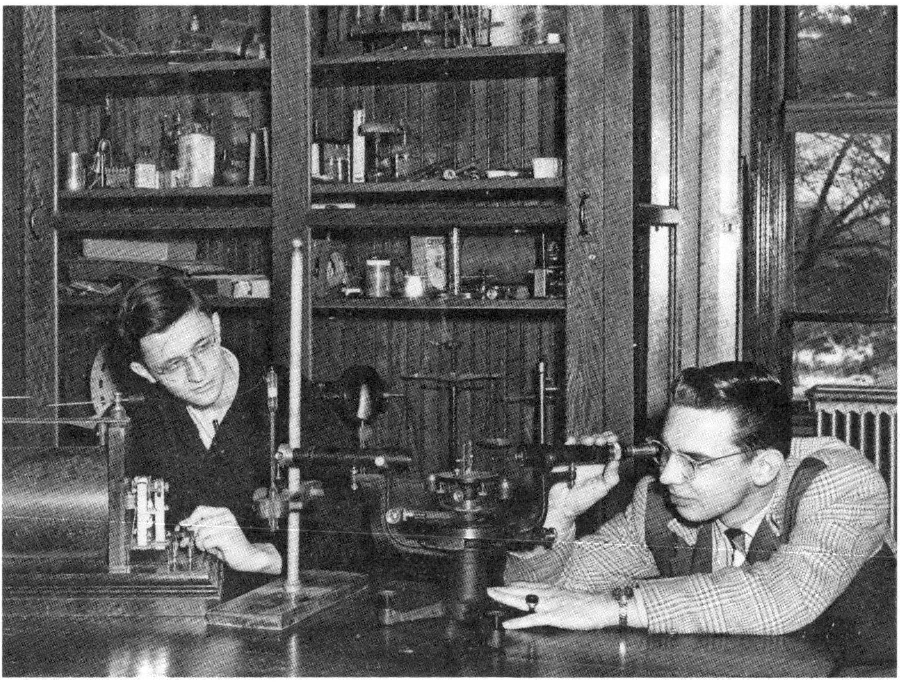

Using a spectrometer (at right) and an induction coil, these two students carry out a physics experiment in a college laboratory during the 1940s. *Courtesy of Alma College Archives.*

Curricular changes were made as the need was perceived. Graduation requirements instituted in 1919 reflected the goal of the college to provide liberal training. The kindergarten program was abandoned, and the coursework in the junior and senior years was strengthened. Two majors were now required of each student. The new grouping system of curriculum demanded a shifting of graduation requirements. The plan, designed primarily by faculty, changed the direction of the academic program.

A problem that required much discussion was how to deal with students who cut classes. Faculty enacted a modified set of absence regulations. A degree of credit was deducted for each absence in a class, and if the absences exceeded twice the number of weekly recitations, the student was dropped from the class. Three cases of tardiness equaled one absence.

The faculty also tried to become consistent in using letter grades, abandoning the old one-hundred-point scale. The stiffness of Alma's grading system was appreciated by professors at the University of Michigan, where Alma graduates often went for postgraduate training. Between 1900 and 1935, 74 of 897 alumni had earned graduate degrees at the university. This compared favorably with graduates from other small Michigan colleges.

President Crooks resigned in 1937 and was replaced by an Alma graduate, John Wirt Dunning, who found the college's financial situation to be tentative. Recognizing that the college would survive only if it met students' needs, new courses were instituted in fine arts and physical training for women. Incoming freshmen were now required to present more credits, and if they were deficient, they made up the lack through additional college classes. The Freshman Days program demanded that frosh attend fifteen one-hour periods on Fridays during first semester. Subjects taught in these special sessions included reading, study, library, health and hygiene, table etiquette, social contacts, educational guidance, vocational guidance and personality development. President Dunning also instituted a strong core experience in American democracy.

Six months before Dunning left for health reasons in 1942, the country was drawn into war by the Japanese attack on Pearl Harbor. The man who saw the college through the difficult years of World War II was former vice-president Roy Hamilton, who had been at Alma since 1919. During his presidency, the government's V-12 program, training navy men and marines, kept the school open.

Following the war, an influx of veterans seeking higher education prompted the building of temporary housing and the placing of numerous house trailers for accommodations. A new business major was added, and inter-departmental majors were developed. Classes that would train men as foremen and industrial managers were put in place. Men in this program also were required to experience factory work.

The early 1950s under Presidents Dale Welch and John Stanley Harker saw little advancement in curricula. Changes, however, were on the horizon. Robert D. Swanson was inaugurated in 1956. This bundle of energy immediately appointed a Long Range Planning Committee, which inevitably affected the curriculum. As a result of the committee's findings, a number of new professors were hired. Many were PhDs, and they were frustrated by the lack of commitment of many students. Athletes sometimes disappeared from the campus and only returned in time to play in the next season. Tightening up the criteria for admission and retention, the school triggered "Black Thursday." In January 1958, more than 60 students were dismissed for poor scholarship. Another 134 were put on probation.

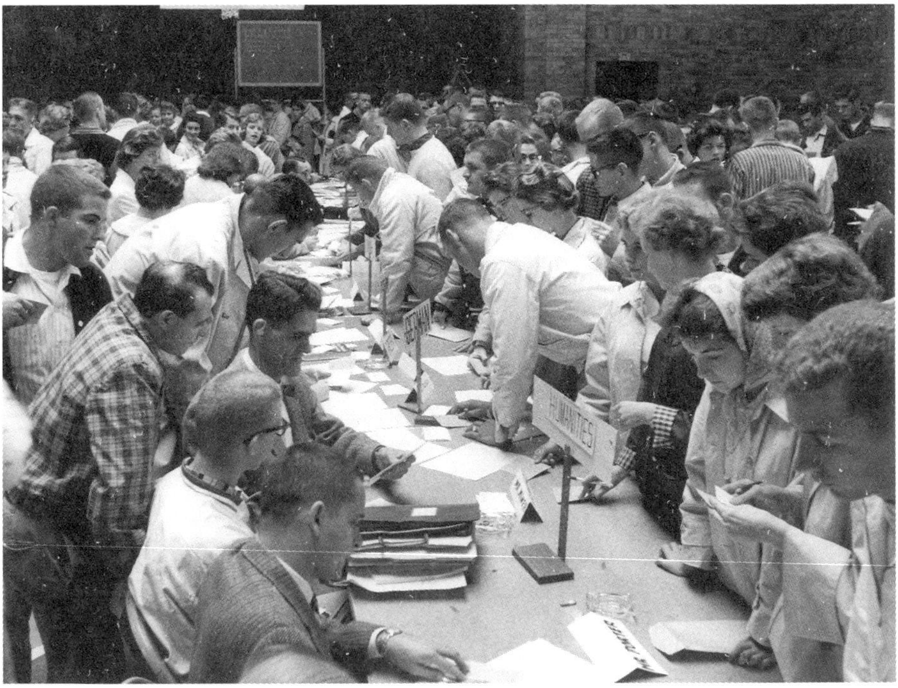

English professor Ray Miner helps students enroll in humanities courses during the frenzy of registration in 1950. *Courtesy of Alma College Archives.*

In 1959, new graduation requirements were instituted. Students were still required to take one course in religion, two courses in laboratory science, three courses in social science and four courses in foreign language. But now a bold new course appeared—Western Civilization. It was an amalgamation of English, history, philosophy and religion courses designed to create an overview of who we are as Americans and how we got here. In addition, seniors were given more intensive exams in their majors, and a senior project, such as a thesis, essay, research project or creative work, was demanded. With the dropping of secretarial courses, the minor in home economics and the bachelor in music education degree, Alma College drifted back to being a college of the liberal arts.

In the 1960s, student enrollment increased substantially and new faculty members were hired. A whirlwind of changes swept the college, improving its reputation in academic circles. Some departments were strengthened. New departments were created. Within a few years, the enthusiasm for the Western Civ program declined as faculty members questioned whether some Western Civ courses wouldn't better serve in majors, cognates or electives. Eventually, the highly touted core curriculum, along with all-campus reading and the senior thesis, proved difficult to administer. In keeping with the general changing of standards and mores during the 1960s, the faculty made major changes in loosening the curriculum.

A new schedule of three eleven-week terms replaced the two-semester plan. Course requirements in mathematics, speech, foreign language, social science, humanities and natural science could be satisfied through proficiency exams. The senior thesis was dropped, as was the all-campus reading program. The Western Civ core curriculum faded away.

In 1969, the chief academic structure, Old Main, burned. This disaster seemed to herald more changes in curriculum. New educational requirements were being implemented. Ronald O. Kapp was appointed to the newly created position of provost. President Swanson appointed a President's Commission to take a fresh look at the purpose of Alma College. It concluded that the academic program should focus on two goals: educating responsible human beings rather than merely educating students and concentrating on students as learners rather than centering on departments or disciplines. Thus, the old requirements were relaxed.

New challenges in the 1970s resulted in the addition of the bachelor of fine arts, the bachelor of music and the bachelor of social work degrees. The Department of Business Administration saw phenomenal growth,

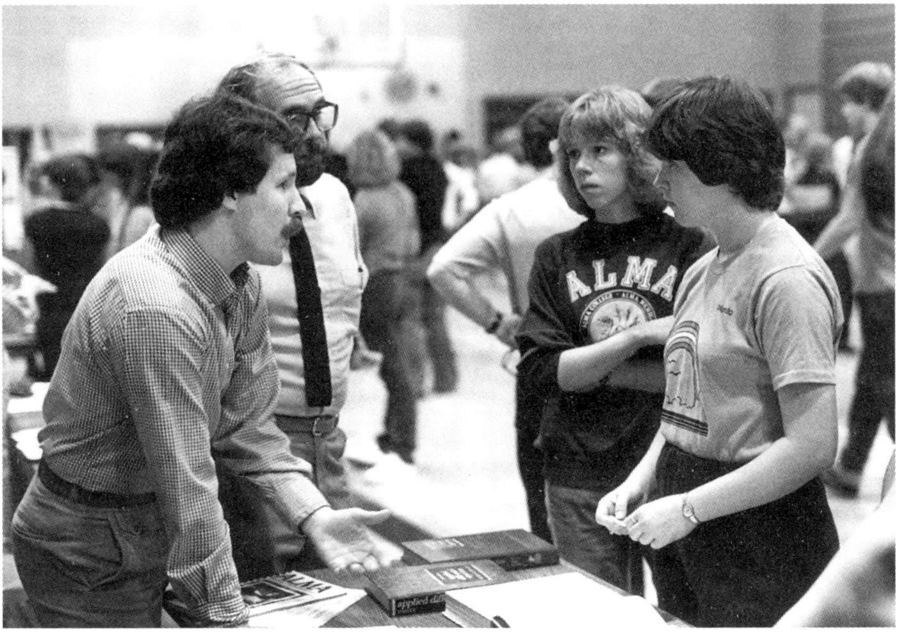

Professors Tim Sipka and Mel Nyman advise students regarding math course selections during an academic fair held in the early 1980s. Each department set up a table advertising its discipline, and freshmen visited the tables to learn about that department. *Gordon Beld photo; courtesy of Alma College Archives.*

with nearly one-third of students enrolled in that program. Reflecting the strength of the curriculum, the college was granted a Phi Beta Kappa charter in 1979.

President Swanson retired in 1980, having overseen major changes in the physical plant and the curriculum during his tenure. To his successors came the responsibility of preparing Alma College to enter the twenty-first century.

In fulfilling this demand, several curricular changes are evident. A freshman preterm was offered and proved popular. The traditional three terms of the 3-3-3 schedule were replaced by a 4-4-1 system with two longer terms and a single-class, month-long spring term in May. Many of the spring term classes involve travel that takes students abroad.

A variety of changes keeps the college curriculum up to date. New majors in anthropology, biotechnology, healthcare administration and others have been added. For the Education Department, constant changes in the state curriculum require constant changes in education classes for prospective teachers. Recognizing the need for excellence in writing, the college requires students to take four classes that demand writing in several disciplines. An international component may be fulfilled by foreign language study or by international travel.

In striving for excellence, Alma College adapts its curriculum to meet the needs of students in a constantly changing world.

—David McMacken

Chapter 13

ALMA ABROAD

Since an early goal of the college was to train Presbyterian missionaries, it was only natural that several early graduates would take trips by steamship to faraway lands carrying the gospel to the heathen. Thus began the school's international outreach.

One of the first to go was Bernice Hunting, daughter of the first college president George F. Hunting. She graduated in 1891 and sailed to Tripoli, then part of Syria, on an investigative trip. Once she understood the country's needs, she began establishing schools there. In 1900, she wrote home that work around Tripoli was different this year from the former years in Syria. Illness in the city had closed the boarding school, and she had moved to a village called Fia, where she organized a school for girls. She was there two weeks and then moved on to other villages. She wrote home, "I should be glad of the prayers of friends in Alma, for I am in some sense your representative here."

Numerous other students represented the church and the college in worldwide missionary work. They would write letters updating their college friends on the progress of their ministries. Claire Booth-McKee wrote from Siam, "The land…has great possibilities…were it not overshadowed by the darkness of heathen superstition and sin." Some missionaries would return to campus when on furlough and speak in chapel of their work and their adventures.

As years passed, students continued to go forth with the gospel to faraway places, but a gradual change of emphasis in church and college stressed

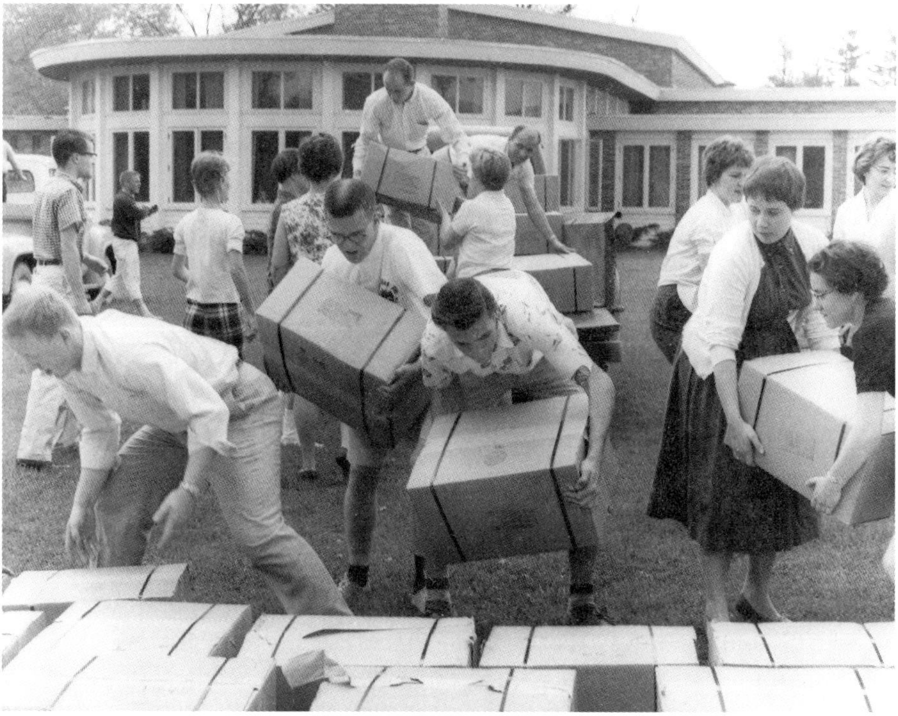

When the Books for Africa project mushroomed across the state in 1959–60, many truckloads of books arrived on the Alma College campus. Here, boxed books are being carried to the lawn of the chapel and stacked in the shape of the African continent before the dedication ceremony. *Courtesy of Alma College Archives.*

helping the natives of various countries more than deliberately spreading the gospel. During the 1920s, '30s and '40s, few students traveled abroad as a result of college programs. The '50s and '60s saw the beginnings of travels that would enhance students' skills—often by increasing proficiency in a foreign language and living in a different culture.

Alma College students were alerted to another culture when the Books for Africa program occurred in 1959–60. A Presbyterian International Youth Leader, Dr. James Robinson, conceived the project that would inspire high school and college students across Michigan. He shared it in the summer of 1959 at a Presbyterian conference on the campus of Alma College.

The concept was to collect children's books to supply a library in Kenya. During 1959–60, the suggestion exploded into reality when young people began collecting books of wider appeal, and the Books for Africa program was underway. Alma College served as the headquarters for the project.

Books were collected by youth in the Michigan Synod. The volumes were sent to the college by the truckload from all over the state. Eventually the influx of books outgrew the library basement and old arts building. The collection was moved to the science building basement, where volunteers boxed the sixty thousand books for shipment to Africa. Several companies joined the project by donating boxes and by offering both trucking and ocean shipping. An estimated five thousand volunteer hours went into getting the books to Africa.

In May 1960, a dedication ceremony drew to the college nearly five hundred Michigan young people, college students and guests. The 1,600 boxes of books were stacked on the lawn near the chapel in the shape of the African continent, and people stood next to this symbol as Dr. John Karobi of Kenya accepted the books. Guests surrounding the "continent" heard him explain that the books would constitute the first lending library in that part of Africa, and it would serve around one million people. The Kenyan

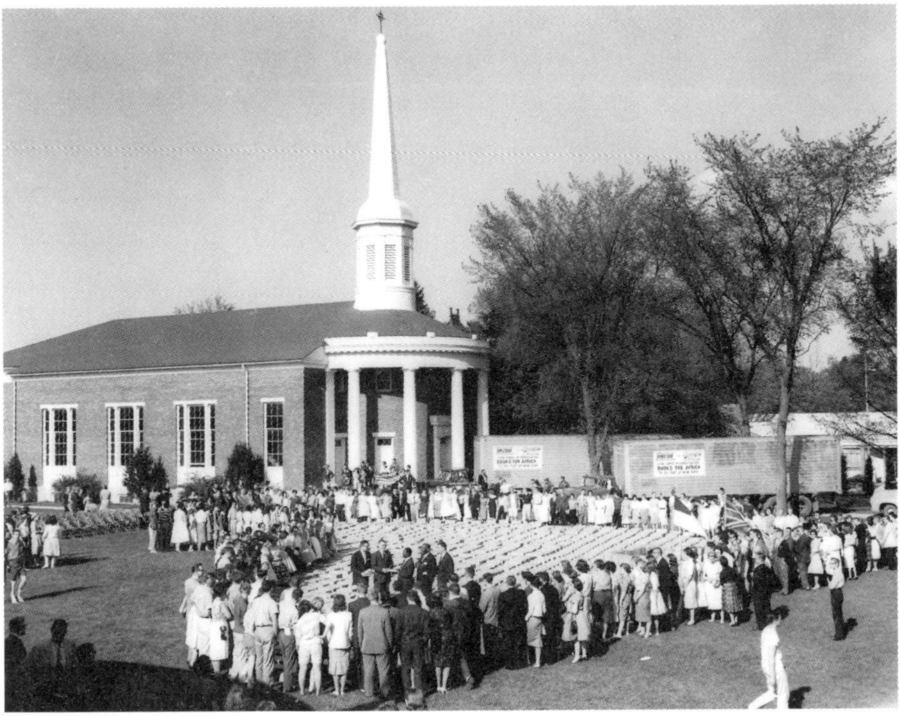

As students and guests surround "Africa," Dr. John Karobi accepts the boxes of books for his country. He and other officials are standing in the continent for the ceremony. *John N. Scholl photo; courtesy of Alma College Archives.*

government had donated a building to house the library, and the Agha Khan had given $5,000 to decorate the building and install shelving and lighting. He assured the crowd that he would be back in Nairobi, Kenya, ready to receive the books when they arrived by ship.

This project was covered by *Life* magazine, press services and television stations and was the first of several educational connections that Alma College established with African nations. The need for students to adjust their worldview prompted the establishment of numerous foreign study programs that took students abroad.

The Studies in France program began in 1963. Alma College, in cooperation with L'Ecole de l'Alliance Francaise, made its first attempts to send students abroad for study during their junior year. The Studies in France were designed to increase language skills and to allow students to experience the French culture.

Kay Tack, along with other Alma College students, spent a year in Paris. She discovered that many Parisians spoke English, and she had to resist the temptation to speak English when her purpose in being there was to improve her French-speaking skills. Studies did not occupy all of her time. She enjoyed the Luxembourg Gardens, which was a favorite of the eleven Alma College students in the program at the time she was in Paris. Kay met French families, was invited to dinner and was put in social situations where she would need to speak French.

Jane Davison spent her junior year attending the University of Madrid under a program through New York University. She boarded in the homes of Spaniards and learned that they lived life to the fullest. She also learned social practices when several American girls went to a dance. It was the custom for an unescorted female to dance with only one gentleman for the entire dance. These girls danced with numerous men, embarrassing their host families.

She and three other girls rented a car and camped their way through southern Spain. The camping areas had no fireplaces, so the girls lived on sandwiches. She also reported that her art class in Madrid met three times a week at the Prado, one of the world's great art museums. In the late 1970s, Alma College developed its own program of studies in Madrid.

The junior year abroad program took JoAnn Eschelman to the University of Heidelberg in Germany in 1965–66. She found that the German professors were more relaxed than those at home. As did many foreign students, JoAnn took classes in the language department to hone her German reading and speaking skills. She traveled to France and to Berlin, where she observed the infamous Berlin Wall. She reported that the students in her group peered at the East German guards, who peered right back.

The success of the junior year abroad program also inspired studies in Mexico, South America and Spain. By 1979, in collaboration with the University of Aberdeen in Scotland, students could have a foreign experience in an English-language culture.

Perhaps the major cross-cultural experience sponsored by Alma College was the Africa Fellowship, which ran from 1963 to 1993. Each year, a student was chosen to travel to Nigeria, where he or she would teach at the Mayflower School in Ikenne. The school had been founded in 1956 by Tai Solarin, who worked with Alma provost Ron Kapp to set up collaboration between the schools.

An anonymous donor funded the first fellows to go to Nigeria. The funding supplied the student with round-trip transportation, a monthly subsistence allowance and money for travel in the country. The student was expected to spend the year teaching in his area of expertise. The goal was to improve conditions for Nigerians, but often fellows found that the greatest influence was not on what they did but on what they learned.

The first fellow, Jerry Smith, went to Nigeria in 1963. Each week, he taught fifteen periods of chemistry and nine periods of biology to tenth- and eleventh-grade students. He volunteered to sponsor fifteen students for two hours a week in societies studying agriculture, landscaping and music. He pointed out that cobras, army ants, malaria and the steaming heat and torrential rain of the jungle were unpleasant, but he concluded, "We have received more than we have given."

Thomas Fegley, the fellow for 1968–69, gave advice to future fellows not to buy a lot of things to take to Nigeria as virtually everything they would

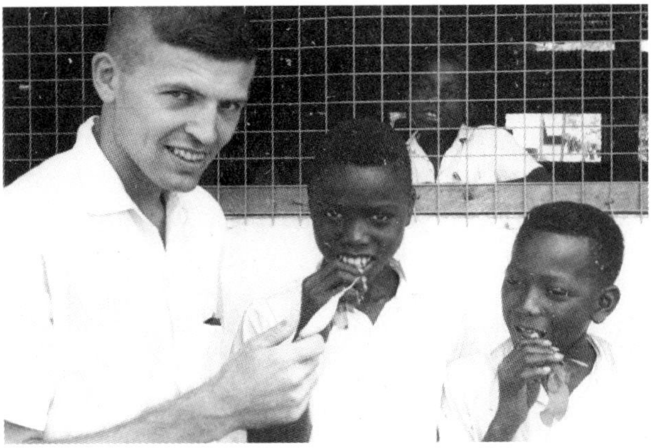

Alma College's first Africa Fellow was Jerry Smith, who traveled to Nigeria in 1964 to teach at Mayflower School. Here, he's introducing two of his students to radishes. *Courtesy of Alma College Archives.*

need could be purchased there. He said to take a camera, one change of clothes and some money. He also suggested taking personal gifts for the school's principal and his family.

He taught English, but he felt he did it very poorly because he didn't know what he was doing. He had not been trained to teach English as a second language. He also found the native Yoruba language very challenging, as did virtually all the fellows over the years of the program.

Fegley admitted to culture shock, but he concluded that the only way to counter his mixed feelings was to socialize. He advised that future fellows should not hole up with a book but accept invitations to go to town for a drink of palm wine.

He revealed that fellows should be sensitive to Nigerian culture and expectations. He wrote, "A missionary zeal from an American kid who is rich and who will return to America in one year can be very offensive." He suggested that the Nigerians would judge the fellows not on how well they taught but on how well they got along with the students.

Fellow Susan Buchan, 1969–70, arrived in September in a war-torn Nigeria. The war ended in January 1970, and she and others became involved in relief work in addition to teaching. They obtained a jeep and a large truck, which they loaded with medical supplies. They left at four or five o'clock in the morning and drove to a river where the bridge had been blown up. They slept that night on the sand and then in the morning crossed the river on a very rickety ferry and began delivering their cargo to hospitals.

In 1975, Tom Rademacher, the thirteenth fellow, ran into difficulties in obtaining a visa. He applied in April, but it had not arrived by the time school began, and he was put in the awkward position of not being able to take classes or settle into employment as he waited for the visa to arrive. When it finally arrived, it was too late for him to travel to Nigeria, and he declined to be re-nominated for the program. In the past, visa problems had delayed Mark Wangberg and Craig Carpenter from arriving in Nigeria on time.

At homecoming in 1986, fourteen of the twenty-four former fellows arrived on campus for a reunion with the founder of Mayflower School, Tai Solarin, who had been the primary link between Alma College and the Nigerian school. They were excited to see him and exchange news and reminiscences. Solarin had been a prisoner of conscience in Nigeria, having been arrested and jailed numerous times. He felt the key to the future of Nigeria was good education. In 1971, he was Alma's commencement speaker, and the college gave him an honorary doctor of letters degree.

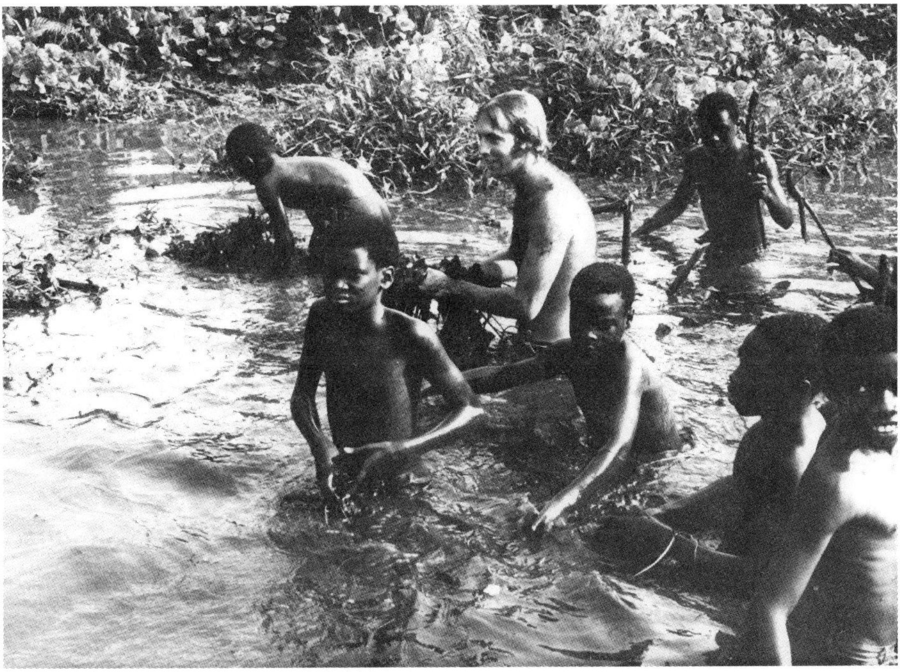

Gary Klepper, 1972 Africa Fellow, helps students clean weeds from the river near Mayflower School in Ikenne, Nigeria. *Courtesy of Alma College Archives.*

Most of the fellows revealed that their experience in Nigeria had changed their lives. After graduation, many went into professions designed to help the poor and needy. David Eyer and his wife, Dodie, went to Nigeria in 1970–71, and their experiences changed their perspectives. They saw Nigerians who were starving as a result of the civil war. The Eyers saw a sharp contrast when an *Almanian* arrived reporting that students back home were upset because the food service offered only two flavors of ice cream. David described these complaints as petty. Later, David and Dodie served as teachers of the Inuit in northern Canada.

In 1973, the Africa Fellowship was renamed to honor the late Dr. Jerry G. Smith, who had been the first fellow. The Africa Fellowship continued for thirty years before being discontinued, not because it had failed but because political unrest in Africa became a safety issue for the fellows.

Eventually, students from Mayflower School studied at Alma College. The first Nigerian student to come to Alma was Olugbenga "Benga" Oredein in 1966. He was the second young man from his village to go overseas, and his departure caused much excitement among his people. Various school

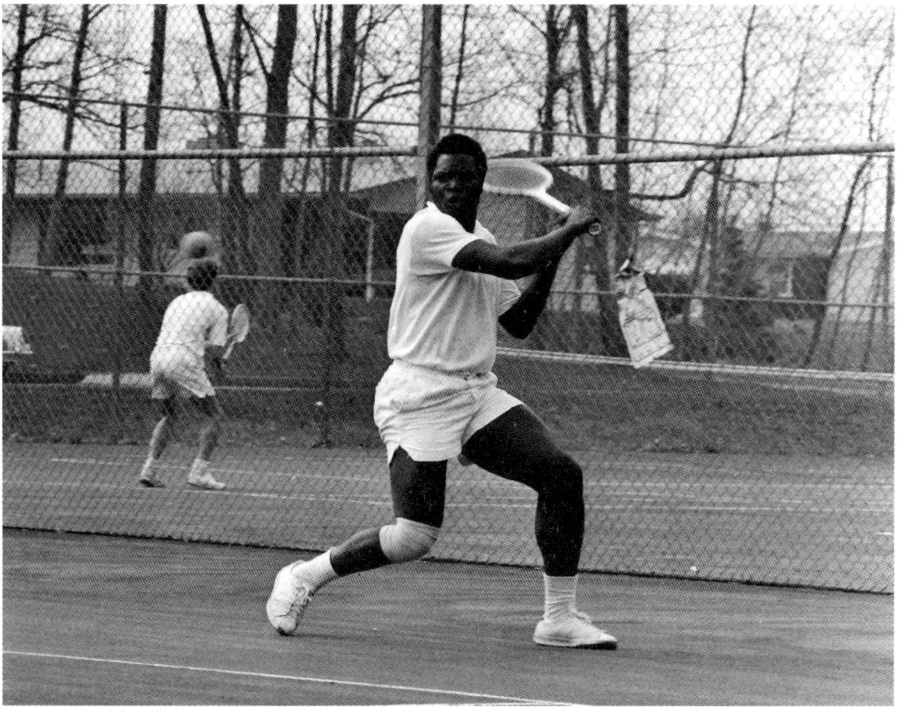

The first student from Mayflower School to attend Alma College was Olugbenga Oredein, who earned an impressive 3.5 grade point average and captured the number one singles spot on the men's tennis squad, though he had never played the game before coming to America. *Gordon Beld photo; courtesy of Alma College Archives.*

organizations and a church in Flint provided funds to bring him to America. He experienced an exceptional four years at Alma College, graduating with a 3.5 grade point average. He was accepted into the premed program at Howard University in Washington, D.C. Benga also excelled at tennis, which he had never played before coming to Alma. In his senior year, he nailed down the number one singles spot on the tennis team.

By the 1960s, students from other countries were coming to Alma College. They were required to be proficient in English and have the funds to pay their way. They heralded a stream of foreign students who have come each year to study at the college. Likewise, cross-cultural experiences by Alma students have become the norm, with numerous yearlong and spring-term sojourns in countries around the world.

—David McMacken

CHAPTER 14

GREEK LIFE

The earliest Greek organizations at Alma College were not fraternities and sororities but literary clubs whose chief goal was to educate students in areas not covered in the regular classical curriculum. These activities included writing stories, essays and poems as well as learning correct parliamentary procedure.

The fraternal groups met on Monday evenings in their clubrooms on campus. After 1902, the fourth floor of the new Wright Hall was plastered and made into fraternal rooms. Each society consisted of fifteen to twenty-five students.

Zeta Sigma started as a men's literary society in 1889. The Adelphic Literary Society was organized by men in 1898, becoming Phi Phi Alpha in 1901. Female students could belong to Alpha Zeta, which dated from 1890 and was the literary society for women of the Collegiate Department. The Philomathean was open to ladies of all departments. The Froebel society was designed for women of the kindergarten department. Besides offering instruction, the literary societies served as the social centers of college life.

Zeta Sigma and Phi Phi Alpha evolved from literary societies to fraternities during the 1910s and '20s. The college curriculum now met the needs in writing, debate and other disciplines. Thus, the clubs became fraternities and sororities in the social sense.

Phi Phi Alpha was the first frat to rent a house for its men. Its first house was on State Street, several blocks from campus. Then the Phis lived in

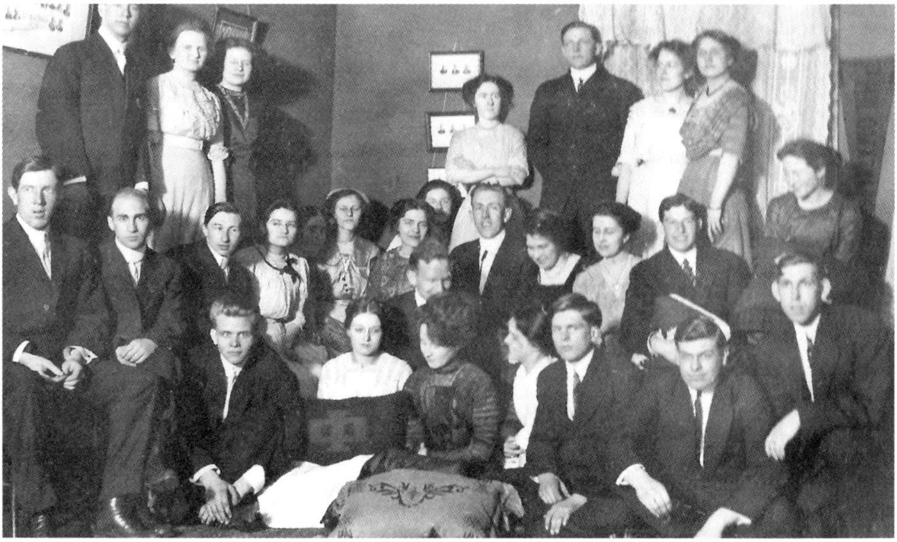

The Philomatheans and Phi Phi Alphas became affiliates, and in 1912, the Philo girls entertained the Phi boys in their beautiful society room at Wright Hall. They served cake, and some of the men read papers they had written. Then the girls staged a stunt contest. Boys and girls were matched up for the two-course luncheon. *Courtesy of Alma College Archives.*

two other houses. In April 1932, they were driven from their house by fire. The house was rendered unfit for habitation, and the men found housing downtown at the Wright Hotel. Some men lived in private homes. Finally, they bought the Fred Hooper house, a large edifice on Philadelphia Street across from Wright Hall, better known later as the TKE house.

World War II posed a serious challenge to the frats. Both Phi Phi Alpha and Zeta Sigma were suspended during the war for lack of male members. Delta Gamma Tau had been chartered locally in 1939 and was the only fraternity to stay active during the war.

As soon as the navy's V-12 officer training program left campus in October 1945, Alma College began moving students back into their original dorms. In a ten-day fury of activity, Wright Hall was prepared for the women's return. Male students returned to Pioneer Hall, although some continued to live off campus. Other men and women took up residence once again in the Greek houses.

During World War II, when Phi Phi Alpha was deactivated, the college took title to its house, and the dean of women lived there with her husband and children. After the war, the fraternity resumed normal operations and bought the house from the college. The Delts reconditioned their house at

603 West Center and moved back in. Zeta Sigma completely redecorated its house at 323 West Superior and planned to reopen in September 1946.

The *Scotsman* yearbook in 1946 said, "It has been said that the value of a college education is not determined by the amount of acquired book learning alone, but also by the associations and friendships made. Fraternity life supplies these."

Once again, the excitement involved in pledging gripped the Alma campus. In 1946, "rush" was held on March 11 and March 25, followed by the period of silence. On April 2, rushees gave their choice, and on April 3, bids were placed under the doors of those who had been accepted.

Each fraternity and sorority, by tradition, gave both open and closed parties. Sigma Philo, the newest sorority, dating from 1943, emerged when the Philomathean and Pi Sigma Nu combined. This sorority was known for its scholastic excellence as well as its enthusiasm for softball. The girls also gave successful parties. One day, they hiked off with their dates to a closed party at Turck's Park across the river. Eventually they wound up at the cinema downtown. A few days after their formal initiation and banquet, they spent a weekend at Crystal Lake and later held a formal dinner dance on May 24.

Alpha Theta, the oldest sorority, sponsored the first dance of the year shortly after the V-12 men left campus. It also sponsored Club Alpha Theta in January, creating a nightclub décor. A few years earlier, in 1942, it had started the custom of sorority house parties when the members packed their swimsuits and took off for a lake near Clare. In 1946, the swimming party was held at the Rosedale cottage at nearby Crystal Lake.

The Kappa Iotas sponsored a Sno-Ball Dance in December 1945 and a South American Swing Dance the following February. Their chief project was redecorating their sorority room and getting new furniture.

Over the years since World War II, a number of fraternities and sororities have gone national, and some have dropped national affiliation. In 1957, the Phi Phi Alpha fraternity petitioned the national Tau Kappa Epsilon fraternity to become a chapter. A delay in acceptance was in part because of a penalty Phi Phi Alpha received for an "exuberant smoker." Alma College asked the national organization many questions before TKE was allowed to grant the charter.

The house on Philadelphia Street was purchased back from the college, and an apartment was added, providing space for about six men and the housemother, who was now required by the college. The chapter was chartered in October 1957 with a church service and a chartering banquet

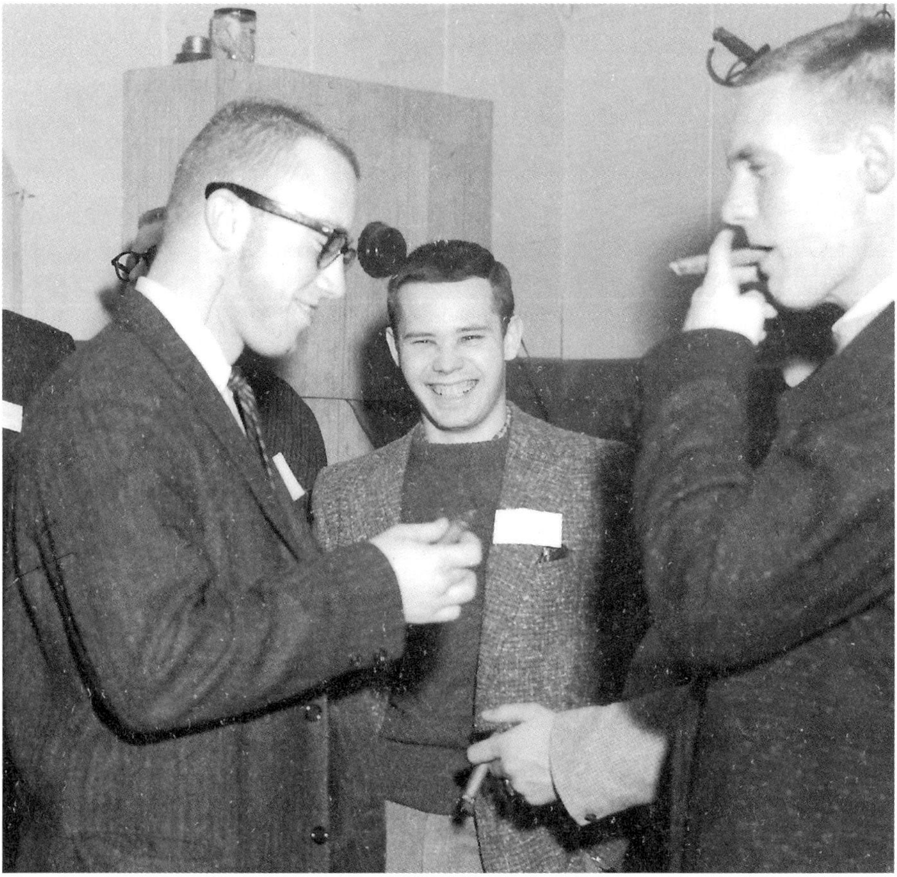

After men signed a rush list, they were invited to frat smokers, traditional gatherings where they smoked cigars. Each frat offered a meal and a presentation to acquaint prospective members with the organization. *Courtesy of Alma College Archives.*

featuring guests and speakers. Phi Phi Alpha became Tau Kappa Epsilon, Zeta Delta Chapter. The TKEs soon established a reputation for having the most athletes and winning the All-Sports trophy. Hazing took place, but it was kept under control.

In 1976, because of transgressions that crossed the line on March 27, the chapter was suspended by President Swanson. His memo to faculty and administrators referred to the "culmination of many years of unsatisfactory relationship between the fraternity and the college." The TKE house closed on April 17, 1976.

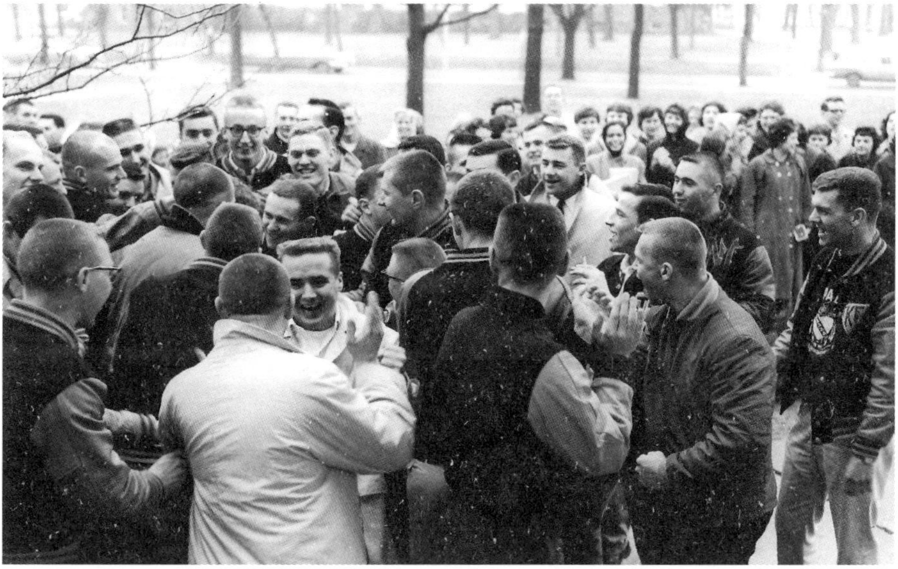

Having received and opened their bids in the chapel, these men came out the door to greet the TKEs, who welcomed and congratulated them with embraces and backslapping. *Courtesy of Alma College Archives.*

Some students thought the move was an attempt to phase out the entire Greek system at Alma College and that the administration was trying to preserve the image of the college. The TKEs understood otherwise. They had been on probation, and they knew that what had happened on March 27 had triggered Swanson's decision. One student expressed the regrets of others when he said, "There will be a definite change in the campus next year. The TKEs always added a little excitement."

To redeem themselves and reestablish the chapter, the TKEs had to establish a "colony" of respectable members with an advisory committee to be in control of the colony. If all went well, the chapter could be reactivated in July 1977.

In 1997, English professor Dr. Eugene Pattison, a TKE and longtime TKE advisor, reflected that a man joined a fraternity "to toughen up, to knock about and learn how to deal with the rough edges of life." He recalled that, when he was honored by the chapters that "bid" him, it was as if every man in the fraternity had said, "I like you, and I hope you like me. Let's eat together, live in the same quarters together, plan our activities together."

Those activities, said Pattison, might include building homecoming floats, sponsoring open houses and dances, running fundraisers and even getting together during the summer. It also meant favors like getting a ride from a far-off bus station when you missed your connection. It meant sympathy in times of loss and defeat as well as congratulations in moments of success.

The 1950s, according to Pattison, emphasized gracious and courteous living. "Friends and parents often encouraged Greek membership as a way to develop those skills," he said. "However you define gracious and courteous living, such values abide more deeply than any of us could have imagined when we picked up that bid after chapel one Friday morning in February."

As the "attention-getting" fraternity, the TKEs received attention they had not intended when their house on Philadelphia burned in March 1985. By the time the firemen headed for the fire, they could see the flames from downtown. Twenty-two men were living in the house when the smoke detector sounded. Five or six used the fire escape. Five jumped from second- and third-story windows. Others ran out. No one was hurt. Little was saved. The campus and community came to the rescue of the TKE men with clothing, books, emergency loans and housing. The men were moved into Bruske Hall for the rest of the semester.

Sororities, likewise, affiliated nationally; Alpha Theta joined Gamma Phi Beta in 1984. The early literary society, the Philomathean, through several

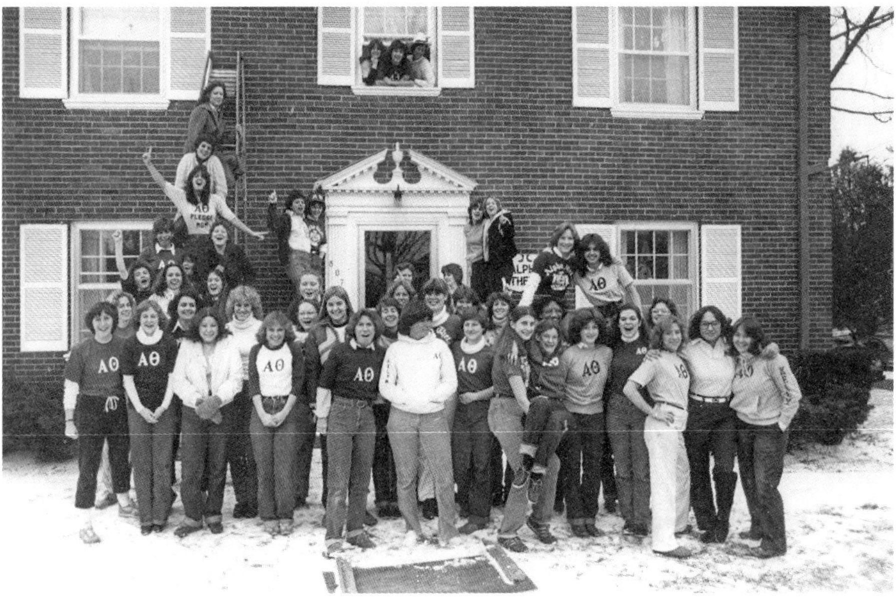

Alpha Thetas gather in front of their house on Superior Street on a chilly day in 1980. *Courtesy of Alma College Archives.*

name changes became a chapter of Alpha Sigma Tau, the first national affiliation for an Alma sorority.

In addition to traditional Greek organizations, several national service-oriented fraternities have organized chapters at Alma College. In March 1947, under the guidance of biology professor Les Eyer, a chapter of Alpha Phi Omega was formed. This chapter eventually faded but was reestablished in May 1965 as Omicron Tau. After eight years, it, too, faded. Still, in those active years, it had provided service-oriented activities on campus and in the community.

In addition to their traditions, fraternities and sororities have also had their philanthropies. Big Brothers/Big Sisters of Gratiot County has benefitted over the years from volunteer service by the Greeks of Alma. So have Habitat for Humanity, the Red Cross and many other nonprofits.

Students have had varied opinions on Greek life. Inter-fraternity rivalries sometimes developed. Some fraternity brothers would be friends with a man until rush, when he pledged a different fraternity. Then the friendship ceased. While some were critical of the Greek system, others supported it because of the cooperation, leadership, brotherhood and teamwork that the fraternities developed. Whatever the opinion, "rush" was always an exciting time when fraternities and sororities attempted to attract good men and women into their chapters.

At one time, the ceremony of "bidding" was conducted after chapel, when the fraternities gathered outside the various doors, and the men inside opened their bids and went through the doors out to the sidewalk to accept the bid and the plaudits and backslapping of their new brothers. The ceremony was later moved to the west lawn outside the chapel and then into the field house. What had been a subdued, polite greeting of the pledges had turned into an emotional "tribal" ritual attended by the entire campus.

Recently, the annual fraternity runouts and the sorority walkouts have taken place in January in the Stone Recreation Center. Membership in the Greek organizations slid in the 1960s and 1970s, but it bounced back after that. At this writing, five sorority houses cluster on the southwestern corner of campus, and five fraternity houses are located on the southeastern corner of campus.

From the early days when the Greek organizations on campus were literary societies to more recent times, Greek life at Alma College has evolved into a social and historic part of the Alma College scene.

—David McMacken

CHAPTER 15

TWO FOR THE TOP, ALMOST

Excitement was hardly the word for it when Claude Watson, Los Angeles attorney and vice-presidential candidate for the Prohibition Party, came to Alma in October 1936. After all, he was a friend of many in the city, had been an exceptional student at the local high school and college and now was getting national recognition.

There were a few, of course, who figured his campaign stop wasn't anything particularly special. This was the second time in as many months that a familiar face had come back to Alma in quest of the nation's number-two office. In September, Frank Knox, publisher of the *Chicago Daily News* and Republican vice-presidential nominee, had rolled into town in a six-car campaign train to make a Labor Day address at Alma College's Bahlke Stadium.

Though thirty-eight years had passed since Knox was an Alma student, many in town still remembered him—not only for his postgraduate achievements but also for his curricular and extracurricular activities on and near the campus. They knew his wife, too. Frank met Annie Reid when both were students at Alma College.

The 1936 election, of course, had been a topic of conversation on Alma streets and throughout the country long before the campaign was underway. By July 1935, Knox was considered one of the leading candidates for the GOP's presidential nomination. The *Literary Digest* suggested the nomination of Knox for the nation's top office "would be geographically perfect."

In August, *Newsweek* reported that a poll of 2,600 county chairmen ranked Knox behind Idaho senator William Borah but ahead of Kansas governor Alfred Landon.

Fortune declared in November that Knox "has no rivals, only potential rivals…To an extent which the public at large does not recognize, Frank Knox is politically far ahead of the field."

However, as the June 1936 Republican convention in Cleveland approached, Landon took the lead and wrapped up the nomination. Among those who stepped to the microphone to congratulate him were Knox and Michigan senator Arthur Vandenberg.

Landon wanted Vandenberg as his running mate, but the senator wasn't interested. Knox left the convention and started back to Chicago with Annie and his secretary, John O'Keefe. When they stopped at a Michigan City, Indiana hotel, they learned from a radio broadcast that Frank had been selected as the party's vice-presidential candidate.

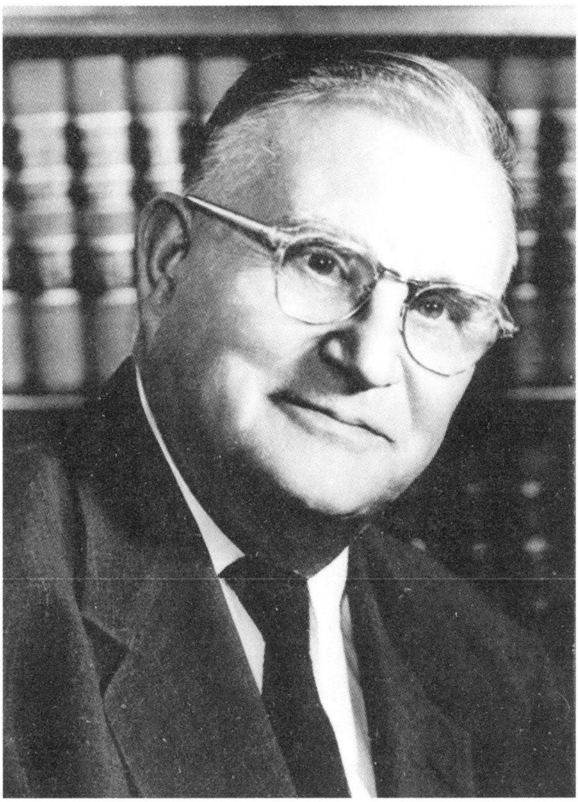

Claude Watson, Prohibition Party candidate, was one of two former Alma students seeking the vice presidency in 1936. In 1944 and '48, he was his party's presidential nominee. *Courtesy of Alma College Archives.*

Before the major party's hoopla took place at Cleveland, the Prohibition Party had convened at Niagara Falls, New York, to nominate the first presidential ticket of the 1936 campaign. Compared to the big Republican bash, this convention in early May was a decidedly tame affair. There were only 172 delegates and a half dozen reporters.

After nominating nationally known Prohibition leader D. Leigh Colvin for president on the first ballot, the delegates drafted Sergeant Alvin C. York as his running mate. York, a national hero after single-handedly killing 25 Germans and taking 132 prisoners, was not a member of the party and refused to accept.

The convention ended without a vice-presidential nomination, and a month passed before party officials selected a nominee. On June 16, just hours before Democrats nominated President Franklin D. Roosevelt for a second term, the Prohibition Party announced that its executive committee had chosen Watson for the second spot on its ticket.

A Michigan native, Watson was born in a frame and log cabin near the Wexford County community of Manton in 1885. He moved with his family to Alma, where he attended high school. After a year at Alma College, he worked as an accountant and auditor for a subsidiary of United States Steel Corporation. In 1912, he became a Free Methodist minister and, in 1928, a lawyer in California.

Despite their simultaneous runs for the vice presidency, Watson and Knox were not acquainted. Watson had attended Alma College during the 1906–07 academic year. Knox was an Alma student in the 1890s.

Knox entered the college's preparatory school as a junior in 1893. Besides taking an accelerated program and working many part-time jobs, he participated in extracurricular activities. A member of the college's first football team in 1894, he was its captain the following year. He also was involved in debate and oratory.

He took part in extracurricular activities of a less legitimate nature, too. Most fellow students considered him the mastermind of a prank that was recalled at alumni reunions as the "Nellie Affair." Nellie, the horse of Professor Joseph Ewing, was kidnapped by students one night and painted with zebra-like stripes. The next morning, her release was timed to coincide with the school's chapel service, and her homeward trot took her past the open windows of the chapel in Old Main. The chapel service ended abruptly, and Nellie was captured—but not before students managed to keep her galloping around the campus for a while.

Knox, who came to Alma with only twenty-five dollars in his pocket, worked to pay for his schooling—often with his own business ventures. His most notable and least successful was the production and sale of a coffee substitute called "anti-coffee." It had been developed by an Alma attorney, and Knox bought him out with an offer of seventy-five dollars and his nearly new bicycle. He hired other students as salesmen, and soon loads of the product were being shipped out of Alma. But no money came in, the product started coming back and the business ended.

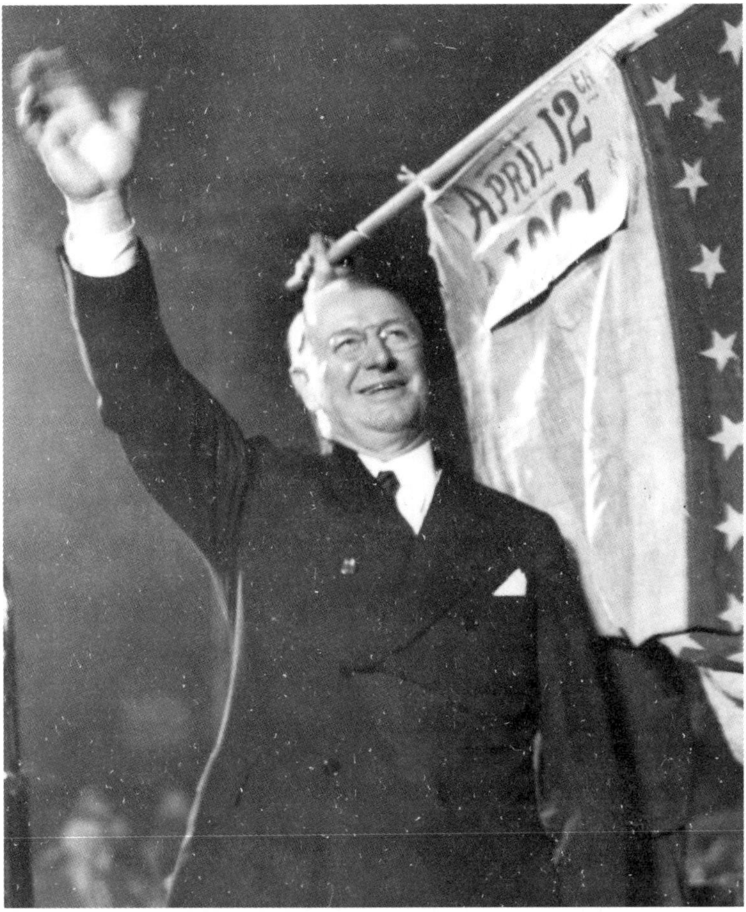

During the 1936 campaign, Frank Knox traveled twenty-two thousand miles through thirty-six states in an effort to secure votes for himself and Republican presidential candidate Alf Landon. Knox's Democratic counterpart, Vice President John Nance Garner, made just one speech during the campaign. *Courtesy of Alma College Archives.*

Knox was just weeks away from graduation in 1898 when the United States declared war on Spain. Determined to do his part, he bicycled sixty miles from Alma to Camp Eaton at Island Lake to enlist in the army. When told fifteen more men were needed, he returned to Alma and immediately arranged a meeting of nearly all the college's male students. He succeeded in recruiting fifteen who returned to Camp Eaton with him. Later in the war, Knox joined Theodore Roosevelt's Rough Riders in Cuba and began a wartime association with the fiery colonel that had a tremendous impact on his life.

It wasn't until 1912 that Knox received his degree from Alma. Trustees then conferred a bachelor of arts certificate, noting that he was "a member of the class of 1898 who was prevented by the Spanish-American War from completing the course and later supplemented the work done by specified readings."

When the war ended, he became a reporter for the *Grand Rapids Herald*. The door to that job opened when William Alden Smith, a congressman and owner of the paper, was running for Congress and felt that advocacy by a war veteran would be helpful. Speaking on behalf of Smith was the beginning of Knox's involvement in politics. In 1910, he helped Chase Osborn become governor, and two years later, he worked tirelessly, but unsuccessfully, for Teddy Roosevelt in his efforts to get the Republican presidential nomination and then a bid for the presidency on the Progressive Party ticket.

At the *Herald*, Knox was quickly promoted to city editor and then circulation manager. In 1902, he formed a partnership with John Muehling, operator of a Grand Rapids printing and bookbinding shop, and purchased the *Lake Superior Journal* in Sault Ste. Marie. After eliminating their competition and expanding their operation, they sold out in 1912 and started a new paper in Manchester, New Hampshire. Though the Manchester partnership lasted through the lifetimes of both men, Knox was for a time general manager of the twenty-seven newspapers owned by William Randolph Hearst. The relationship between Knox and Hearst was stormy, and Knox resigned in 1930. Soon after that, Knox became editor and publisher of the *Chicago Daily News*.

Setting aside his duties at the *News* in 1936, he accepted the nomination for the vice presidency in a July rally at Chicago Stadium. On the Sunday afternoon before Labor Day, his campaign train pulled into the depot at Alma. He and Annie weren't arriving for just another political rally. They were coming home—to the place where they had met and become college sweethearts. After greeting the crowd, they were led by a color guard of

World War I veterans to the college campus, where they spent the night at the home of President Harry Means Crooks.

During that holiday weekend, the city's streets were decorated with flags, bunting and pictures of Knox. The old rocking chair he had used during his college days and the bicycle he had traded for the anti-coffee business were on display. After a mid-afternoon parade, twenty thousand people gathered at Bahlke Field for the political rally. Senator Vandenberg introduced the candidate, who began his nationally broadcast speech by declaring:

> *The New Deal is not wicked. It is just unsound. It is not planning a dictatorship; it just has delusions of grandeur. It is not relentlessly determined to reorganize our country; it just has got started and does not know where to stop. It is not attempting to destroy the Constitution; it just hasn't had time to bother with the Constitution. It is not bent on bankrupting the treasury; it just doesn't know the value of a dollar. It is not deliberately creating deficits; it just doesn't know how to keep books. It is not a Samson pulling down the pillars of the temple; it is just a goose in a thunderstorm.*

Six weeks after Knox's visit, Watson came to town for a Prohibition Party rally that was considerably less dramatic than the grand Labor Day gala held by the Republicans in Bahlke Stadium. Watson spoke at Alma College's Sunday morning chapel service and again in the afternoon at East Superior Street Christian Church. In the latter message, entitled "Old John Barleycorn Runs Amuck," he told his listeners that the Prohibition Party had advocated more than twenty of America's most advanced movements before they were promoted by other parties. Among them were women's suffrage, old-age pensions and government regulation of natural resources.

In another address on Monday, he compared trends in the United States at that time to the fall of the Roman Empire. Citing mockery of religion, increasing vulgarity of comedies, growing divorce rates and declining moral values, he feared that "we are becoming the same thrill-crazy people that the Romans were before they lost their identity."

In November 1936, voters returned President Roosevelt and Vice President Garner to office with the most lopsided victory since James Monroe's 1820 defeat of John Quincy Adams. Landon and Knox carried only Maine and Vermont for 8 electoral votes. Roosevelt and Garner captured 523. Watson and Prohibition presidential candidate D. Leigh Colvin won less than 1 percent of the votes and trailed the Union, Socialist and Communist Parties.

Even in Alma, the favorite sons didn't do well. Landon and Knox led in only two of the city's six precincts. The local paper didn't publish results for the Colvin-Watson ticket or those of other minor parties.

Claude Watson was the Prohibition Party's candidate for president in 1944 and 1948.

After the 1936 election, Knox didn't again seek elective office. Between 1940 and his death in 1944, he served as President Roosevelt's secretary of the navy.

—Gordon Beld

Chapter 16

THE MODEL UN

What if you as an Alma College student had a class that absorbed all your spare time as well as time that wasn't "spare"? What if the class challenged you, inspired you, drove you and required more commitment than you ever thought you had? What if the class had a professor who pressed you and demanded the very best you could offer? What if the class changed your life?

That has been the case for many student participants in the Model United Nations program that has flourished at Alma College since its inception in its present form in 1992 and has been a life-changer for many. It continues to bring honors and recognition to Alma College as this small school consistently tops all competitors—both large and small, unknown and prestigious—in the annual Model UN Midwest competition in St. Louis and the national competition in New York City.

Model UN replicates the United Nations in deliberations, proposals and policy adoption. Students in colleges worldwide participate in the program, which began as the League of Nations Model Assembly in the 1920s. In May 1930, nine Alma college students traveled to Kalamazoo College for the third-annual Michigan League of Nations Model Assembly. The league's program transitioned into the Model United Nations after the development of the United Nations in 1946.

At Alma College, the program began as a club years ago sponsored by various professors. In 1985, under the direction of Robert Johnson, professor of political science, the Alma delegation to the St. Louis Midwest competition represented the country of Jamaica. The eight students developed a paper clarifying Jamaica's stand on various issues.

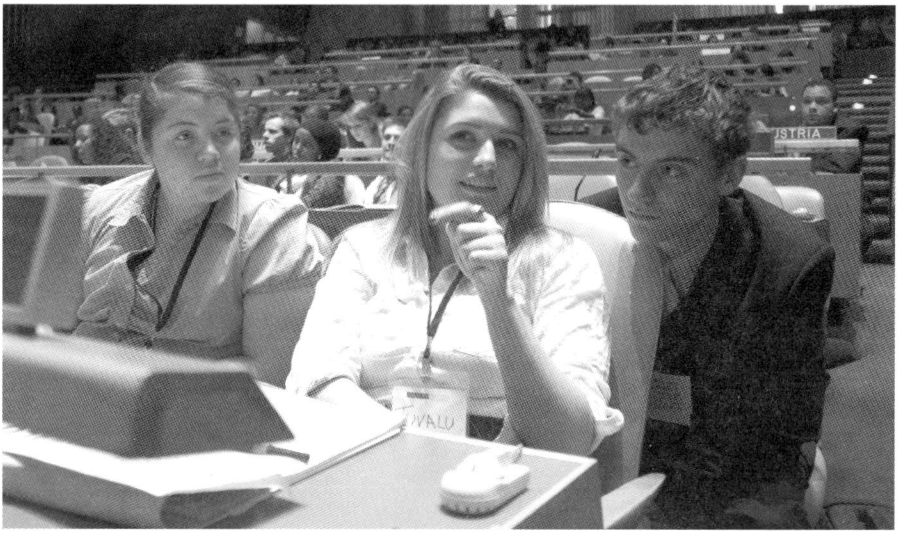

At the 2011 Model United Nations in New York City, Rebekah Miller, Allison Oswald and Chris Bilski plan their next move. As it had for years, the Alma contingent took top honors at the conference. *Courtesy of Alma College Communication and Marketing Office.*

Now Model UN is based on a winter semester class taught by Dr. Derick "Sandy" Hulme, who arrived at Alma College in 1992 and was handed the program. The class is a winter semester political science course open to all students. It requires no prerequisite and may be taken for credit throughout all four years at Alma.

In 1994, their first time at the New York conference, members of the Alma team took the second-highest award given a delegation. The next year, they received the highest award. In 1996, they took the second-highest award again. But in 1997, the Alma contingent moved into first place, and it has not looked back. Since that time, Alma has won the Outstanding Delegation award for seventeen consecutive years.

Known as a demanding and inspiring teacher, Hulme has developed the program at Alma to the point that Alma students have won thirty-nine Outstanding Delegation awards at the Midwest Regional Competition and thirty-two at Nationals, the most for any college or university in the ninety-year history of the conference. In addition, members have earned more than $700,000 in scholarships. In competition, Alma's team has been described as a "superpower."

Model UN works like this. Students are assigned countries in November, based on an October application. They begin researching their country only after they have been assigned to specific committees. This happens the first night of class in January. They investigate and research their country so extensively—the geography, the politics, the people, the needs and the weaknesses that need to be addressed—that they can present themselves as UN representatives for that country. The goal is to pass resolutions and policies that will improve the standard of living in their country and also to address needs from a global perspective.

To become a citizen of a country and be able to advocate for that country requires an immense amount of research. Participants spend an inordinate amount of time at the library and researching online. Hulme suggests that the Model UN class alone could compare to taking a full load in a term, considering its demands on time and energy.

Those very demands have had a transformative influence on many students. Some, whose academic commitment could be described as lackadaisical, suddenly ignite as they become immersed in intense research of their country. Consequently, their whole academic performance improves. Former participant Lauren Shaw from Saginaw said, "It's not a class where you can slack off, and I am absolutely a better student because of it."

Students not only commit time and energy to the Model UN mission, but they also become committed to their fellow committee members and the ultimate success of the group. They draw together to critique one another and hone their skills for the common good. When Hulme holds his famous grilling sessions, pairs of students meet with him in his office. There he challenges one student's knowledge of the assigned country while the other takes notes on areas where the student is weak. The weakness gets worked on. Hulme credits this devotion to the group for the success of much committee work. He points out that the team dynamic often results not only in prize-winning performances but in lifelong friendships as well.

In imitating the real UN, students learn that while national and international problems—whether HIV in sub-Sahara Africa or the Israeli-Palestinian conflict—are truly serious and challenging, few of these issues are solved easily. These complicated matters require discussions and compromises, strategies and negotiations. Developing students' abilities in these areas is a major goal of Model UN.

Helping the program at Alma is the Model UN house at the edge of campus. Seven Model UN students live there, offering a haven for other Model UN students and allowing for both social and academic pursuits.

The college is very supportive of the Model UN, which serves as a formidable recruiting tool. The record of the Alma delegation at the

National Conference in New York City is unmatched. More than five thousand students from 250 colleges and universities worldwide congregate for deliberations, and as of 2013, Alma College has come out on top with Outstanding Delegation honors for seventeen years running.

The delegations are judged by conference officials who take into consideration oral arguments, written essays and personal presentations. Hulme supplies students with a guidebook detailing skills they will need to impress judges. They practice various kinds of speech-making and methods of moving committees forward. They also learn the importance of effective eye contact and how to dress appropriately so that they will stand out and be identifiable. The Alma delegation has practiced and rehearsed all of these details to the point that they feel confident they are well prepared for the competition. That confidence has been justified year after year.

Each spring, the team flies to New York City for the five-day conference, and the excitement begins. Recently, the Model UN competition has been held at the New York Sheraton. Here teams meet in committees and work on specific problems. Committee work begins at 7:00 a.m. and typically ends between 1:30 and 2:00 a.m. In recent years, the Alma teams have represented Antigua and Barbuda, Malawi and St. Vincent and the Grenadines.

Teams also spend two days in the United Nations headquarters itself. They interact with UN officials and experts during committee sessions and also attend a briefing by senior foreign service officers at the U.S. State Department's Mission to the UN. Being in the UN General Assembly Great Hall is an impressive experience, and team members love having their pictures taken at the speaker's lectern. A delegate dance is held the evening of the last day of the conference, for until then delegates have had little interaction except in committee work.

Model UN has long-term effects in the number of postgraduate fellowships its members have been awarded. The program has produced four Truman Scholars, nine Fulbright Scholars and two Gates-Cambridge Scholars, an unusually high number for a school the size of Alma College. In all, Alma College has had more than forty winners.

Ultimately, Model UN students have developed a foundation that will stand them in good stead in their future endeavors. They have learned the art of research, the ability to form an argument, the skill of speaking confidently in public and the aptitude for developing a clearer view of the world and its problems.

—David McMacken

CHAPTER 17

HARD ACTS TO FOLLOW

Almost from the beginning, Alma's performing arts program has been both an exporter and importer of exceptional talent. Student musicians, dancers and actors have thrilled audiences not only in Michigan and the Midwest but also throughout the United States, as well as overseas. At the same time, outstanding professional performers have come from afar to counsel, train and entertain Alma students.

During the college's early years, choirs and orchestras entertained nearby audiences, but the closest thing to a band was the Mandolin Club, which, during a weeklong tour in 1899, presented concerts at Big Rapids, Clare, Edmore, Evart and Howard City. Back in Alma that year, it didn't march during halftime of football games, but it did present a concert to raise funds for the Athletic Association.

The college's first band, according to the *Almanian*, was organized during the 1914–15 academic year. In its report on the final football game of the 1914 season, the *Alma Record* said, "The 12-piece band, decorated with maroon and cream sashes, furnished lively music during the afternoon." In January 1915, the *Almanian* reported that the band had ordered uniforms with white trousers and coats and caps of dark maroon. According to the 1915 student yearbook, "a number of men from the town" helped to swell the ranks of the band.

A new group, formed in 1922 and called the Maroon and Cream Band, had thirty members, who wore maroon capes and what the *Almanian* called military caps.

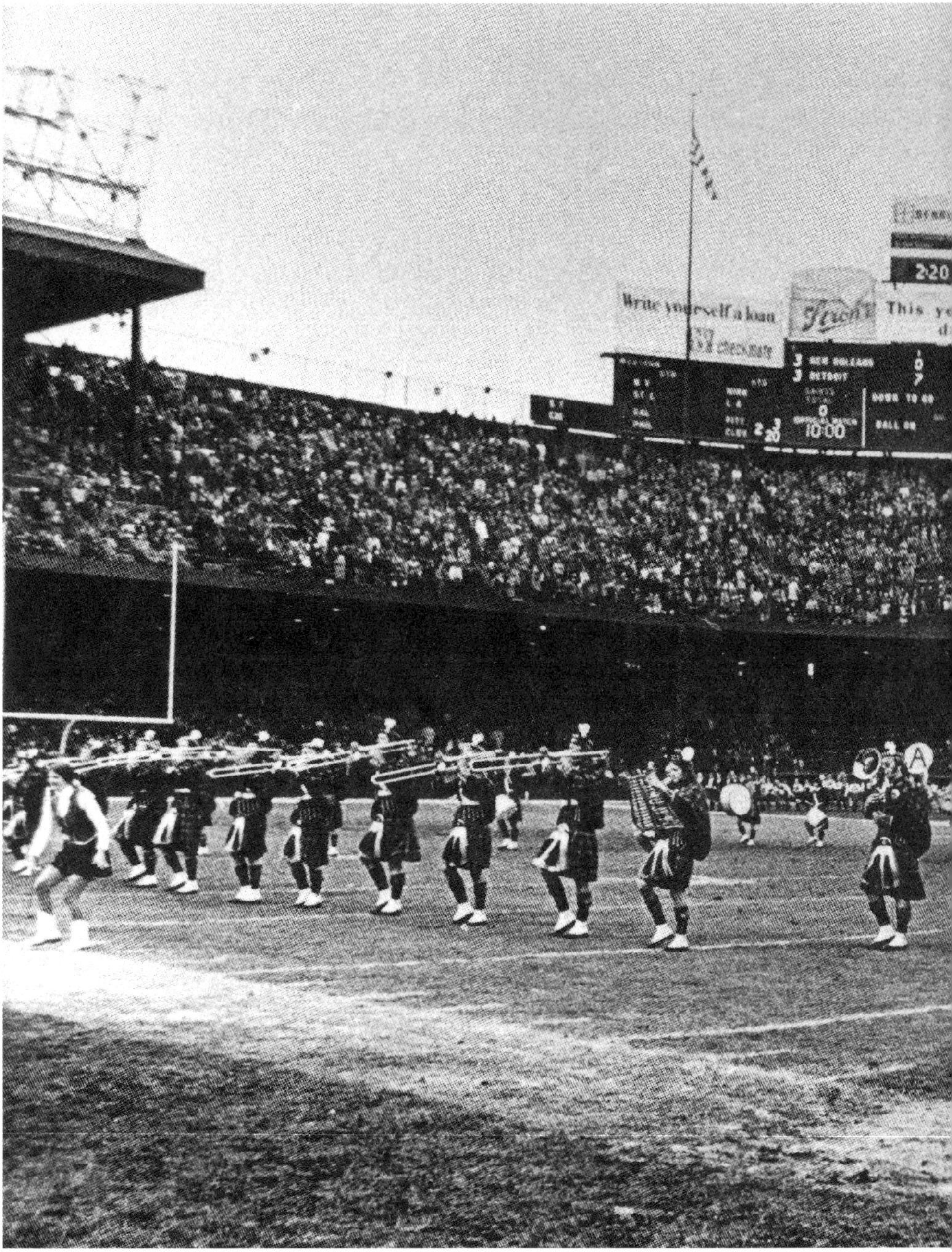

Alma College's Kiltie Band dazzled spectators during pregame and halftime performances at the 1972 Detroit Lions–New Orleans Saints football game in Tiger Stadium. Three years earlier, the band made another Tiger Stadium appearance when the Lions battled the St. Louis Cardinals. *Courtesy of Alma College Archives.*

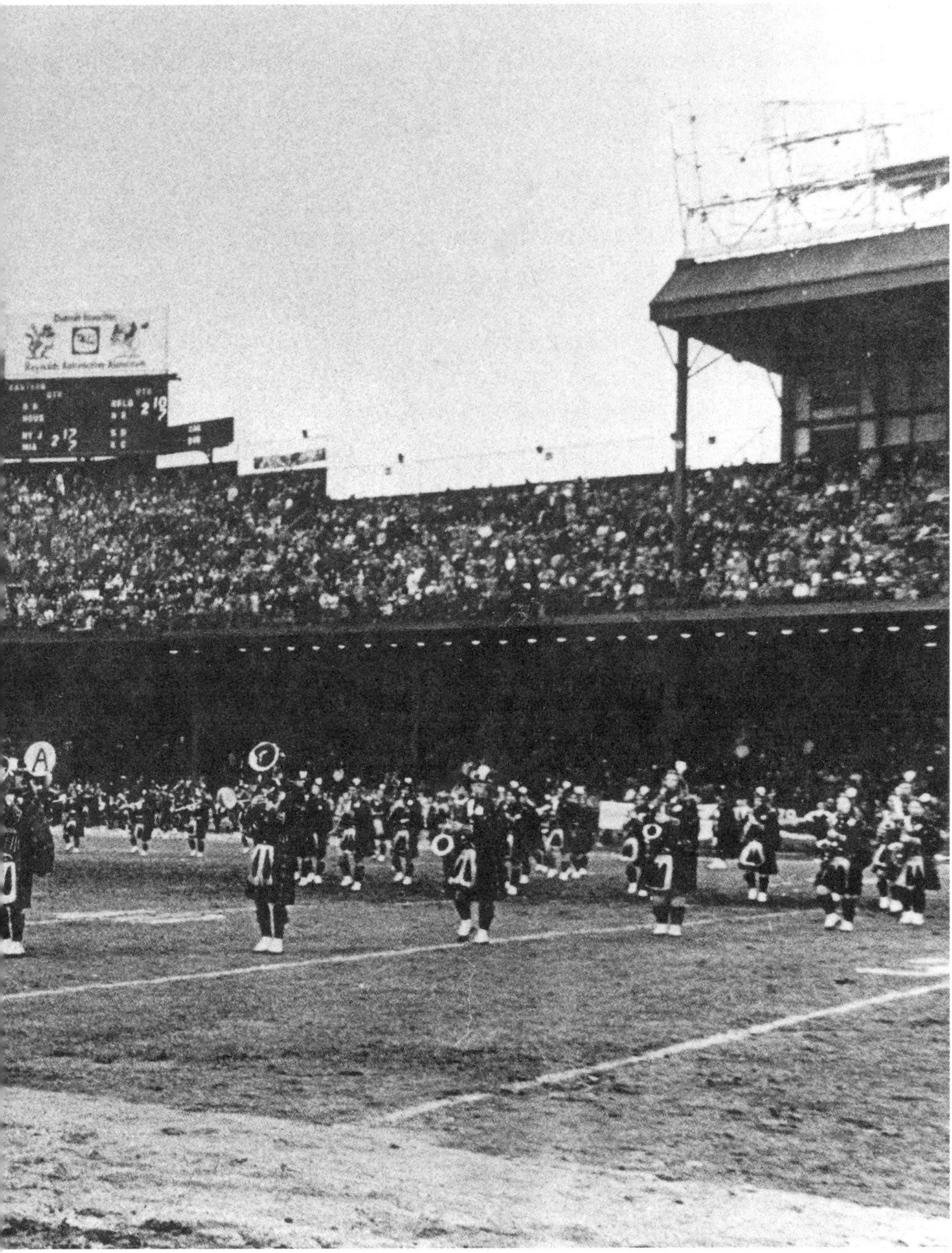

In 1937, six years after Alma's athletic teams first became known as the Scots, the college band acquired uniforms featuring kilts and became the Kiltie Band. Instigator of the kilt-clad band idea was Reverend William Malcolm, pastor of the Presbyterian Church in Three Rivers. He recommended MacPherson tartan for the kilts because he liked its flashy red-and-blue pattern. The college's Alumni Association raised funds for purchase of the new uniforms, and they were first worn during a pep rally at Bahlke Field in October 1938. The *Almanian* noted, "The boys are trying to learn how to sit in kilts. They are taking lessons from the girls."

Today, band members wear kilts made of the official Alma College tartan.

Among the band's many performances through the years were several in Detroit, especially during the 1960s, '70s and '80s. It presented pregame and halftime shows at Tiger Stadium when the Detroit Lions hosted the St. Louis Cardinals in the fall of 1969 and was back again in 1972 when the Lions took on the New Orleans Saints. Appearing with the Kiltie Band in the second Tiger Stadium event were seven pipe bands and more than 150 highland dancers from throughout the Midwest and Canada. The band also marched in the 1984 and '85 Thanksgiving Day parades at the Motor City.

Among other appearances of the Kiltie Band during that period were ones at Disney World in Florida, Town Hall in New York City, the John F. Kennedy Center in the nation's capital and a joint concert with the U.S. Naval Academy Band at Annapolis.

More recently, a pipe band of about twenty pipers and drummers has added a new dimension to Alma's musical program. In the 2013 competition at the Alma Highland Festival, the Alma College Pipe Band was the winner in Grade Four of the U.S. Open Pipe Band Championships.

From the college's earliest days to the present, vocal music groups have also provided fulfilling experiences for Alma students and inspiring concerts for audiences throughout the United States and abroad. The 1931 merger of men's and women's glee clubs formed what has become the college's most prestigious singing group. Professor Jesse Ewer led what then became the A Cappella Choir. In 1984, it was renamed the Alma Choir.

The choir's tours have taken it to both coasts and many communities between, and recently it has made trips to Europe every two years. When the choir toured Scotland and England in 1981, its female members became another college group with a touch of tartan in their attire. They wore skirts of Royal Stewart plaid that had been tailored by Dao Tak Lim, a Cambodian refugee whose family's resettlement in Alma had been made

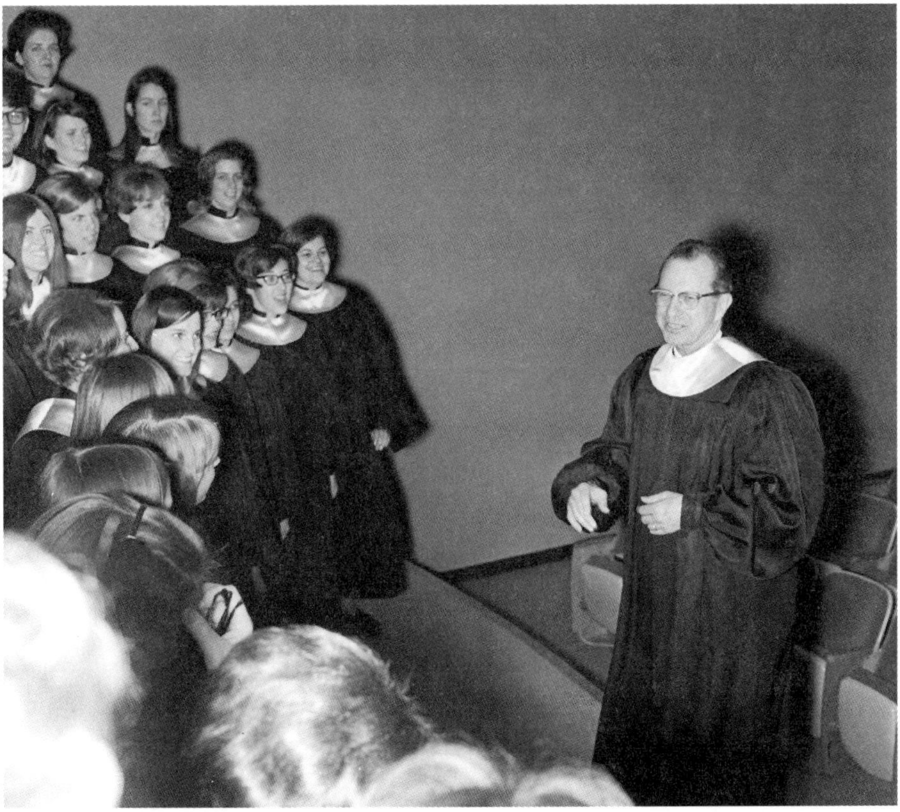

Ernest Sullivan directs the college's A Cappella Choir at a 1960s warm-up session. He and present choir director Will Nichols have produced talented vocal music groups for fifty-six of the last sixty years. Sullivan led Alma's singers from 1953 to '79, and Nichols has been the director since 1983. *Gordon Beld photo; courtesy of Alma College Archives.*

possible by members of the United Methodist Church, several of whom were on the college staff.

Formation of the performing dance group Orchesis in the early 1960s provided opportunities for many more talented students to thrill audiences. In the 1990s, the name of the organization was changed to Alma College Dance Company.

Under the leadership of Dr. Joe Sutfin of the English Department, a troupe of student mimes entertained audiences, including children at the Lutheran School for the Deaf at Dearborn, during the 1970s and early '80s.

Members of Alma literary societies began staging dramatic performances during the college's early days, initiating the theatrics that have amazed

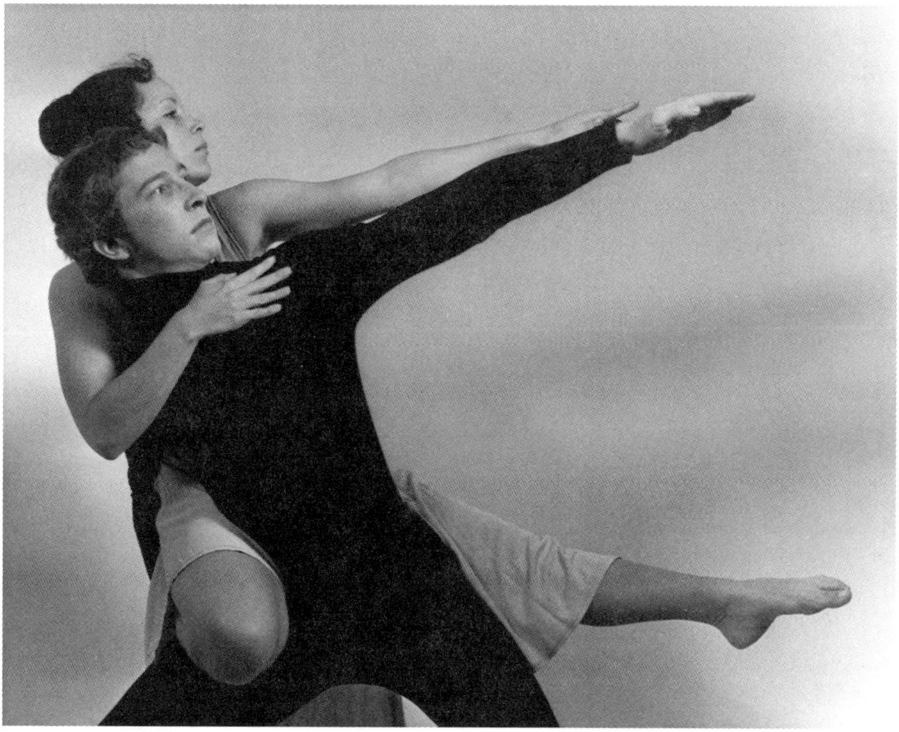

Before they came to Alma, neither Angie Leaver nor Ed Kain knew how to dance. Ed stood on the sidelines at dances in Bad Axe High School, not knowing what to do. Angie didn't even go to the dances at Fruitport High School. But they learned quickly and thrilled audiences at productions of Orchesis, the college's modern dance group. *Gordon Beld photo; courtesy of Alma College Archives.*

audiences for many years. Many of the student actors and actresses have continued to perform on the stage after graduation. One of them is Kathy Ferrand, a 1966 grad whose hometown was Rockford.

After her freshman year at another Michigan college, she transferred to Alma, where she was well along in her studies for a career in education when Albert Katz, an associate professor of speech, remarked, "You don't really want to be a teacher, do you?"

"No," Kathy replied, "but I don't know if I dare go into acting."

"Well, you'll never know if you don't try," Katz responded.

She did try, and in three years on the campus, she had roles in six productions of the Alma Players. During her Alma years, she also had summertime experience in theater. In 1964, she was an apprentice at the Houghton Lake Playhouse, and in 1965, she appeared in four Shakespearean dramas as an associate with the Great Lakes Shakespeare Festival in Ohio. But that was just the start. She went on to become well known across the country for her performances on the stage and screen.

Kathy's last performance as an Alma student was in *Spoon River Anthology*, staged the month before she received her degree. But that wasn't her last theatric contribution on the campus. She returned in 1975 as an artist in residence and appeared with students in three performances of *She Stoops to Conquer*.

By that time, she had earned a master's degree in speech and theater at the University of Michigan and completed six seasons on the stage of the Guthrie Theater in Minneapolis, one of the most prestigious regional theaters in the country. She also had performed in educational films and narrated several broadcast commercials.

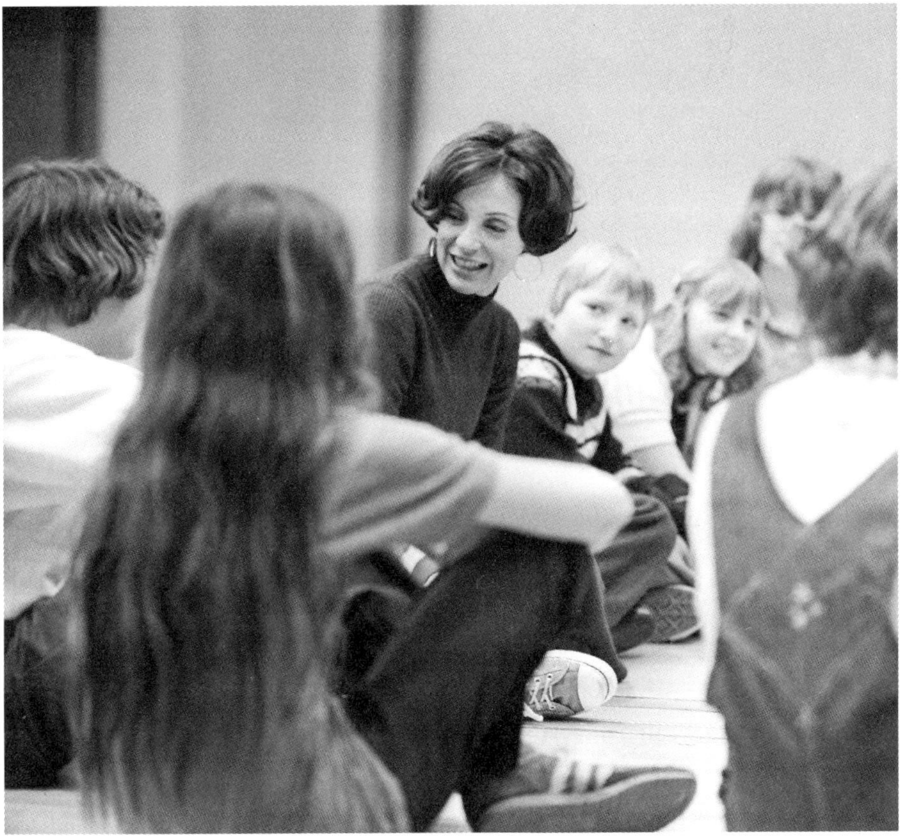

Kathy Ferrand, an Alma alumna and later a performer on stage and screen in the United States and abroad, shares her theater experiences with area schoolchildren during her 1975 return to Alma as an artist in residence. *Gordon Beld photo; courtesy of Alma College Archives.*

While back in Alma, she provided instruction and counseling for student drama participants on the campus and in nearby schools. That, she noted, was a plus—not only for those students but also for herself. "It made me realize," she said, "how crazy I am about acting and how much it is a part of my life.

"As a student here," she added, "I would have loved to have had somebody who'd really been out there and done it come and work with me."

Subsequently, Kathy performed on Broadway, at the Floating Theater in Seattle, Arizona Theater in Tucson, the Pasadena Playhouse and the Playbox Theatre in Melbourne, Australia. She also was on stages of several countries in Africa. Her feature-length film appearances were in *North Country* (2005) and *The Horrible Flowers* (2006).

An artist in residence for a longer period at Alma was Mary Beth Peil, an accomplished lyric soprano with the Metropolitan Opera National Company during the three years when she frequently was on the campus. She came to the college six times each year, from autumn of 1967 through spring of 1970, for periods of a week to ten days. Besides performing on the campus during each visit, she spoke and sang in classrooms, counseled individual students and made appearances before school and community groups.

Arrangements for her appointment at Alma were made through Edward Warner, executive director of Affiliate Artists, Inc., who pioneered the affiliate artist idea when he began a period of service at Beloit College. Mary Beth was the first of many other affiliate artists who eventually signed agreements with colleges.

Before her first trip to Michigan, she had received plaudits from several critics for her concert and oratorio performances. Her roles as Mimi in *La Boheme* and Susanna in *The Marriage of Figaro* prompted Miles Kastendieck of the *New York World Journal* to note that she was "a singing actress of great potentiality and should find herself on the threshold of a notable career."

Allen Hughes of the *New York Times* praised Mary Beth and Harry Theyard, who played Rudolfo in *La Boheme*: "They were young, they were attractive, their acting was so convincing that it scarcely seemed like acting at all, their voices were well matched in amplitude and timbre, and their diction was exemplary."

Bob Pennington of the *Telegram* in Toronto criticized other performers in *La Boheme* and then added that "the Mimi of Mary Beth Peil, however, was quite remarkable…I have seen *La Boheme* performed over thirty times in eight countries, but never have I seen a more convincing Mimi."

Typical of Mary Beth's many appearances in the Alma area was one in February 1970 when 450 fourth- and fifth-graders from Alma schools filed into the Luce Road School all-purpose room, sat on the floor, heard Mary Beth talk about opera and watched presentations of scenes from *Carmen*, *Hansel and Gretel* and the *Marriage of Figaro*. Probably for the first time, these children saw and heard opera—and they liked it. To most of their parents, opera was a lot of noise in a foreign language through a radio loudspeaker on a Saturday afternoon. Mary Beth introduced it to the children as "a play in which the actors sing their lines."

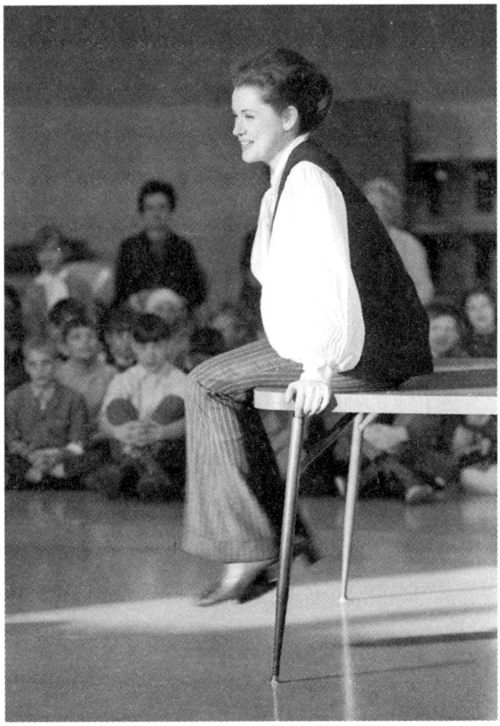

Alma's affiliate artist Mary Beth Peil tells Luce Road Elementary School students about opera during one of her many presentations at area schools during her three-year appointment. She also spoke and sang in college classrooms and counseled students interested in music. A talented young lyric soprano, she later switched to acting and was a well-known performer on the stage, big screen and television. *Gordon Beld photo; courtesy of Alma College Archives.*

A year after her days as an affiliate artist, Mary Beth won national acclaim for her performance as Alma Winemiller in Lee Hoiby's opera *Summer and Smoke*, based on a Tennessee Williams play. Then a role in *Kiss Me Kate* took her to Broadway, and in 1983, she began a national tour as the final Anna Leonowens, playing opposite Yul Brynner in a revival of *The King and I*. The production came to New York in 1985 and concluded after 191 performances at the Broadway Theatre shortly before Brynner's death. He received a Tony Award for his role as the king, and Mary Beth was a Tony nominee for best performance by a featured actress in a musical.

As she moved further from singing and into acting, she performed in several big screen productions, including *The Odd Couple II* with Jack Lemmon and Walter Matthau. She has acted in many television productions and was Evelyn "Grams" Ryan in 74 of the 128 episodes of the teen drama *Dawson's Creek*. Besides the four young stars of the show, she was the only actress to appear throughout its six-season run. Later she was Jackie Florick, mother-in-law of main character Alicia Florick, in the CBS serial *The Good Wife*.

Another talented young vocalist was also at Alma during the period of Mary Beth's affiliation with the college. He, however, was on the campus only to entertain during three one-night stands in 1969, '70 and '71. The first of those came about when a late cancelation made it necessary to book another show for students. The agent through which programs were scheduled recommended a young man with a lot of talent who was going to do really well. His name was John Denver.

The college decided to take a chance. His fee was only $750. Denver had been a member of the Chad Mitchell Trio, but in 1969, he left it and set out to establish himself as a solo performer. Some sources state that his appearance in Alma was "the first" of his solo career. Others say it was "among the first."

For both Alma students and the up-and-coming Denver, it was love at first sight. And it lasted. When he came back in 1970, he treated his audience to a song that hadn't previously been played on a college campus—"Take Me Home, Country Roads." When he came again in early 1971, the journey wasn't easy. The country roads near Alma were clogged with snow, and his car broke down. He trudged through drifts for two miles and, just as his audience was about to give up and depart, he and his snow-covered guitar appeared.

—Gordon Beld

Chapter 18

THE COMMUNICATION ARTS

From its earliest years, Alma College hoped its students would become gifted communicators, and the curriculum reflected this goal. The school encouraged debate and oratory, the standard skilled oral discourse of the time. Accomplished speakers were admired, and many students aspired to be regarded as excellent oral communicators.

Debate was considered significant, especially when Alma College debate teams entered intercollegiate competition. Debate was introduced in 1901, but it was considered appropriate for male students only. In 1910, the debate class met three hours a week. The debate topic that season was: "Resolved that the U.S. government should levy a progressive income tax." In debates with Olivet and Hope Colleges, the Alma team won the debate, defending the opposite sides of the question. The *Almanian* boasted, "Alma's debaters have reached a standard during the past year that has seldom been attained before, and their record pays a high tribute to the Department of English Speech." Because the thinking and speaking skills needed in debate are useful in many situations, it became a standard offering at the college over the years.

Both men and women practiced oratory. This method of colorful and exaggerated speaking had a long history in Congress and among local politicians who entertained at Fourth of July gatherings. In college oratory, special attention was given to eulogy and popular address, as well as platform reading. Each student was required to give an evening public recital. The oration of Hurd Drake, "The Beacon Light of Men," took him to the state meet in Lansing in 1910. Female orator Mrs. Laura Sebring took first place that year with a brilliant oration and eulogy about Giddings, a pre–Civil War politician.

Written communication was also important. The magazine *Almanian* was published monthly during the early years, featuring essays and articles by students and faculty as well as a page or two of the latest campus news. Eventually, the magazine grew into a weekly newspaper that has been published for more than a century. The *Almanian* faithfully recorded campus activities and the latest concerns of students, including conflicts with administration, rebellion regarding various rules and youthful reactions to local, national and international events. Student-produced with an advisor, the *Almanian* enjoyed a great deal of editorial freedom. Presently, the newspaper is issued on Mondays and maintains a web presence.

To record the events of the year, the *Maroon and Cream* yearbook was established in 1910 and published by the junior class. In 1938, it became the *Scotsman* and, since 1995, the *Scot*. Also student-produced, the yearbook in its early years pictured student activities, faculty photos and student photos—all in a traditional format. In the 1960s and '70s, creativity reigned, and the *Scotsman* issued forth in a variety of formats and themes. One issue consisted entirely of photos without captions. No matter the design, the yearbook has faithfully recorded the Alma College experience year after year.

The school's literary magazine has been published from time to time under several titles. It was known as the *Pine River* for a few years, but in recent years, it has been the *Pine River Anthology*, a collection of artistic work, both writing and art, that reflects the creativity, talent and hard work of many Alma College students.

Alma College first "went on the air" in the fall of 1938 when WBCM in Bay City aired a series of half-hour broadcasts featuring the college each Friday evening. It also did a play-by-play of the college's first night football game, when lights had been installed on Bahlke Field and Mrs. Mary Bahlke threw the switch to illuminate the gridiron. It would be a decade, however, before the college became involved in local radio.

In 1948, the new local radio station, WFYC, began broadcasting Alma College programs produced by students. The first program was a drama, *Johnny Appleseed*. The broadcasting thespians performed in the radio chamber of the speech department. A *News from Alma College* radio show aired weekly on WFYC.

A radio club was formed in 1952. The club produced two half-hour broadcasts a week each Tuesday and Thursday from 3:00 to 3:30 p.m. on

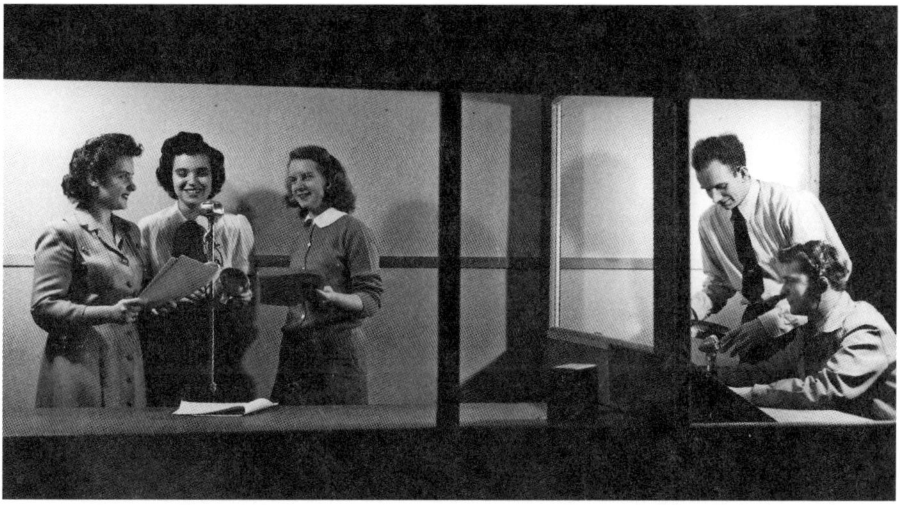

Girls prepare to present a radio drama complete with sound effects in the late 1940s. The program was broadcast over the Alma-area station, WFYC. *Courtesy of Alma College Archives.*

WFYC. Broadcasting to the central Michigan community, the Tuesday program featured news and drama; the Thursday broadcast was entirely recorded music. These broadcasts allowed students practice in engineering, writing, directing, sound effects, announcing and acting, and all this was accomplished by volunteers.

It would only be natural that Alma College would set up its own radio station, as was common among many smaller colleges in the 1960s. In 1966, a campus radio station using telephone lines was completed. Frank Tefft, radio engineer at Central Michigan University and consulting engineer for WFYC, helped students set up the equipment. The station was to broadcast from 7:00 p.m. to midnight on weeknights and Saturday and Sunday afternoons. This setup was not successful and was later abandoned, but the need for a campus station was not forgotten.

In January 1979, another college station, WABM, began broadcasting just to the campus using electric lines to carry its signal at 590 AM. The station had been in the works for fifteen years. The student-run AM station carried top forty music and college sporting events. Many students, some with broadcasting experience, volunteered to work at the station. Still, this station faded away, leaving a gap in the college's communications scheme.

This gap was filled in March 1979 when WQAC, "The Duck," went on the air. This low-power radio station broadcasts at 90.9 FM and can

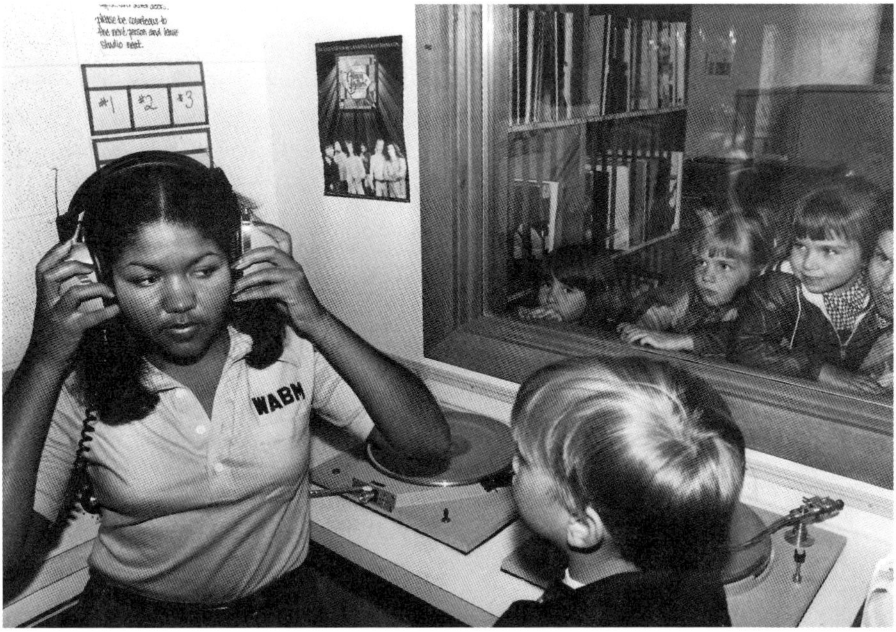

A WABM staffer explains the finer points of being a radio disc jockey to children who are visiting the studio. *Courtesy of Alma College Archives.*

be picked up in nearby towns and as far away as Carson City and Clare. WQAC is student run, has a paid staff of nine and a faculty advisor. The station streams on its website. Student DJs send out the tunes, and both paid and volunteer staff can create their own shows, whether talk, music or news. They are required to attend a training session to learn how to use the equipment and which FCC rules apply. The studio is located in Tyler-VanDusen Student Center and broadcasts twenty-four hours a day.

A new media studies major reflects the seriousness with which Alma College continues to regard the need for skilled communicators.

—David McMacken

Chapter 19

From Calamity to Cleanup

Professor Ed Lorenz, teacher of history and political science, came to Alma College in 1989. He was vaguely aware of an environmental disaster in Alma's sister city, St. Louis, but oddly, he only learned of the details when attending a conference the following year at Massachusetts Institute of Technology. When he introduced himself as from Alma, Michigan, an agrichemist from North Carolina told him about the disaster in St. Louis, Michigan. Ed's interest was piqued, but he had no idea that the chemical mess left by the Michigan Chemical/Velsicol Chemical Company would occupy his attention for the next twenty years.

His involvement really began when a Service-Learning Committee at the college received a Kellogg Foundation grant. Committee members pondered how the grant should be used. Ed suggested that students could become involved in the St. Louis chemical debacle by interviewing people about what had happened. The committee decided to concentrate the grant dollars on this project for a year, and the students began their work.

The story of the disaster was commonly known. The Michigan Chemical Company, a major manufacturer of the pesticide DDT, had dumped chemicals into the Pine River for years, seriously polluting the river. The greater disaster occurred in 1973. The company had begun manufacturing a fire-retardant product marketed as Fire-Master and a cattle feed supplement known as Nutri-Master. Workers at the chemical company mistakenly shipped bags of Fire-Master instead of Nutri-Master to the state Farm Bureau elevator, where the fire-retardant became mixed into cattle feed. Herds of cows sickened and had to be destroyed and buried in mass graves. People statewide who had ingested milk from the cows also had the chemicals in their systems.

The Environmental Protection Agency (EPA) stepped in, and the chemical plant, now part of the Velsicol Chemical Company, was shut down, leaving a heavily polluted site. Years of litigation followed. The plant was dismantled. Parts of the plant were trucked away to landfills. The rest was buried on-site and covered with a thick blanket of clay to prevent the diffusion of the remaining chemicals. The EPA finished its work and secured the site, surrounding it with a chain-link fence and setting a tombstone etched with a warning declaring that the site was hazardous.

It was this mess, both chemical and bureaucratic, that Ed Lorenz and other Alma College faculty members would deal with for many years. Joining him were chemistry professor Melissa Strait and geology professor Murray Borrello, along with alumna Jane Eyer Keon, whose father, Lester Eyer, was a professor emeritus of biology at the college. They were to become authorities on the plant site, the polluted river and the challenges of dealing with defunct companies, government agencies and the bureaucracy involved in cleaning up a site of major chemical pollution.

Whenever Ed and Murray took students to the river near the abandoned plant site to take sediment samples, the students were guaranteed a rich mixture to analyze. The professors jokingly referred to the site as their "Velsicol Laboratory." Students' samples often included petroleum from Alma's Total Refinery, as well as DDT and other elements left by the Michigan Chemical/Velsicol Chemical Company. It was commonly known that aquatic life was scarce near the plant site and that fish in the river contained an unsafe level of DDT. Signs warned fishermen not to eat the fish they caught.

Invited to be presenters in Alma's Evening in the Park summer lecture series, Ed and Murray described the plant site and then set fire to their sample of river mud. This flare-up made a distinct impression on the audience that evening.

In 1997, the EPA returned to St. Louis. It was time to begin cleaning up the polluted Pine River. A public meeting was held at the St Louis Senior Center. Ed and his students were there, as were a large number of angry St. Louis citizens. It was standing room only. To placate irate citizens and to end the rancorous four-hour meeting, EPA officials announced that by law, a Citizens' Advisory Group (CAG) could be formed. The pad was passed, and many people signed up.

A month later, in December 1997, the CAG met for the first time. The group officially was known as the Pine River Superfund Citizen Task Force.

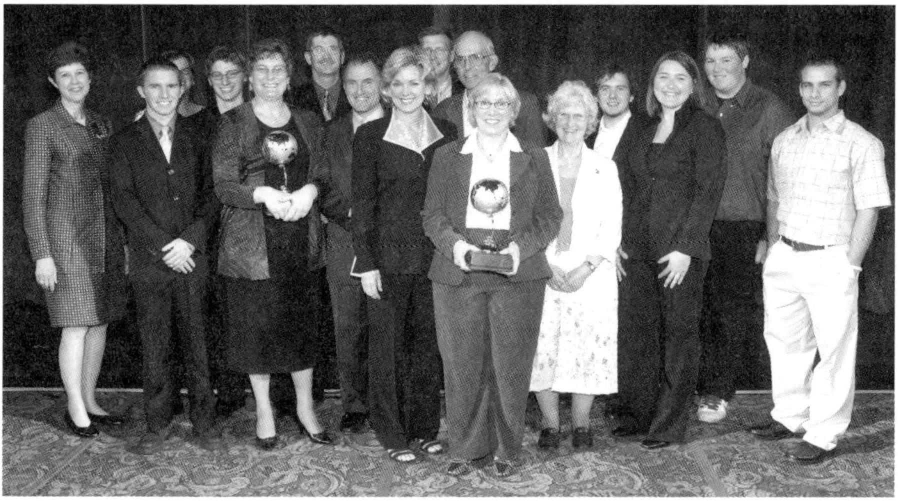

At the Fox Theater in Detroit, the Citizens Advisory Group and Alma College received the 2008 Carter Partnership Award of $10,000 for their collaboration in helping generate the EPA cleanup in St. Louis. College president Saundra Tracy is at far left. Holding trophies presented to the college and the CAG are Professor Melissa Straight (left) and Jane Keon. Among those between them is Governor Jennifer Granholm. *Courtesy of Michigan Nonprofit Association.*

Ed was chosen as chairperson, and Jane, Melissa and Murray at once became active in the group. A number of determined St. Louis citizens joined as well. At the beginning, the group had no idea of the bulldog tenacity it would demonstrate as it fought for the site to be thoroughly cleansed.

As the $100 million cleanup of the river progressed, more problems surfaced. Chemicals were oozing from under the clay cap. Yards near the site had been dusted with chemicals for years and were polluted. It appeared that workers or neighbors of the plant site might be suffering from an unusual number of cancers. In addition, a chemical had migrated into one of the city's water wells. No one knew if this chemical was dangerous or not, but the well was shut down. How many months or years might it take before this chemical drifted through the aquifer to the other city water wells?

St. Louis was used to bad news. It was acknowledged to be one of the more polluted towns in America. Now, while it was struggling to recover from the general disaster and to market itself as a good place to live, the purity of its water sources was in doubt.

The CAG, however, never gave up. The volunteer members continued to meet for an hour and a half once a month as they had for fifteen years to deal with seemingly insurmountable challenges. The members included some formidable individuals. In his award-winning book *Civic Empowerment in an Age of Corporate Greed*, Ed Lorenz enumerated the members: labor union members from the local Total Petroleum refinery, active church members with a sense of how to steward the world, college personnel who encouraged students to become involved, a number of working and retired individuals from the community and two well-trained retirees from the Dow Chemical Company. They were Fred Brown, former head of the Michigan United Conservation Clubs, and Gene Kanaga, a world-class expert on DDT. Kanaga befuddled neophyte EPA "experts" on DDT who did not expect to be challenged by a member of the CAG. The CAG, by any standards, was a diverse, devoted and dynamic group, and its freedom from regulation empowered it. The CAG was soon to make a fortuitous discovery.

Velsicol had been absorbed by the conglomerate Fruit of the Loom, the underwear manufacturer. Both Velsicol and Fruit of the Loom had gone bankrupt. In making a claim against the company, the CAG boldly asked for $100 million, expecting to receive little or nothing. The companies, however, had taken out environmental insurance policies, and once this was known, the CAG went after money to fund a new water system for St. Louis.

In a David-slays-Goliath scenario, the adversaries met in federal court in Bay City. Attorneys from the U.S. Justice Department, the EPA and the Velsicol/Fruit of the Loom Trust were prepared to massacre the attorneys representing St. Louis. Ultimately, in a shocking and surprising turn of events, the persistence of the CAG paid off. A settlement gave the City of St. Louis $26.5 million to fund a new city water system. Needless to say, St. Louis city officials and members of CAG held a victory party.

Furthermore, a long-term cleanup of the plant site, other related contaminated sites and the Pine River to its confluence with the Chippewa River has been scheduled by the EPA. None of this would have happened without the determined efforts of the CAG. Other cities, left in the same contaminated state by Velsicol, have chain-link fences but no cleanup plans.

Student involvement in the cleanup mission was strong. Shannon Finnegan at one time served as secretary of the CAG. She moved on to receive her master's in public administration and become a senior analyst in the Government Accountability Office in Washington, D.C. Cardell Johnson developed innovative plans to help high school students become involved in environmental issues, and he presently serves as senior policy analyst of the U.S. Environmental Protection Agency. He is also the youngest member of the Alma College Board of Trustees.

Jane Keon reflected that none of the CAG's members received wages for their work in St. Louis. In fact, many contributed both time and money in the interests of the project's success. They persisted because they believed in the cause. Now they are waiting for the day when their to-do list has all items crossed off.

Without the expertise of Alma College professors, alumni and students, it is doubtful this major environmental cleanup would have ever come to fruition. Their dedicated efforts have not gone unnoticed by the Alma and St. Louis communities. Ed Lorenz and Murray Borello received the City of Alma's highest award, the Order of the Tartan, and Jane Keon was honored by receiving the Spirit of St. Louis Award. For sponsoring the Eugene Kanaga International DDT Conference in 2008 and for their years of cooperation, the CAG and Alma College received the Jimmy & Rosalyn Carter Campus-Community Collaboration Award of $10,000.

—David McMacken

CHAPTER 20

FOR THE LOVE OF THE GAME

Just a year after Alma College held its first classes in 1887, its students began organizing athletic teams. Efforts were underway in the fall of 1888 to form baseball, football and wrestling teams, as well as a gymnastics class.

The first baseball squad played a team known as the Maple Leafs and lost, 14–9. There is no evidence of football competition that year. Perhaps that's because students seemed to have no idea about what kind of weather would be conducive to gridiron action. "After Christmas, they will entertain challenges from other colleges," the *Alma Record* reported.

There were wrestling contests that year but on an intramural basis. Then, in 1889, instruction and practice opportunities in gymnastics were provided, and baseball took off in a big way. Spring competition on the diamond was followed by a summer schedule that took the team on a twenty-five-game, thirty-day tour of northern Michigan. Professionalism wasn't a concern in those days. A pitcher and catcher from Carleton were hired at thirty dollars per week to pad the roster.

A colorful baseball series began in 1894 when Alma played the first of several annual games against the Indian team of the government school at Mt. Pleasant. That year, the contest was a feature of field day on the campus, and Fred Avery was the big winner of prizes offered by local merchants. For participation on winning teams in the three-legged and lock-step races, he received a necktie and dinner at the Wright House. His first-place finish in the two-hundred-yard dash earned twelve shaves by Nick Davidson.

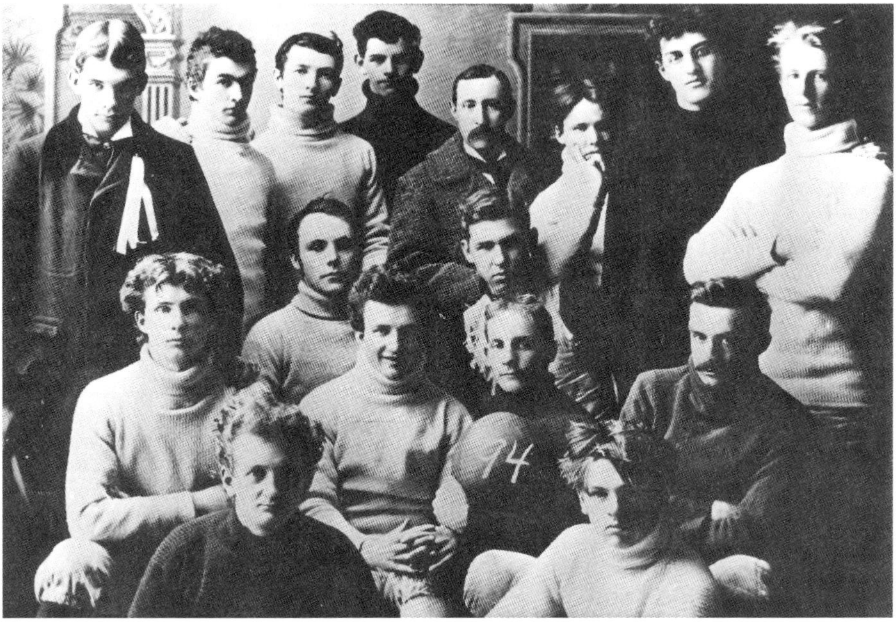

Alma's first football team was this 1894 squad coached by Professor John T. Ewing (back row, fourth from right). Captain of the team was Edward Siegfried (holding ball), who had three years of experience with Susquehanna College and University of Pennsylvania teams. Frank Knox, who later became well known for his accomplishments in journalism and politics, is at the right end of the back row. *Courtesy of Alma College Archives.*

Both male and female students competed in a tennis tournament that spring. Paul Bruske teamed with Kendall Brooks to win the men's doubles, each of them earning two tennis balls. Then Bruske played alongside Esther Marsh in the mixed doubles. Her prize was a three-dollar hat.

Football, the sport that was to bring the most excitement and notoriety to the campus in future years, kicked off in the fall of 1894. Alma won its only two games that year with 6–0 and 10–0 triumphs over the Saginaw Athletic Association's team.

Not everyone was enthused about the accomplishment. Another passenger on the train that took Alma's men home after the second contest sent a letter to an area newspaper complaining about the exuberance of the team when it arrived at the depot. He contended that people "stood around and kicked because they made so much noise. Some of the businessmen thought the young fellows ought to be arrested. It was the first time, no doubt, that there had been anything stirring in the sleepy place, and it was a shock to the somnolent natives."

Playing left tackle on that team was Frank Knox, who later found excitement as a member of Teddy Roosevelt's Rough Riders, head of several newspapers, Republican nominee for vice president and secretary of the navy.

The college's first affiliation with an athletic league was as one of three members of the short-lived Central Michigan Athletic Association. The other two were Central Normal School (now Central Michigan University) and the Indian School. In its early years of athletics, Alma also competed against members of the Michigan Intercollegiate Athletic Association (MIAA), though it didn't become a member until 1902. The MIAA is the nation's oldest athletic conference still in existence.

Amos Alonzo Stagg, the University of Chicago's famous football coach, came to the college as a lecturer in 1901, and that fall, one of his protégés assumed coaching responsibilities at Alma. He was Theron Mortimer, identified by the *Alma Record* as "the famous Chicago tackle." Another player for Stagg, Jesse Harper, coached at Alma in 1906–07 and later was head coach at Notre Dame.

Most exciting of the 1905 baseball games at Alma was one against the University of Michigan. The Wolverines were on the way to Chicago, and Alma enticed them to make a detour by guaranteeing seventy-five dollars. The home team whipped the university, 4–1.

An MIAA record that will stand forever was registered by Alma's basketball team during the 1918–19 season. The squad established the best single-game defensive effort in league history, shutting out Olivet, 27–0. Perhaps another member could tie it—though that's extremely unlikely—but none will ever beat it!

The men's basketball team was unstoppable in its first two seasons of play at the college's new Memorial Gymnasium, completed in 1923. Paced by Captain Arthur "Red" Carty, who later played professional ball with the Detroit team of the American Basketball League, Alma annexed MIAA championships in 1924 and '25. Carty also was a catcher on the Alma baseball team, and in a 1924 game at Grand Rapids, he caught the ceremonial first pitch from William Jennings Bryan.

Alma's football teams, which had piled up four MIAA championships during the 1910s, did it again in the decade of the '20s. But in 1926, they were robbed of a victory by the Detroit police squad. When Alma punted and the ball was in the air, a referee whistled one of the team's players for holding. According to rules of that time, play should have stopped. But the receiver for the cops ran the ball into the end zone. The official brought the

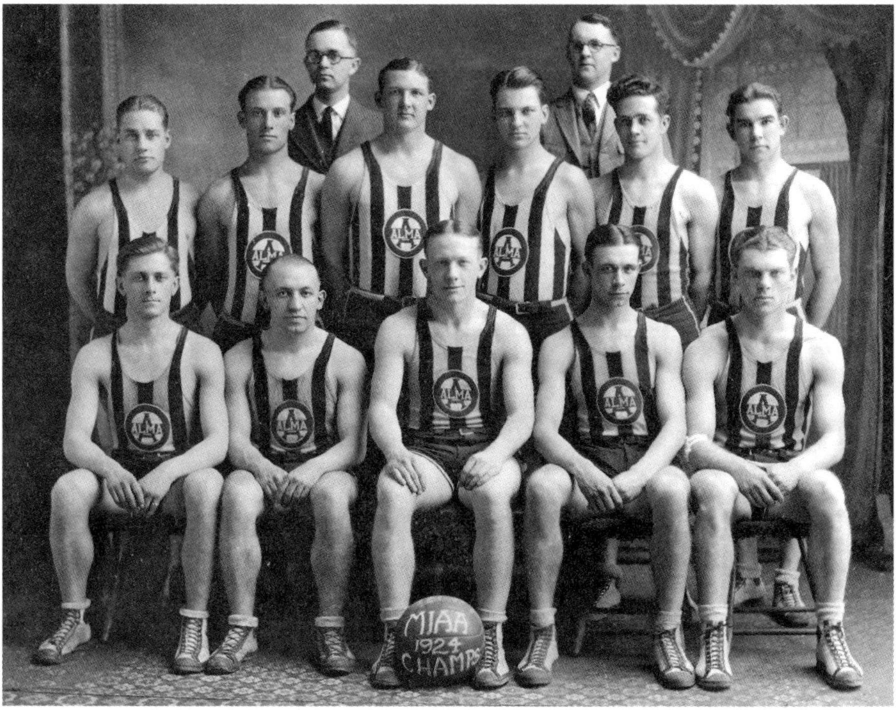

Art Carty (middle of front row) was captain of Alma's 1924 basketball team, the first Scot five to win an outright basketball championship. During the following season, he played for the Detroit Pulaski Post Five team, one of the initial members of the American Basketball League, first professional basketball league in the nation. *Courtesy of Alma College Archives.*

ball back to the spot of the violation and was about to walk off fifteen yards. When the lawmen complained, however, he put it on the three for an extra point try. Alma protested, but the official, according to the college's student newspaper, said the police "threatened to quit the field if the touchdown was not allowed." The game ended in a 13–13 tie.

In 1931, Alma's athletes—known by a variety of nicknames, such as Maroon Sox and Fighting Presbyterians—became known as the Scots. The winning selection of three choices in a student election had been submitted by freshman Herb Estes, later a trustee of the college.

Alma's 1935 football team was one of eight undefeated and untied football teams in the nation. Six members of the squad had played on Alma High School's 1931 state championship team—the Block brothers, LeRoy "Riley" and Wilson "Wadge"; Max Dean; Melvin Fuller; Al Fortino; and Leo Washburn.

The Scots' 1941 football season opened with a game against Grand Rapids University, which was coached by George "Potsy" Clark, previously the headman of the Detroit Lions. His assistant was Gerald R. Ford, later president of the United States. Despite their opponents' impressive coaching staff, the Alma men were victorious with a 12–0 shutout.

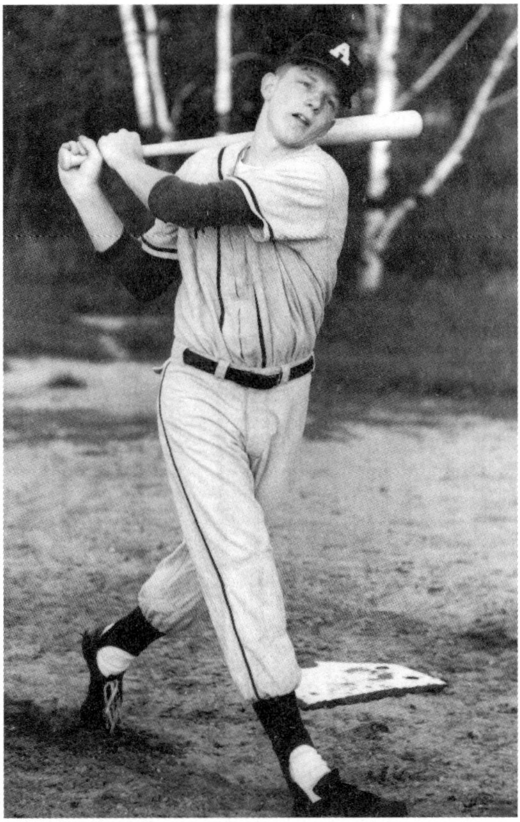

Detroit Tiger outfielder and 1968 World Series hero Jim Northrup, shown here in the batter's box as an Alma athlete, was better on the mound than at home plate for the Scots. An All-MIAA quarterback in football, he turned down pro football offers from the Chicago Bears and New York Titans (later the Jets) to play baseball for the Tigers. *Courtesy of Alma College Archives.*

Alma's 1940–41 MIAA basketball champions were invited to participate in the National Intercollegiate Basketball Tournament at Kansas City, where they topped the Panhandle Aggies of Oklahoma before being eliminated by Murray State Teachers College of Kentucky. In another postseason contest, Alma was edged, 45–43, in overtime by the Harlem Globetrotters at Ithaca High School's gymnasium.

Alma's baseball teams were powerful during the decade of the 1950s when the Scots piled up the MIAA's longest string of championships—eight from 1951 through 1958. The 1953 season had hardly begun when pitching ace Bob Bruce was called up by the Detroit Tigers. After hurling for farm clubs, he played at Detroit from 1959 through '61, then with the Houston Colt 45s, which became the Houston Astros (1962–66) and the Atlanta Braves (1967). In 1958, Jim Northrup—Detroit Tiger batting hero of the World Series ten years later—was more help to the Scots on the mound than at the plate. He had three wins and no losses as a pitcher, but he ranked sixth on the team in batting.

The longest dry spell in Alma's impressive football history came to an end in 1967 when the Scots captured the MIAA championship for the first time since 1951. Denny Stolz, a former Scot quarterback, took over the coaching duties in 1965 and registered Alma's only consecutive undefeated seasons in 1967 and '68.

The 1967 game against Olivet was Michigan's small college game of the era. Both teams were undefeated with 6-0 records, three of the wins in the MIAA. Olivet was even more hungry for a championship than the Scots; it had been fifty-three years since the Comets last finished at the top of the association. Bahlke Field was a sea of mud after a foot of wet snow fell the day before and was churned into slush during a high school game that night. Seven thousand fans, the most ever to see a game at Alma, were on hand when the Scots kicked off to Olivet. And it didn't take long for every one of them to become astounded.

Their first surprise was that Stolz had his team punt on third down, then even on second down. That was the technique he used to move the ball ever nearer the Olivet goal. Then, when the breaks came, his gridders turned

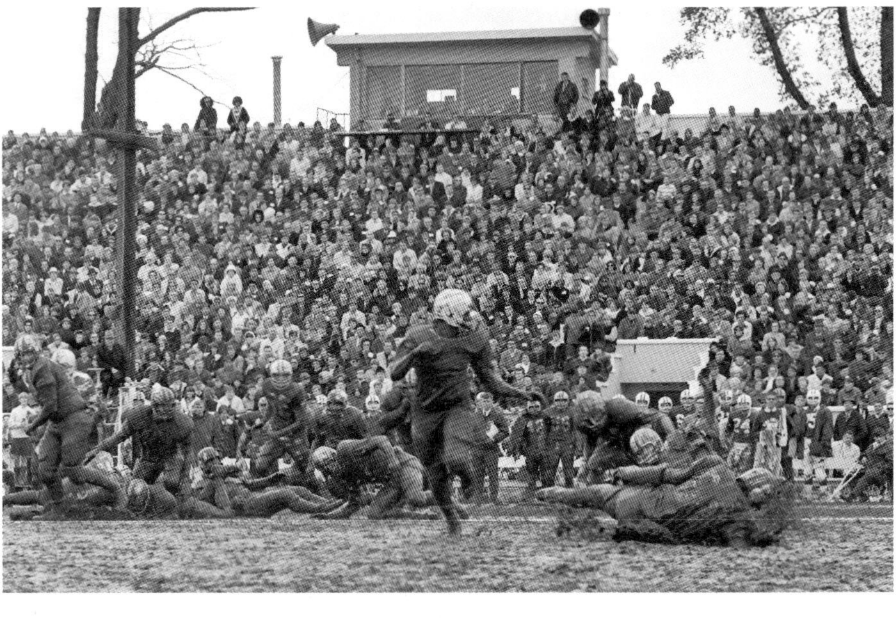

Identification of players, and even determination of which team they were on, became difficult soon after the first kickoff when Alma and Olivet, both undefeated, battled at Bahlke Field in late October 1967. With at least a share of the MIAA championship at stake, Coach Denny Stolz's clever strategy led to a surprising 34–0 Scot victory. *Gordon Beld photo; courtesy of Alma College Archives.*

them into touchdowns. It wasn't even close. Alma had a 20–0 halftime lead and was on top, 34–0, at the final gun. The following week, Alma wrapped up the MIAA title in a snowy game at Kalamazoo.

Alma won its first cross-country championship in 1969 when Coach Charlie Gray's squad tied Calvin for the honor. The Scots' Don Yehle was the first across the line at the MIAA meet. He covered the four-mile Lenawee Country Club course at Adrian in record time and did the same a year later at Albion when Alma clinched the title outright. At the end of that season, he became the first Alma athlete to be designated an All-American when he finished among the top runners in the National College Division Championships of the NCAA.

Scot runners also were impressive in track during the spring of 1970, posting their first MIAA track championship while sweeping through dual meets undefeated and then overpowering opposition at the association meet in which they finished forty-six points ahead of second-place Hope College.

In 1977–78, Bill Klenk coached Alma teams to championships in two sports. His basketball squad ended a thirty-six-year drought when it tied Albion for the MIAA crown, and his baseball team earned a title in 1978 with an 11-1 association record. More titles were added in 1980, '81 and '83 as the Scots continued to dominate MIAA diamonds.

In football, a 1971 game at Kalamazoo produced the wildest finish ever in Alma football. The Scots had a 12–10 edge with only eleven seconds to play, but the home team kicked a field goal for a 13–12 lead and obvious victory. There were seven seconds left when the Hornets kicked off. But Terry Phipps, a substitute back, took the ball on Alma's thirty-three-yard line, weaved through the entire Kalamazoo eleven and crossed the goal after the clock ran out. Excited Alma players and fans flooded the field as the scoreboard registered an 18–13 Scot triumph.

The games Alma's gridders played in 1980–81 at Pontiac's Silverdome Stadium, home field of the Detroit Lions, didn't match that excitement, but they were interesting. Both years the Scots took on Michigan Tech's gridders in football doubleheaders known as the Michi-Dome Football Classics. Each game pitted Lower Peninsula and Upper Peninsula teams against one another. Wayne State University competed against Northern Michigan in the second contest each year.

After leading all NCAA Division III teams in total offense during 1984, the Scots traveled overseas for football competition the following summer. They defeated the Finnish Northern Lights, 72–0, in the Arctic Bowl at Oulu and the Finnish National All Stars, 53–0, at Helsinki.

In 1981, Alma ruled as kings of MIAA wrestling by halting Olivet's nine-year reign as champions with a stunning 24–19 victory over the Comets, who had piled up forty-three straight dual meet wins. The Scots repeated as champs in 1982 and '83.

During the past century and a quarter, many scholar-athletes have made Alma proud—but none more so than quarterback Josh Brehm who in 2006 won the Gagliardi Trophy, an annual award to the most outstanding football player in the NCAA's Division III. That year Brehm set new MIAA records for total offense, most passes completed and most yards passing. In classrooms where he majored in business and psychology, he posted a 3.78 grade point average.

But he's not a rare example. Hundreds of outstanding Alma scholar-athletes have performed magnificently through the years, both in academic and athletic efforts. Nevertheless, not many of Alma's athletes have dreams of making a name for themselves as sports heroes. They're on the field just because they love the game.

—Gordon Beld

CHAPTER 21

IRISH 196, SCOTS 0

Most serious football fans can rattle off the names of the coaches whose innovations have modified, and usually improved, the game. But ask them about Wilfred Bleamaster, and they'll come up blank. No, he didn't invent the sucker shift or the single wing. He's the guy who invented the suicide schedule.

Bleamaster became Alma's football coach in 1912 when Dennis Grady, the prior mentor, took the head coaching position at Northwestern University. Bleamaster's first season as head of the Maroon and Cream gridders went well. After an opening loss to Michigan State (then Michigan Agricultural College), his team conquered the next six opponents, including Central Michigan Normal (now Central Michigan University) and the University of Detroit.

Then, however, he made a big mistake. He booked Notre Dame for the third game of the 1913 season, and his team suffered a 62–0 thrashing. A week later, the powerful Irish humbled Army in the game that popularized the forward pass. It was in that contest that Notre Dame confounded the football world by humbling the Cadets, 35–13, with its Gus Dorais–Knute Rockne aerial attack.

Bleamaster took his 1914 and '15 teams to South Bend, too, and those were the years of the suicide schedule. Alma opened both seasons against the Irish and then took on Michigan State a week later.

The blame may not have been all Bleamaster's, though. Jesse Harper, who had been the Alma mentor in 1906 and '07, had taken over as head coach

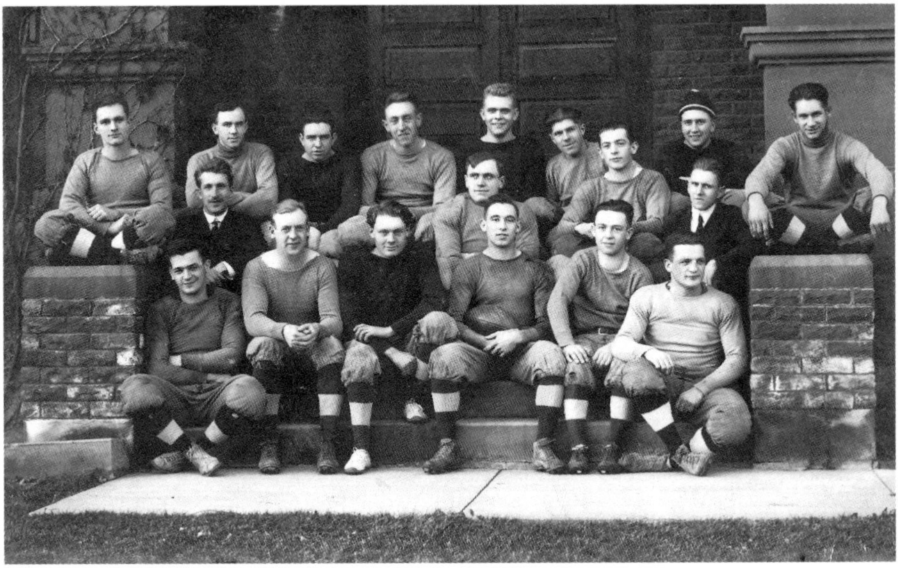

With coach Wilfred Bleamaster (left end, second row) are members of the 1913 Alma football team that tangled with Notre Dame at South Bend. A week later, the Irish amazed football followers by drubbing favored Army. Though the Irish whipped Alma 62–0, Notre Dame coach Jesse Harper had kind words for the visitors. "I've never seen such a bunch of game fighters in my life," he said. *Courtesy of Alma College Archives.*

of the Irish in 1913, and he may have initiated the idea of the South Bend get-togethers among old friends.

There may not have been much Bleamaster could do about Michigan State either. Both Alma and the Spartans were members of the Michigan Intercollegiate Athletic Association (MIAA), and they had competed against one another regularly since 1896.

Of course, Notre Dame and Michigan State weren't quite the powers they are today. But Alma was no giant either. In 1914, the college had only 144 students—64 of them men and fewer than 20 of them football players. One Alma player who competed against the Irish still recalled the whippings at South Bend more than a half century later. Once, when Bleamaster sent in a substitute for him, he intentionally went off the field on the Notre Dame side so the coach couldn't send him right back in.

Another Alma gridder claimed until the day he died, sixty years later, that he was robbed of a touchdown. He said he caught a pass and took off for what would be a sure score. However, an official blew his whistle and halted play. When Bleamaster protested, the ref said he stopped the action because he thought the Alma receiver wouldn't have survived if the three pursuing Irish giants had pounced on him.

After a 56–0 thumping by the Irish in the 1914 season opener, the Scots were shut out by Michigan State, 60–0, the following Saturday. Then, in the second year of the suicide schedule, Notre Dame tallied only 32 points, and Alma actually scored against the Spartans—but lost, 76–12.

Two years of opening against the Irish and Spartans were enough for Bleamaster. He left to become coach at the University of Idaho, and Harry Helmer took over at Alma in 1916. At least he didn't have to play Notre Dame in his opener. It was the last game on the schedule. But the result was the same as those of the first three contests in South Bend. The Irish were 42–0 victors, and the scoring total for the four seasons of insanity in Indiana became Notre Dame 196, Alma 0.

Alma's revenge of a sort for the slaughters in South Bend finally came in 1975 when a former Alma player and coach, Denny Stolz, was in charge of the Michigan State football program and finally conquered the Irish, 10–3. A quarterback at Alma in the 1950s, he returned in 1965 as head coach. In six seasons, he piloted the Scots to three MIAA championships.

Harper, Bleamaster and Stolz weren't the only men whose early steps on Alma's fields of play led them to impressive positions in university and professional athletics. When Stolz was a player at Alma, his coach was Lloyd Eaton, later head coach at the University of Wyoming and then director of player personnel for the Green Bay Packers. When Eaton went to Wyoming in 1962, he replaced Bob Devaney, who moved on to Nebraska.

Devaney, an All-MIAA end at Alma in the 1930s, is considered by many to be one of the best college coaches ever. He led the Cornhuskers to consecutive national championships in 1970 and '71.

Steve Sebo, who preceded Eaton at Alma, later was athletic director at the University of Virginia.

George Allen, coach of the Los Angeles Rams and Washington Redskins, was a student at Alma in a navy V-12 program during World War II and may have seen football action with the Scots in 1943.

Jim Northrup, slugging outfielder for the Detroit Tigers and hero of the 1968 World Series, was an All-MIAA quarterback for the Scots in 1959.

Early in the college's gridiron history, there was another dedicated coach who has been all but forgotten—intentionally so, perhaps. Edwin Steele was his name, and he came to Alma in 1920. That fall, his football team lost the first six games on its schedule and then traveled to Holland for the season finale against Hope College. There, more than one hundred miles from Alma where nobody knew him, he suited up and played the whole game against the Dutch alongside his younger charges while an older student stood on the sidelines and pretended to be the coach. Alma won, 7–6.

His kind of determination might have been just what the Scots needed in their battles against Notre Dame. But Steele arrived at Alma just a few years too late.

—Gordon Beld

The Man Who Made a Difference

Of the many coaches and players who contributed to Alma's impressive football heritage, one in particular stands out. Pete Schmidt, a stellar performer on Denny Stolz's undefeated 1967 and '68 teams, went on to make impressive contributions as a coach in high school, college and university athletic programs. But, more importantly, Pete was a man who made a difference. With his guidance and encouragement, his players were better on their fields of play, in their classrooms and throughout their lives.

At Alma, his 1960s contributions helped to enhance the college's gridiron reputation, but in the 1980s and '90s, Pete became a thorn in the side of the Scots.

Throughout most of the Michigan Intercollegiate Athletic Association's history, either Alma or Albion College has claimed bragging rights for winning the most championships. Albion's Britons took two trophies

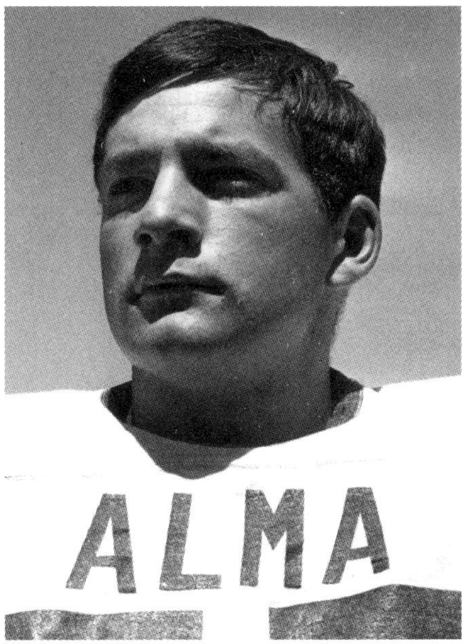

Pete Schmidt was an impressive man. An outstanding player on Alma teams of the late 1960s that went undefeated two years in a row, he later was football coach at Albion College, where his teams assembled a string of eight straight MIAA championships (1989–96). Four years after becoming assistant head coach at Indiana University in 1996, his life was cut short by lymphoma. *Gordon Beld photo; courtesy of Alma College Archives.*

before the Scots entered the league in 1902, and when Pete graduated and left Alma in 1970, each team had eighteen trophies. After ten years as a highly successful high school coach, he joined the Albion staff in 1982 and, a year later, became head coach. At that time, Alma had a one-trophy edge on the Britons in MIAA competition, 21–20. At the end of the decade of the '80s, the Britons and Scots each held twenty-two championships.

Then, in the early '90s, the roof fell in on the Scots. After tying Adrian for the MIAA title in 1989, Pete's gridders registered seven straight outright championships, leaving Alma far behind in the dust. At the end of the 1996 season, the Britons had twenty-nine trophies to Alma's twenty-two.

Pete's record at Albion is exemplary. His nine championships tie him with Ray Smith, former Hope College coach, for the most trophies ever in MIAA football. Each led teams to nine titles, but Pete did it in fourteen seasons. Smith was at Hope for twenty-five.

Pete's Albion teams went to the NCAA Division III playoffs five times, and in 1904, they captured the national championship. His 1996 squad led the country in total offense with a 538-yards-per-game average.

During his fourteen seasons as head coach at Albion, Pete's teams compiled a record of fifty-four wins, eleven losses and a tie. Even more impressive were the academic performances of his players. During those fourteen years, every single Albion player earned a degree.

In December 1996, Pete was invited to join the Indiana University staff by Cam Cameron just a few days after he took over as head coach. As assistant head coach and quarterback coach, Pete developed one of the Big Ten's most-improved offenses. The 1999 Hoosiers averaged 405.9 yards in total offense and scored thirty or more points in each of six games.

In October of that year, Pete was diagnosed with lymphoma. He died at Bloomington Hospital on September 20, 2000, and when the Hoosiers took the field for their next game, there was a tiny sticker on each helmet. "Pete" is all it said.

However, his colleagues had more words. Cameron commented, "Pete was a great husband, father, coach and most importantly a man of great faith. It's not often you get an opportunity to hire one of your idols, yet I was fortunate to be able to do that four years ago when I hired Pete. He will always be an inspirational and motivating force in my life and the lives of many others."

In honor of the former Alma player and Albion coach, the MIAA created the Pete Schmidt Memorial Scholar Athlete Award that is given each year to an exceptional graduating senior player.

—GORDON BELD

Chapter 22

LATE STARTERS, BUT STRONG FINISHERS

Opportunities for women to compete in intercollegiate athletics were few and far between in Alma College's early days. During the late nineteenth and early twentieth centuries, many believed ladies should not participate in contact sports. The idea that girls were to be thought of as "sugar and spice and everything nice" threw cold water on any hopes they may have had for sharing in the glory men found on fields of play.

Until rather recent years, their athletic opportunities went little beyond standing on the sidelines and cheering for the men, especially at football and basketball games. But they were really good at that, and their enthusiasm spread to teams on the field and fans in the stands.

At first, the rare athletic opportunities for coeds were intramural, but one did compete against representatives of another college as early as 1900. That was Faith Brooks, who placed second in Indian club swinging at a track meet with Olivet College held at Ithaca.

When Alma was admitted to the Michigan Intercollegiate Athletic Association (MIAA) in 1902, girls were able to play tennis at the league's twice-a-year field days. That probably was permissible because the competitors stood on opposite sides of the net. Injury was a possibility, of course—but not collision. Records of the MIAA show that champions for women's tennis were crowned from 1939 to the present, except for the World War II years of 1943–45.

However, competition in other sports awaited Alma's 1941 participation with other MIAA colleges in establishment of the Athletic Federation of

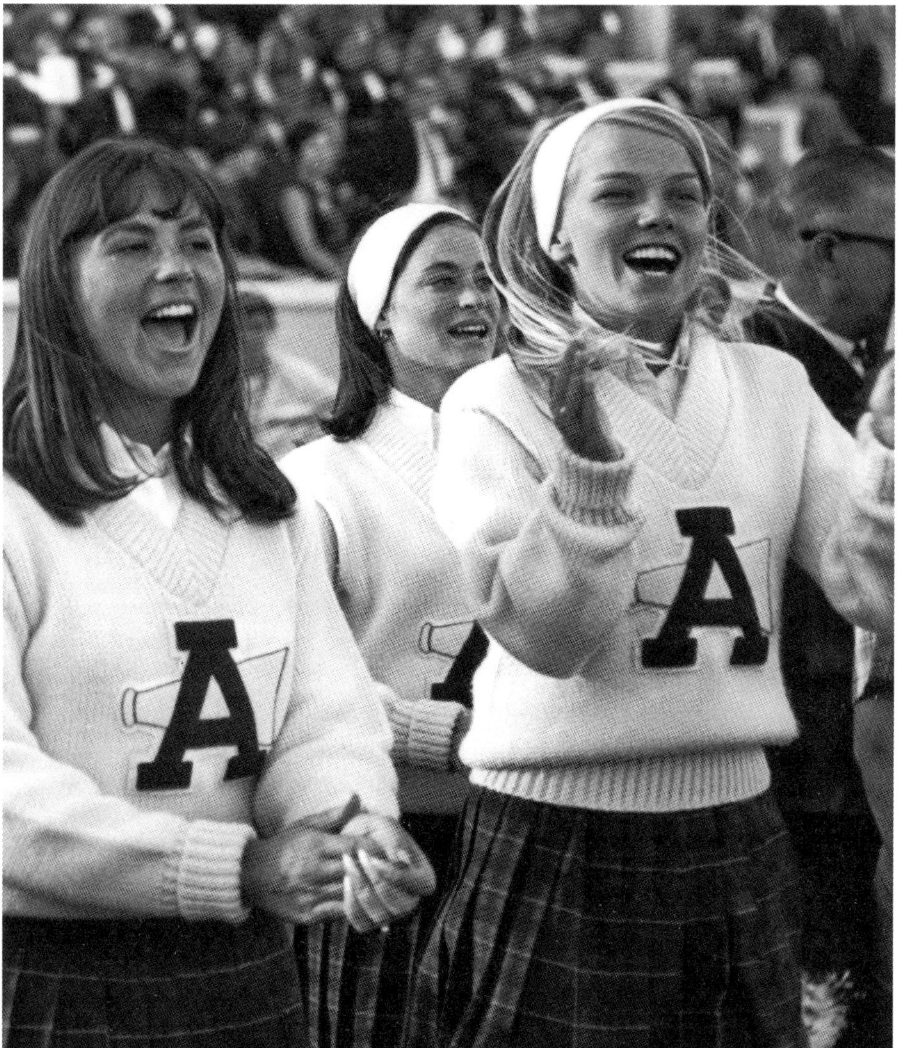

During the years before athletic opportunities for women became equal to those of men, Alma coeds cheered on male athletes from the sidelines, and that continues today. It was three cheers for Alma in 1965 when this enthusiastic trio reacted to a touchdown. From left, they are Randy Norris, Beth Bultema and Casey Cummings. *Gordon Beld photo; courtesy of Alma College Archives.*

Michigan Women. A few years later, its name was changed to Women's Michigan Intercollegiate Athletic Association (WMIAA).

In 1952, archery was added to tennis as an official WMIAA sport. Since competitors stood next to each other and aimed at distant targets, that, too, was not a contact sport. Alma's lasses turned in outstanding performances with their bows and arrows, especially during the 1970s.

Beginning in 1962, the league presented its Jo Dunn Outstanding Archer Award to the year's most accurate competitor, and Ann Giebel's performance first brought the trophy to Alma in 1966. Then, during the 1970s, six other Scot ladies captured the prize: Mary Lou Fortmiller, 1971; Sher Hansen, 1974; Karen Dosson, 1975; Judy Vasseliu, 1977; Marilyn Ennis, 1978; and Martha Rosner, 1979.

During that decade, Alma's archers also took home MIAA championship trophies three straight years—1971, '72 and '73—and added another in 1979. In leading the Scots to that championship, Ennis shattered the league's record for individual high score with 2,258 points. The sport was discontinued after the 1981 season.

Basketball has long been popular with Alma's women, but there is little information about competition in the early days. Women's basketball originated in the 1890s, but it probably didn't arrive on the Alma campus until the 1920s. It became a WMIAA sport in 1972.

Except for the fact that competitors attempted to throw a ball into a basket, there weren't many similarities between women's and men's versions of the sport at first. The court for women was divided into zones, three at

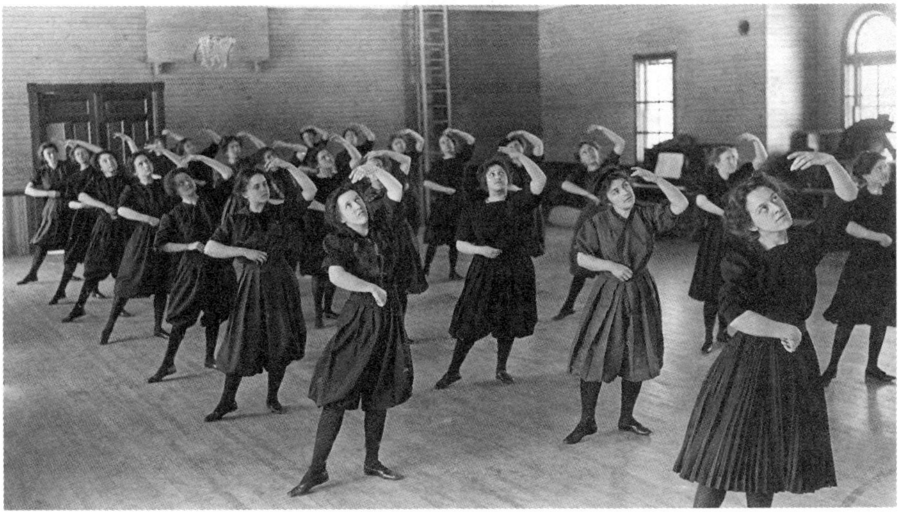

Female participants in Alma's early physical education classes, such as this one in 1912, wore uniforms that permitted no more visibility of skin than that on arms and faces. The same was true for those who took part in basketball and the few other sports in which young ladies could compete. *Courtesy of Alma College Archives.*

first and then changed to two, and players assigned to one zone could not enter another. Only three dribbles were allowed before passing or shooting, and from 1910 to 1913, dribbling was prohibited. To further reduce contact, there could be no steals. Placing a hand on the ball while it was held by an opponent resulted in a foul.

Women's uniforms ensured that all skin was covered. Typical attire included pantaloons, divided skirts that met below the knee; long stockings; and long-sleeved shirts. Even though the girls were covered to that extent, men were prohibited from watching early women's games.

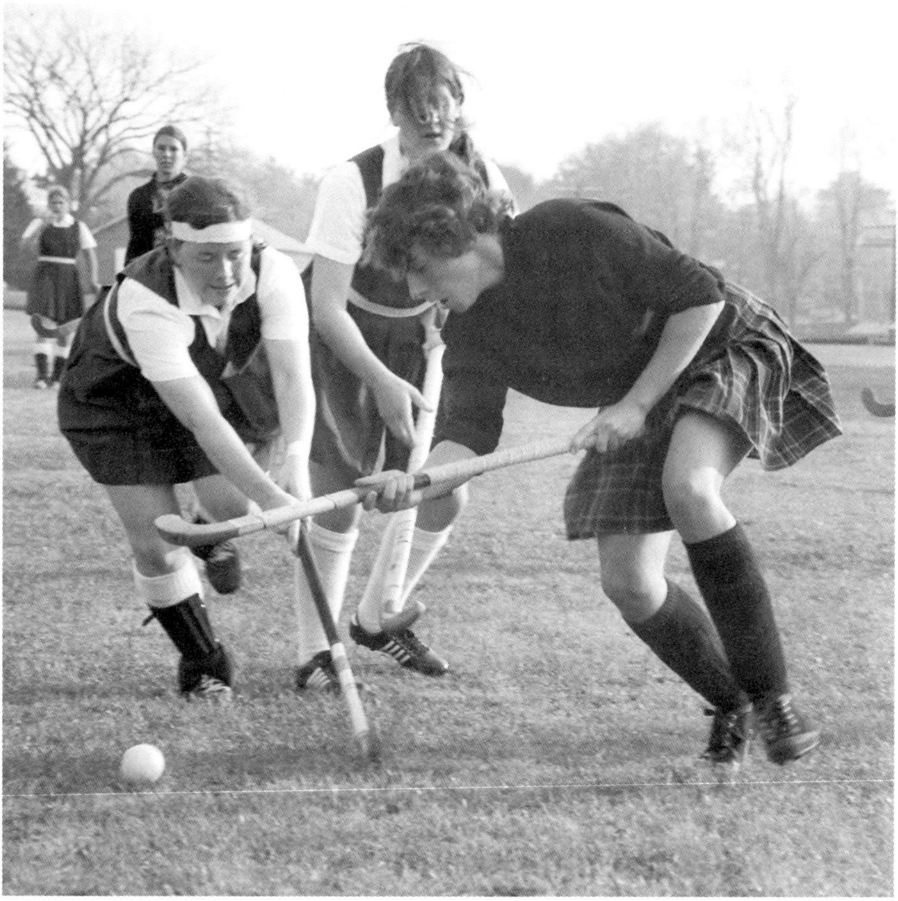

Carolyn Sachs (at right), a star performer on Scot field hockey teams of the early 1970s, beats opponents to the ball. Alma women began competing in the sport on an intramural basis soon after World War I, when a field was developed behind Wright Hall. *Gordon Beld photo; courtesy of Alma College Archives.*

The first known women's hoops conflict between MIAA schools took place in Alma on March 20, 1943, when the Scot ladies defeated Kalamazoo, 20–12. It was also in 1943 that the same two schools competed in the first known softball game between WMIAA teams. In that contest, Alma posted a 15–10 victory over the Hornets.

The WMIAA sanctioned field hockey as early as 1968, and Alma's first really impressive season was 1970, when the team was victorious in all league contests and compiled an overall record of eight wins and a tie in eleven games.

Finally, in 1972, women were given opportunities for competition equal to those of men when Title IX became law and prohibited discrimination in athletics on the basis of sex. Suddenly, the list of sports in which women could compete was lengthened. Today, Alma's women participate in basketball, bowling, cheerleading, cross-country, golf, lacrosse, soccer, softball, swimming and diving, tennis, track and field and volleyball.

In 1977, the WMIAA was incorporated into the MIAA, and in 1981, the league began including results of women's competition with those of men in tabulating points for its all-sports trophy.

After the acceptance of women in the restructured MIAA, Alma's ladies quickly moved to the top in nearly all the sports sanctioned by the league. Their first championship after the restructuring was the 1978 field hockey crown. With a record of four wins, no losses and two ties, the Scots shared the crown with Albion.

In 1981's first MIAA competition for a cross-country championship, Alma and Albion also shared the trophy. Scot runners compiled a 4-0 dual meet record, but they finished second to the Britons at the annual league meet in Alma, despite Lisa Thocher's first-place finish.

The first basketball championship for Alma's women came during the 1981–82 academic year, too, when they won eleven of their twelve MIAA contests. The team participated in NCAA Division III tournament competition but was eliminated by North Central of Illinois, 86–78.

The first volleyball title came the following fall when Alma and Calvin split the honors. To gain a tie for the crown, the Scot ladies needed a win over Calvin in the final game of the season, and they overpowered the Grand Rapids team, 15–7, 15–13 and 15–4.

The cross-country squad finished on top that fall, too, taking the trophy for a second straight year as Thocher set a new MIAA record in the league meet. She placed third in regional competition at Cleveland and was thirty-third in a field of 110 at the nationals in Fredonia, New York.

In autumn of 1983, Alma's women swept all available MIAA trophies—cross-country, volleyball and field hockey—and added another basketball title in the winter. In cross-country, the lady harriers not only captured a third consecutive MIAA trophy but also became the first Alma team of either sex in any sport to win a multistate regional championship. At the NCAA Great Lakes Regional, Alma easily outdistanced second-place Calvin by thirty-two points.

Alma's all-time greatest one-year championship output was the accumulation of six trophies, all won by women's teams, in 1984–85. Besides sweeping the fall sports and basketball again, the Scot women won their first titles in track and softball in the spring. A perfect climax for the 1984–85 accomplishments was the selection of Irenna Garapetian, outstanding goalie for the field hockey team and a summa cum laude graduate, for Academic All-America honors.

The largest collection of trophies accumulated by Alma's women in a single sport consists of the fifteen captured in softball competition. Denny Griffin took over coaching responsibilities in the 1980s and began building the MIAA's most formidable program in the sport. His first championship was in 1985. After recording two more in '86 and '94, his teams really caught fire and recorded nine consecutive titles—the first a tie with Calvin in 1997 and then outright titles from 1998 through 2005. More were added in 2007, 2010 and 2011.

The 1991–92 basketball team brought home a national championship trophy when it swept aside all opposition in the chase for the Division III title of the National Collegiate Athletic Association (NCAA). After nailing down the MIAA title with an 11-1 record, the Scots toppled Adrian in the first round of the NCAA tournament, then eliminated Roanoke of Virginia and Wisconsin Eau Claire in the sectionals, edged Luther of Iowa in the semi-finals and conquered Pennsylvania's Moravian College to win the national championship.

The track team's seven championships were consecutive, running from 1985 through 1991. Amy Doucette came to Alma just too late to perform with those exceptional springtime runners from Alma. She arrived on the campus in the fall of '91 and for four years turned in outstanding performances in both track and basketball. As a freshman, she was one of the Scot cagers who captured the NCAA Division III national basketball title.

And that was just the beginning. On the track in her sophomore year, she set an MIAA record in the 1,500-meter run and qualified for the nationals, where she finished third, enough to make her a Division III All-American.

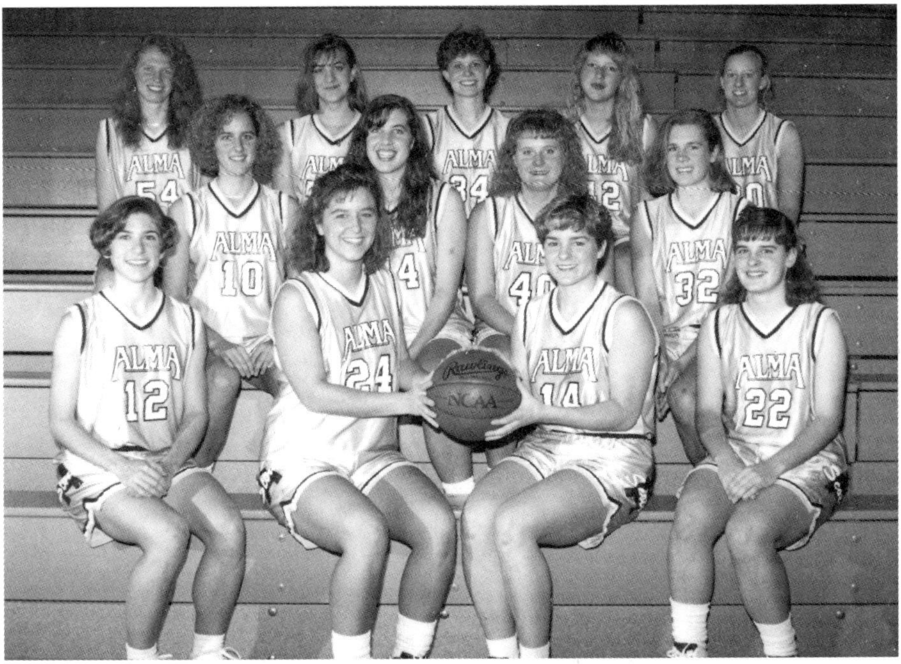

These Scot ladies were the best in NCAA Division III basketball for the 1991–92 season. After winning the MIAA title, they breezed through playoffs to win the national championship. Team members are (from left): first row—Amy Doucette, Susie Kieffer, Laurie La Beau, Terri Hogan; middle row—Jaime McCallister, Kelly Jaster, Amy Elbers, Colleen Wruble; back row—Stephanie Mortensen, Andrea Balliet, Julie Long, Katie Mans, Tara Sherman. *Courtesy of Alma College Archives.*

As a junior in basketball, she was the team's hustler—scoring 239 points and making 84 assists while pulling in 78 rebounds and 65 steals. During her senior year, she became the only Alma athlete, male or female, to win a national championship when she broke the ribbon in the 1,500-meter run at the NCAA Division III national finals.

Alma's women may have gotten a late start on the fields of play, but they don't have to take a back seat to the men when it comes to collecting championship hardware.

—GORDON BELD

CHAPTER 23

ALMA'S ANNUAL SCOTTISH INVASION

It was in the late 1960s that a wee bit of Scotland came to Alma, quickly sprouted and soon put the city on the map as host of one of Michigan's most colorful and exciting festivals. However, neither the heather and hills nor the mountains and moors of Scotland were transplanted here. In fact, other than signs at the entrance to the city proclaiming it "Scotland, U.S.A." there's little else with a Scottish connection. There are few bagpipes, and there aren't many Scottish names in the phone book. Besides that, the flat farmland surrounding the town is hardly a reminder of the rugged terrain of Scotland.

However, for nearly half a century, the Alma Highland Festival has attracted thousands of Scots, and a lot of others who wish they were, to this college town at the heart of Michigan's lower peninsula.

In early efforts to promote the gathering of Scots at Alma, some in the city pointed to Ralph Ely, the first settler in the city, as the connection. Though they proclaimed he was Scottish, he wasn't. He was English, forbid! Ely's ancestors left England's County of Kent in the 1600s and settled in Massachusetts.

Ely's closest link with Scots was during the Civil War, when his Eighth Michigan Infantry Regiment sometimes went into battle alongside the Seventy-ninth New York Volunteer Infantry, popularly known as the Seventy-ninth New York Highlanders. Their uniforms included dark blue Scottish tailcoats with red piping and trousers of Cameron tartan. The unit's seventeen-member brass brand often was accompanied by a piper who wore a kilt. Sponsored by

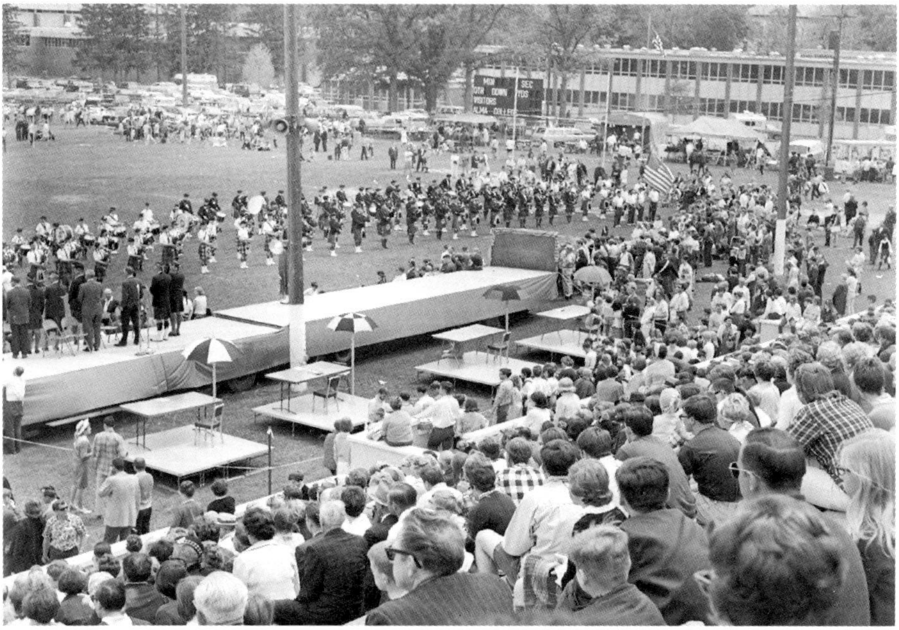

At the first Alma Highland Festival in May 1968, the massed band performed on the old Bahlke Field, to the west of the present stadium. At the opening ceremony that day, ranks of the band were only three or four deep. Even so, the crowd of fifteen thousand was thrilled by the thundering pipes and drums at the opening ceremony. *Gordon Beld photo.*

the Caledonian Society of New York City, it was formed as a militia unit in June 1859 and left for Civil War service in May 1861.

The actual connection between Alma and its Highland Festival is Alma College and its relationship to the Presbyterian Church, which has its roots in Scotland. Though founded by Michigan Presbyterians in 1886, the college didn't emphasize its ties to the Scots until nearly half a century went by.

Because the school's early athletic teams had many nicknames—among them "Fighting Presbyterians"—student editors of the campus newspaper in 1931 announced a contest to find a more suitable name. "According to several sports writers we have encountered," they said, "it is really too bad to have to call a football team by the name of a church." After also considering a few other possibilities, students voted to name the teams "the Scots."

More recognition of the school's Scottish heritage came when its band adopted uniforms with kilts and changed its official name to the Alma College Kiltie Band. At the same time, a group of coeds known as the Kiltie Lassies began performing Highland dances as entertainment at campus events.

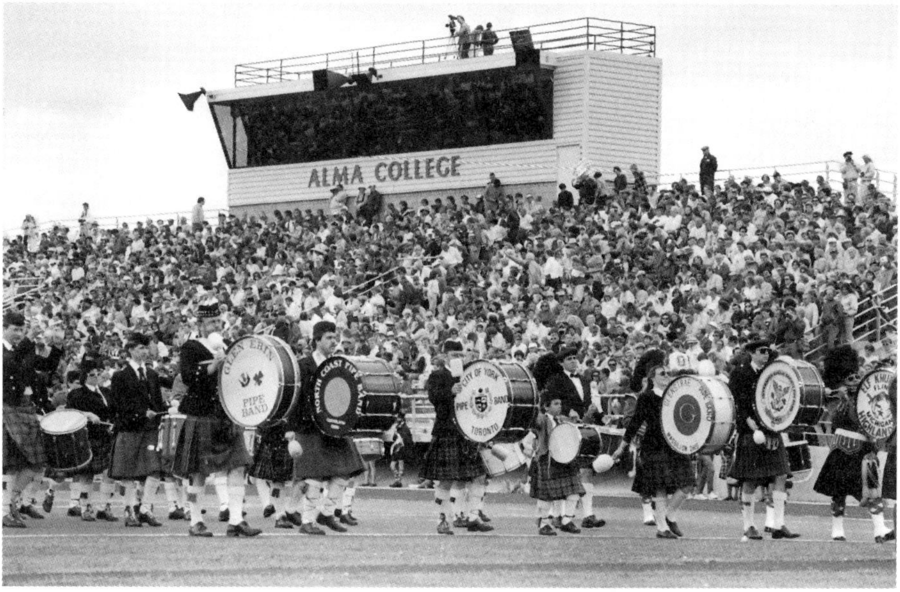

After the festival moved to Alma High School in 1986 while Bahlke Field was being relocated to a new area of the college's athletic complex, pipers and drummers returned to the campus in 1987 and paraded in front of the new grandstand. *Gordon Beld photo.*

However, the Alma Highland Festival didn't come about until later. The seed for today's colorful event actually was planted in Massachusetts, where Ely's ancestors first settled in America. David MacKenzie, an alumnus of the college and a skilled player of bagpipes, attended a Scottish festival at Boston in 1962. Impressed by the thrilling sights and sounds, he told friends back in Michigan, "Having once heard a massed pipe band, one feels this must be shared with the rest of the world."

Unsure how he might bring that kind of thrill to a familiar place in Michigan, he didn't do anything immediately. But in 1967, he arrived in Alma with an idea that could make his dream come true. His first stop was at the office of Guile Graham, the college's director of alumni and community relations. There he suggested that a good promotional tool for the school would be an annual Scottish festival on the campus.

Graham embraced the suggestion but pointed out that the college couldn't afford to divert resources and personnel to bring about an event of that kind every year. Instead, he suggested that MacKenzie talk to officials of the local chamber of commerce who had been searching for ways to make the city better known.

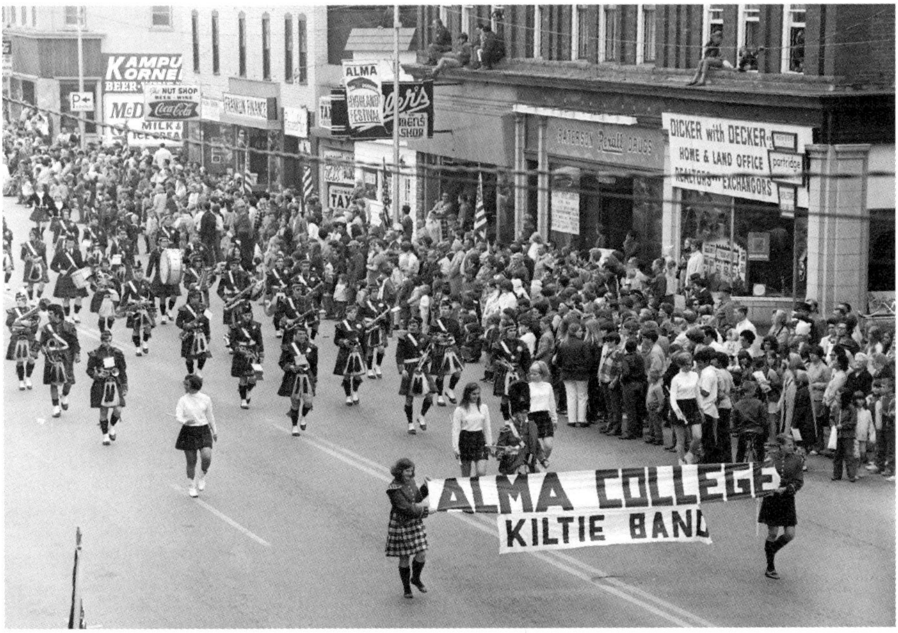

During early years of the festival, Alma College's Kiltie Band marched through downtown Alma and then played the national anthems of Canada and the United States in the opening ceremony at Bahlke Field. A few years later, when the college was not in session during festival weekend, Alma High School musicians took over. *Gordon Beld photo.*

Before making those contacts, however, MacKenzie decided he needed assistance of someone with a better understanding of festival organization and operations. So he asked Kenneth Jones of Okemos, pipe major of the Clan MacRae Pipe Band, to help. The two came to Alma in early November to run their ideas past Graham, and then about a week later, they made their pitch to representatives of the chamber. "We had no opportunity to use our carefully prepared answers to problems and questions that might be raised by the group," MacKenzie said. "There were none."

Three days later, the chamber voted unanimously to establish the Alma Highland Festival and Games, and the first such event was scheduled for Saturday, May 25, 1968. Donald Godfrey, a resident of the city and graduate of the college, was selected to head a committee of volunteers who developed plans for the festival. At its first meeting in January 1968, Jones predicted that the festival might attract five thousand spectators.

During the following months, MacKenzie and Jones came to Alma several times to provide technical assistance and advice. Scores of Alma residents

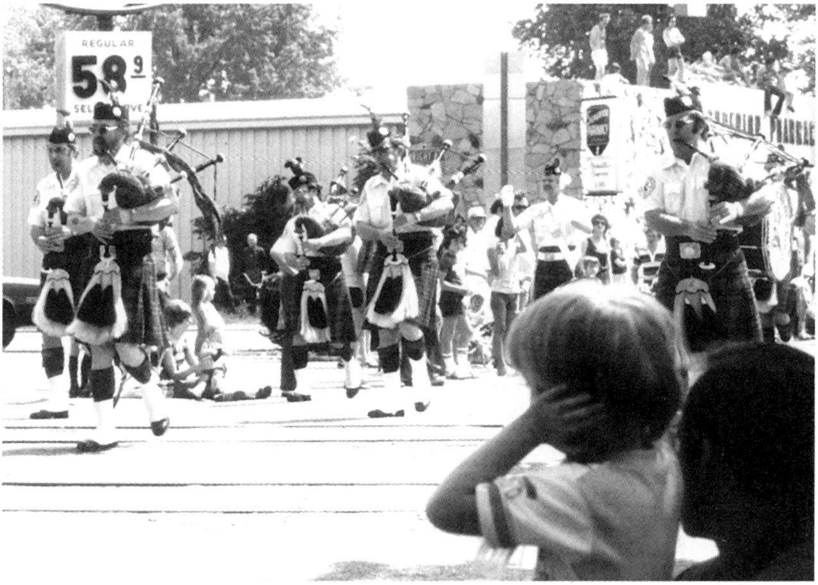

For non-Scots, a wee bit of listening may be required before bagpipe music is really appreciated. This little girl, watching pipers march toward the Alma College campus, hadn't yet developed an ear for the wailing pipes and thundering drums. *Gordon Beld photo.*

soon were scrambling in attempts to handle the hundreds of details involved in preparing for the event.

When the pipers, drummers, dancers and Scottish athletes swarmed into Alma on that springtime Saturday, the weather was perfect. Fifteen thousand spectators dwarfed Jones's prediction. Governor George Romney, speaker at the opening ceremonies, predicted, "If you persist, you can make this the chief Scottish Highland Festival on the North American continent. Indeed, you might even make it bigger than those in Scotland."

Impressed by what happened in Alma that day, *Newsweek* magazine devoted nearly a half page to a report on the festival. "Och," the article began, "but the heart leaped up and the shoulders squared at the brave sound of the massed bands of kilted bagpipers and the sight of the bonnie lassies in their tartan finery delicately toeing and tripping the reels and flings. But last week if these hearts were off in the heathery highlands, in Inverness or Aberdeen, the bodies were at the Highland Games at Alma in the rolling woods and farmlands of central Michigan."

Within the next few years, Romney's prediction seemed fulfilled. In 1969, attendance doubled to thirty thousand; in 1970, fifty thousand;

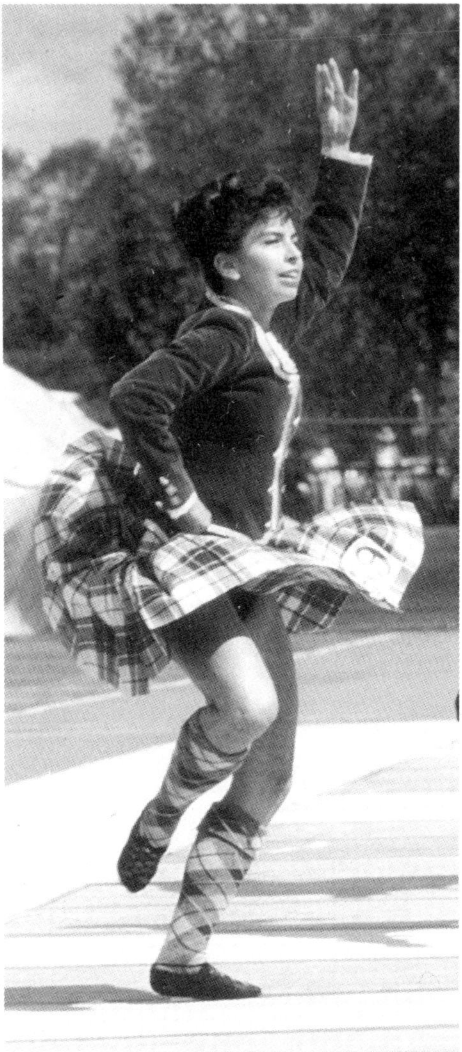

Highland dancers, like this lass, need athletic ability along with stamina and agility as they compete for awards at the Alma festival. Precise and graceful movements, combined with the brilliant hues of swirling kilts, make dancing competition especially exciting. *Gordon Beld photo.*

and in 1971, eighty thousand attended the games. By 1970, the festival was recognized by the National Association of Travel Organizations as one of the top twenty travel events in the United States. *Readers Digest* claimed the Alma festival was "the largest Scottish event held outside Scotland."

Most festival activities take place on the Alma College campus, and that has been the case for all but one of the events to date. The single exception was in 1968, when relocation and rebuilding of the college's Bahlke Stadium forced a move to facilities at Alma High School.

The earliest festivals were scheduled to be the concluding event of Michigan Week, which usually was a week before Memorial Day. In 1972, festival planners moved it to Memorial Day weekend, and the following year, it became a multi-day event with most activities on Saturday and Sunday.

The event attracts many pipe bands from throughout the United States and Canada and, for most in the crowd of spectators, the greatest thrills of the weekend are the sights and sounds of a massed band during opening and closing ceremonies. The wailing pipes and thundering drums of hundreds of kilt-clad musicians then fill the air above the college stadium. From one end of the playing field to the other,

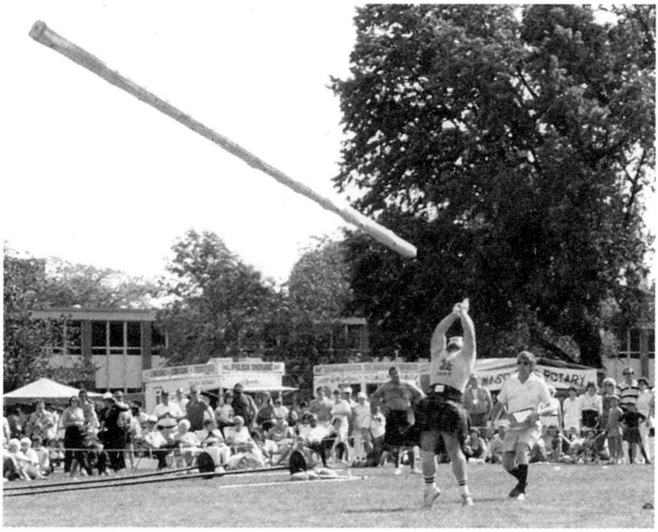

Teasing big guys like this about wearing skirts is risky. They toss these heavy logs called cabers almost as if they were sticks. However, just balancing the timber before running with it and heaving it in the air is difficult. Winners are those who get the log to flip over and land closest to a twelve o'clock position. *Gordon Beld photo.*

large corps of pipers and drummers parade onto the field. After they have assembled as one huge band, the pipe major shouts, "By the center, quick charge!" and his musicians step off toward the east grandstand, pivot at the sideline and retrace their steps toward the west bleachers, all the while rendering the spine-tingling strains of tunes such as "Scotland the Brave," "Road to the Isles" or "Glendaruel."

After Saturday's opening ceremony, the visiting pipe bands compete for trophies and cash awards. Pipe bands also compete Sunday afternoon. Individual pipers and drummers pursue prizes both mornings. Competition in dancing and athletic events continues throughout the weekend.

Seventeen competing bands at the first festival in 1968 were from Michigan, Indiana, Pennsylvania and Ontario. Since then, many have come from other parts of the United States and Canada, and in 2001, the Western Australia Police Service Pipe Band came to Alma and flew home with the top award. Usually, about thirty bands compete for trophies and cash awards at the Alma festival.

Michigan communities that have sent their pipe bands to Alma have included Ann Arbor, Traverse City, Kalamazoo, Royal Oak and Grand Rapids. Among the many non-Michigan competitors have been bands from Kansas City, Atlanta, St. Louis, Minneapolis, Chicago, Milwaukee, Cincinnati, Cleveland and Houston. Some of the many Canadian pipe bands that performed at Alma were from Toronto, Windsor, Guelph, Kingston,

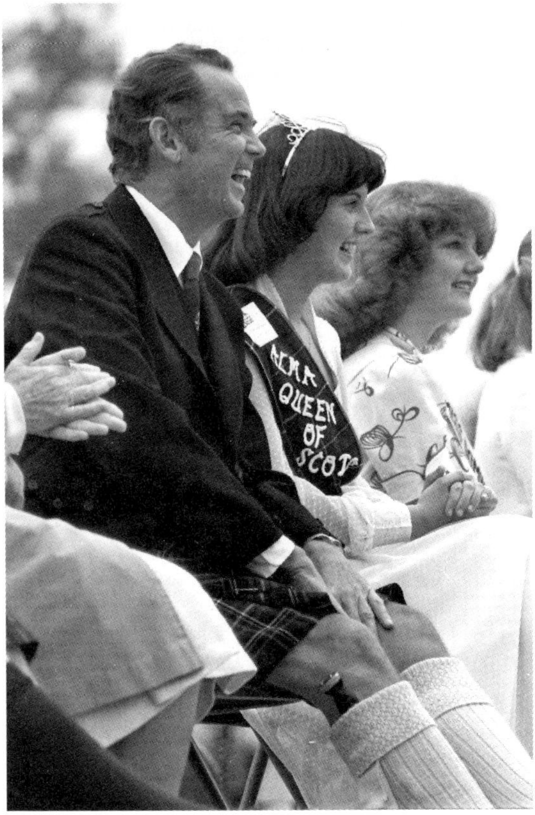

Of several Michigan governors who have participated in events of Alma's festival, only William Milliken has worn a kilt. Next to him at the 1979 festival is Queen of Scots Deirdre Corbett. *Gordon Beld photo.*

Strathroy, Newmarket and St. Johns, Newfoundland.

Each year, hundreds of Highland dancers compete at Alma with precise and graceful movements. The brilliant hues of their swinging kilts make this the most colorful competition of the festival. In the earliest Scottish games, dancing competition was for men only, but today nearly all of the dancers are women.

Making fun of Scotsmen wearing kilts at Alma can be dangerous—especially if they're among the competitors in Scottish heavy athletics. These are big men, and the things they throw around are seventeen-pound stones, twenty-two-pound hammers, fifty-six-pound weights with handles attached and a more-than-one-hundred-pound log that appears to be usable as a power line pole.

The log, fifteen to twenty feet long with a diameter of approximately nine inches at one end and five inches at the other, is called a caber. The tosser, usually with some assistance, manages to lift and balance the pole with the wide end at the top. Then he runs a short distance, straining to keep it from falling prematurely. He stops suddenly and, as the top begins to flip forward, lifts the bottom end in an attempt to throw it so that when the upper end strikes the sod the narrower end falls at a point farthest from him. It is accuracy rather than distance that counts. The best throw is the one that has the narrower bottom end landing closest to a twelve o'clock position.

Another popular festival event is an evening *ceilidh* (pronounced kay-lee). At this traditional Scottish gathering, professional entertainers and individuals from the audience present songs, stories and riddles. Sometimes *ceilidh* guests get to taste haggis, a Scottish concoction made from the heart, liver and lungs of a sheep or goat, mixed with onion, suet, oatmeal, salt and spices. The mixture is boiled in the stomach of the animal and then carried into the *ceilidh* hall by a cook who follows a piper. Typically, a Scotsman with a genuine brogue recites Robert Burns's "Ode to a Haggis" just before the dish is piped in.

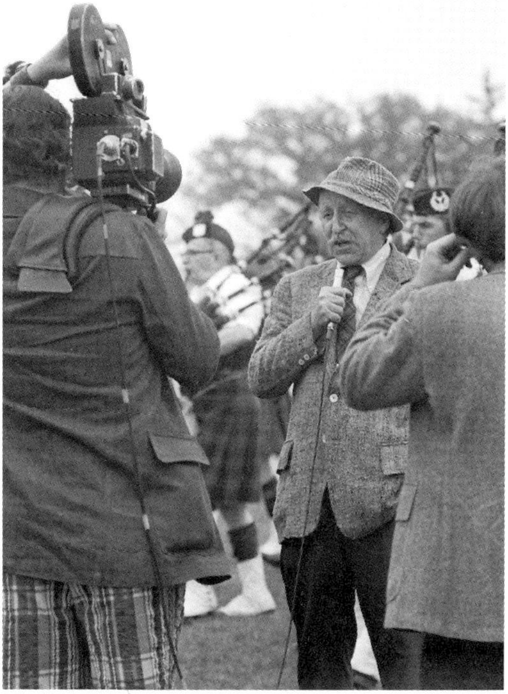

Heywood Hale Broun, sportscaster who was known for his handlebar mustache and colorful prose, was at the 1973 Highland Festival in Alma to report on the event for CBS News. *Gordon Beld photo.*

Other weekend events include exhibitions of Scottish country dancing and border collie sheepherding.

At clan tents, visitors with Scottish heritage can check out their ancestry and learn more about the clans of their forefathers. Vendors sell a wide variety of Scottish goods—tartan fabric, souvenir T-shirts, ties, books, compact discs with Scottish tunes—as well as food of the usual fare at festivals and fairs and bridies and other Scottish meat pies. Visitors yearning to master piping themselves can even purchase bagpipes and a book of lessons. Those who just want to look like Scots can buy kilts and all the accompanying accoutrements.

All who come to Alma on festival weekend discover, before heading home, that they've been transported—in spirit at least—across the ocean to the Highlands and islands of Scotland.

—Gordon Beld

INDEX

R

S

T

V

W

Y

Z

ABOUT THE AUTHORS

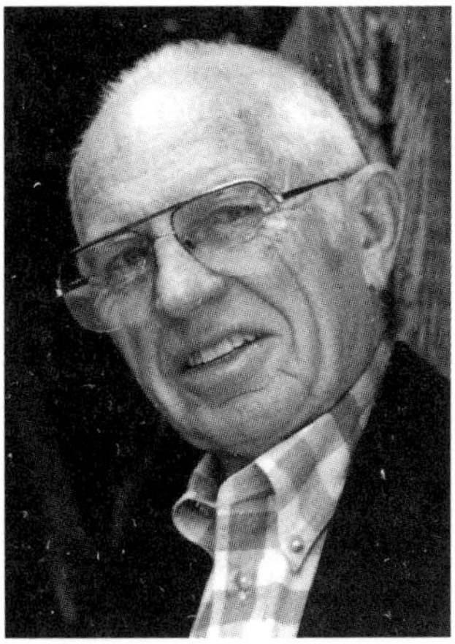

As director of news services and publications at Alma College from 1965 to 1989, Gordon Beld seldom left his office without cameras. In 1976, he received one of four national citations from the Council for the Advancement and Support of Education (CASE) for photography by editors of higher education publications. Alma publications for which he provided writing, editing and design also won awards from CASE as well as the American College Public Relations Association, American Alumni Council and National Association of Intercollegiate Athletics. His redesign of the college's magazine in 1966 earned the Time-Life Alumni Magazine Achievement Award for most-improved magazine in the Great Lakes region. He began writing for the *Grand Rapids Press* in 1944 at the age of sixteen. Two years later, as a trooper in the army's Constabulary force in Germany, his duties included writing Sixty-sixth Squadron news for the *Constabulary Lightning Bolt*. After discharge, he wrote for the *Grand Rapids Herald* until 1959, when the paper ceased publication, and then returned to the *Press*. During most of his years with the *Press* and *Herald*, he taught simultaneously in suburban Grand Rapids schools. He was the first chairman of the Wyoming (Michigan) Historical and Cultural

Commission (1963–65) and a trustee of the Holland Area Historical Society (1997–2003). Since his retirement from Alma College, he has been a regular contributor to *Grand Rapids* and *Michigan History* magazines, author of two books on Grand Rapids history and a historical novel concerning Cambodian refugees. He has been an elder in Reformed Church in America congregations at Grand Rapids and Holland, and he was chairman of the administrative board and several committees of Alma United Methodist Church. In the Alma area, he and his wife, Martha, became involved in resettlement of several Cambodian refugees. Later, they assisted refugees from Vietnam in Grand Rapids and from Kosovo in Holland. For eight years, Gordon was a volunteer teaching assistant in English-as-a-Second-Language classes for immigrants at Holland. For more than twenty years, he provided volunteer editorial services for Exodus World Service, a Chicago-area agency serving refugees. He has degrees from Hope College and the University of Michigan.

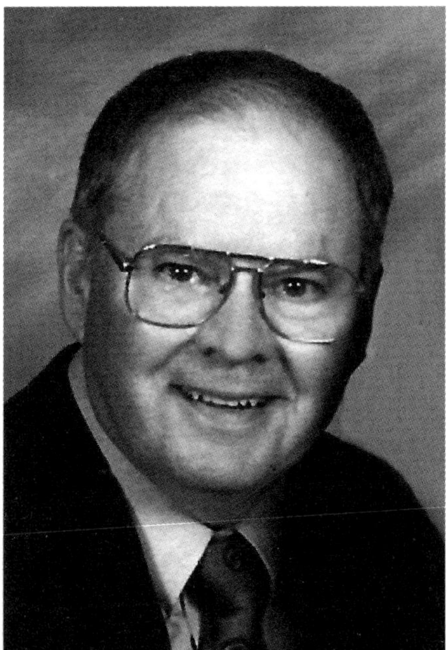

When a student at Alma High School told teacher David McMacken, "You had my grandma in class," he thought it might be time to retire. Two years later, he ended his vocation, after forty years of teaching literature and composition to more than five thousand Alma High School juniors and seniors. In retirement, he has been able to devote more time to his avocation: local history. Born in Alma because it had the nearest hospital, he grew up twenty miles away on the family farm. He attended a one-room country school and later received two degrees from Central Michigan University. A visit to Michigan's Copper Country triggered an interest in Michigan ghost towns, and he investigated those for several years. From his ghost town inquiries, his first article for *Michigan History* magazine emerged, the sordid story of bordello owner, arsonist and murderer Jim Carr. A student once wished to write a term paper on the life of Alma's benefactor Ammi Willard Wright, and McMacken, too, became interested in the life of the lumberman, business tycoon and Alma College founder. This triggered forty years of investigating and sharing Gratiot County history. He has produced more than two hundred history presentations over the years. They ranged from illustrated talks on cemetery art to trolley tours of historic Alma for all of the town's third graders, from scripts for cemetery impersonations to the script for a *Titanic* dinner and program on the hundredth anniversary of the tragic sinking. He is the author of four books on the history of St. Louis, Michigan, where he lives, and five books on the history of Alma and Gratiot County. He has written numerous articles for *Michigan History* and has been a featured speaker in Gratiot County's Evening in the Park series for thirty-five years. He received the Spirit of St. Louis award for his books on that town's history, and he serves on the boards of the Gratiot County Community Foundation, the Theodore Cutler Memorial Library and the Pine River Arts Council. He has served on various boards at Alma's First Church of God. He and his wife, Virginia, are inveterate gardeners with a yard of sprawling flower beds and a productive vegetable garden. They have three adult children and three grandchildren. He says the most important of his historical discoveries was a simple one: the good old days were more old than good.